Voices of
The American People

Volume I

PEARSON
Longman

New York   Boston   San Francisco
London   Toronto   Sydney   Tokyo   Singapore   Madrid
Mexico City   Munich   Paris   Cape Town   Hong Kong   Montreal

Executive Editor: Michael Boezi
Supplements Editor: Kristi Olson
Cover Design: Teresa Ward
Electronic Page Makeup: Lorraine Patsco

Voices of The American People, Volume I

Please visit our Web site at: www.ablongman.com

ISBN 0-321-39590-5

3 4 5 6 7 8 9 10—CRS—08 07 06

Contents

Preface

Selected to complement *The American People* textbook, the documents in this reader are crucial resources in the quest to understand and interpret American history. Their purpose is to introduce some of the voices from the American past, to impart a sense of how historians write history, and to hint at some of the complexities of writing the past.

Several features make the documents accessible and assist in their analysis. Chapter introductions place the selections within a broadly drawn historical context, and each document is accompanied by a headnote which describes the author of the selection and the circumstances under which the document was written. Analysis questions follow each document, suggesting lines of inquiry to help better understand the documents themselves or how they fit into the wider historical context. Study questions at the end of each chapter direct the reader to points of special note and suggest comparisons and opportunities for further inquiry.

PART ONE

A COLONIZING PEOPLE, 1492–1776

One

Ancient America and Africa

This book opens by setting the scene for the intermingling of Europeans, Africans, and Native Americans in the New World, what Europeans called North and South America, by examining the backgrounds of the peoples of three continents and glimpsing the changes occurring with each of their many societies as the time for a historic convergence neared. This allows us to better understand the advent of colliding cultures among societies rimming the Atlantic Ocean. In narrating this historic meeting of societies previously distanced from each other, historians have too often portrayed Europeans reaching the Americas as the carriers of a superior culture that inevitably vanquished people living in a primitive if not "savage" state. Such a view renders Native Americans and Africans passive and static people—so much dough to be kneaded by advanced Europeans. Modern historical scholarship, however, tells us that Africans and Native Americans played critically important roles in a complex intercultural birthing of a "new world." Thus we examine the complexities of West African societies, delve into the societies of some of the peoples of North and South America, and study Western Europeans of the late fifteenth century. In drawing comparisons and contrasts, we equip ourselves to see three worlds meet as a new global age began.

The notion of the Pima people of the modern American Southwest as savages is distinctly at odds with the complexity conveyed in the excerpt from the ancient creation story below. Though they had no written language, the richness of their oral traditions refutes the notion that their culture or society was static. Further proof of this is found in the Dedanawida myth which describes the unification of the Iroquois into the Five Nations, whose constitution has much in common with the U.S. Constitution.

Duarte Barbosa found the same kind of complex and vibrant societies along the east coast of Africa in the sixteenth century. Though explorers such as Barbosa could often communicate their own preconceived ideas and prejudices in these kinds of travel accounts, their works provide crucial first-hand European impressions of Africans in the early stages of contact.

Pima Creation Story
(Traditional—Ancient)

The Pima lived in the Arizona desert along the Gila and Salt Rivers, a remote location that helped them resist European influence. They were named "Pima" in the fifteenth century by the Spanish, who later recorded their first narratives. However, no creation stories were transcribed until the early twentieth century when a Pima named Edward H. Wood met J. W. Lloyd at the Pan-American Fair in Buffalo and asked his help in preserving the legends of Wood's grand-uncle, Thin Leather. The Pima creation story describes a people who favored stability, settlement, and peace and whose artistic traditions were long and rich.

In the beginning there was no earth, no water—nothing. There was only a Person, Juh-wert-a-Mah-kai, "The Doctor of the Earth."

He just floated, for there was no place for him to stand upon. There was no sun, no light, and he just floated about in the darkness, which was Darkness itself.

He wandered around in the nowhere till he thought he had wandered enough. Then he rubbed on his breast and rubbed out moah-haht-tack, that is, perspiration, or "greasy earth." This he rubbed out on the palm of his hand and held out. It tipped over three times, but the fourth time it staid straight in the middle of the air and there it remains now as the world.

The first bush he created was the greasewood bush.

And he made ants, little tiny ants, to live on that bush, on its gum which comes out of its stem.

But these little ants did not do any good, so he created white ants, and these worked and enlarged the earth, and they kept on increasing it, larger and larger until it at last was big enough for himself to rest upon.

Then he created a Person. He made him out of his eye, out of the shadow of his eyes, to assist him, to be like him, and to help him in creating trees and human beings and everything that was to be on the earth.

The name of this being was Noo-ee—the buzzard.

Noo-ee was given all power, but he did not do the work he was created for. He did not care to help Juh-wert-a-Mah-kai, but let him go by himself.

And so The Doctor of the Earth himself created the mountains and everything that has seed and is good to eat. For if he had created human beings first they would have had nothing to live on.

DOCUMENT ANALYSIS

1. How does this creation story differ from the traditions of the Judeo-Christian experience?

2. What are three examples of other cultures' creation stories?

Dekanawida Myth and the Achievement of Iroquois Unity (ca. 1500s)

The document reproduced below is a translation of the story of Dekanawida, the great leader who founded the Iroquois Confederacy, or the Five Nations. Comprising the Mohawk, Onondaga, Seneca, Oneida, and Cayuga people, the Iroquois Confederacy went on to create the Iroquois Constitution, which many historians believe significantly influenced the U.S. Constitution. This story was handed down orally from generation to generation and was not written down until years later. Therefore, the date of its creation is only an estimate.

. . . North of the beautiful lake [Ontario] in the land of the Crooked Tongues, was a long winding bay and at a certain spot was the Huron town, Ka-ha-nah-yenh. Near by was the great hill, Ti-ro-nat-ha-ra-da-donh. In the village lived a good woman who had a virgin daughter. Now strangely this virgin conceived and her mother knew that she was about to bear a child. The daughter about this time went into a long sleep and dreamed that her child should be a son whom she should name Dekanawida. The messenger in the dream told her that he should become a great man and that he should go among the Flint people to live and that he should also go to the Many Hill Nation....

The Ongwe-oweh had fought long and bravely. So long had they fought that they became lustful for war and many times Endeka-Gakwa, the Sun, came out of the east to find them fighting. It was thus because the Ongwe-oweh were so successful that they said the Sun loved war and gave them power.

All the Ongwe-oweh fought other nations sometimes together and sometimes singly and, ah-gi! ofttimes they fought among themselves. The Nation of the Flint had little sympathy for the Nation of the Great Hill, and sometimes they raided one another's settlements. Thus did brothers and Ongwe-oweh fight. The nation of the Sunken Pole fought the Nation of the Flint and hated them, and the Nation of the Sunken Pole was Ongwe.

Because of bitter jealousy and love of bloodshed sometimes towns would send their young men against the young men of another town to practise them in fighting....

In those same days the Onondagas had no peace. A man's life was valued as nothing. For any slight offence a man or woman was killed by his enemy and in this manner feuds started between families and clans. At night none dared leave their doorways lest they be struck down by an enemy's war club. Such was the condition when there was no Great Law.

South of the Onondaga town lived an evil-minded man. His lodge was in a swale and his nest was made of bulrushes. His body was distorted by seven crooks and his long tangled locks were adorned by writhing living serpents. Moreover, this monster was a devourer of raw meat, even of human flesh. He was also a master of wizardry and by his magic he destroyed men but he could not be destroyed. Adodarhoh was the name of the evil man.

Notwithstanding the evil character of Adodarhoh the people of Onondaga, the Nation of Many Hills, obeyed his commands....

Dekanawida requested some of the Mohawk chiefs to call a council, so messengers were sent out among the people and the council was convened.

Dekanawida said, "I, with my co-worker, have a desire to now report what we have done on five successive midsummer days, of five successive years. We have obtained the consent of five nations. These are the Mohawks, the Oneidas, the Onondagas, the Cayugas, and the Senecas. Our desire is to form a compact for a union of our nations. Our next step is to seek out Adodarhoh. It is he who has always set at naught all plans for the establishment of the Great Peace. We must seek his fire and look for his smoke."...

The council heard the message and decided to go to Onondaga at midsummer.

Then Dekanawida taught the people the Hymn of Peace and the other songs. He stood before the door of the longhouse and walked before it singing the new songs. Many came and learned them so that many were strong by the magic of them when it was time to carry the Great Peace to Onondaga.

When the time had come, Dekanawida summoned the chiefs and people together and chose one man to sing the songs before Adodarhoh. Soon then this singer led the company through the forest and he preceded all, singing the Peace songs as he walked...

Then Dekanawida himself sang and walked before the door of Adodarhoh's house. When he finished his song he walked toward Adodarhoh and held out his hand to rub it on his body and to know its inherent strength and life. Then Adodarhoh was made straight and his mind became healthy.

When Adodarhoh was made strong in rightful powers and his body had been healed, Dekanawida addressed the three nations. He said, "We have now overcome a great obstacle. It has long stood in the way of peace. The mind of Adodarhoh is now made right and his crooked parts are made straight. Now indeed may we establish the Great Peace."

"Before we do firmly establish our union each nation must appoint a certain number of its wisest and purest men who shall be rulers, Rodiyaner. They shall be the advisers of the people and make the new rules that may be needful. These men shall be selected and confirmed by their female relations in whose lines the titles shall be hereditary. When these are named they shall be crowned, emblematically, with deer antlers.".…

Each chief then delivered to Dekanawida a string of lake shell wampum a span in length as a pledge of truth.

Dekanawida then said: "Now, today in the presence of this great multitude I disrobe you and you are not now covered by your old names. I now give you names much greater." Then calling each chief to him he said: "I now place antlers on your head as an emblem of your power. Your old garments are torn off and better robes are given you. Now you are Rodiyaner, each of you. You will receive many scratches and the thickness of your skins shall be seven spans. You must be patient and henceforth work in unity. Never consider your own interests but work to benefit the people and for the generations not yet born. You have pledged yourselves to govern yourselves by the laws of the Great Peace. All your authority shall come from it.".…

Then did Dekanawida repeat all the rules which he with Ayonhwatha had devised for the establishment of the Great Peace.

Then in the councils of all the Five Nations he repeated them and the Confederacy was established.

DOCUMENT ANALYSIS

1. What elements of this myth seem familiar to you?

2. How would leaders be chosen in this plan? Who had that power?

3. What was the power, or magic, that finally broke the hold of the evil Adodarhoh?

Duarte Barbosa, Excerpt from *A Description of the Coasts of East Africa and Malabar in the Beginning of the Sixteenth Century* (1518)

Duarte Barbosa was a cousin of Magellan who, like the famous explorer, often worked in the employ of the Spanish government. He remained in the Indian Ocean for sixteen years record- ing with great clarity the political, religious, ideological, military, economic, and social life of the region. His descriptions of the towns along the East African coast provide a unique view of the commercial vitality of the peoples living there at the beginning of the sixteenth century, including Africans (he calls them Gentiles), Moors (Muslims), Christians, and Indians.

Barbosa describes without apology the destruction of many Muslim towns along the coast and the slaughter of the inhabitants if they resisted. The Portuguese made these people captives and took their gold, silver, and other merchandise. His account of the Kingdom of "Benamatapa" in southern Africa is one of the few descriptions we have of the great power and wealth emanating from the gold-bearing regions in the interior and how they were directly connected through trade to the coast. *

SOFALA

Whereon is a town of the Moors called Sofala, close to which town the King of Portugal has a fort. These Moors established themselves there a long time ago on account of the great trade in gold which they carry on with the Gentiles of the mainland: these speak somewhat of bad Arabic (garabia), and have got a king over them, who is at present subject to the King of Portugal. And the mode of their trade is that they come by sea in small barks which they call zanbucs (sambuk), from the kingdoms of Quiloa, and Mombaza, and Melindi; and they bring much cotton cloth of many colours, and white and blue, and some of silk; and grey, and red, and yellow beads, which come to the

---

* From Duarte Barbosa, *A Description of the Coasts of East Africa and Malabar in the Beginning of the Sixteenth Century*, trans. Henry E. J. Stanley (London: The Hakluyt Society, 1866), pp. 4–15.

said kingdoms in other larger ships from the great kingdom of Cambay, which merchandise these Moors buy and collect from other Moors who bring them there, and they pay for them in gold by weight, and for a price which satisfies them; and the said Moors keep them and sell these cloths to the Gentiles of the kingdom of Benamatapa who come there laden with gold, which gold they give in exchange for the before mentioned cloths without weighing, and so much in quantity that these Moors usually gain one hundred for one. They also collect a large quantity of ivory, which is found all round Sofala, which they likewise sell in the great kingdom of Cambay at five or six ducats the hundred weight, and so also some amber, which these Moors of Sofala bring them from the Vciques. They are black men, and men of colour—some speak Arabic, and the rest make use of the language of the Gentiles of the country. They wrap themselves from the waist downwards with cloths of cotton and silk, and they wear other silk cloths above named, such as cloaks and wraps for the head, and some of them wear hoods of scarlet, and of other coloured woollen stuffs and camelets, and of other silks. And their victuals are millet, and rice, and meat, and fish....The Moors have now recently begun to produce much fine cotton in this country, and they weave it into white stuff because they do not know how to dye it, or because they have not got any colours; and they take the blue or coloured stuffs of Cambay and unravel them, and again weave the threads with their white thread, and in this manner they make coloured stuffs, by means of which they get much gold.

KINGDOM OF BENAMATAPA

On entering within this country of Sofala, there is the kingdom of Benamatapa, which is very large and peopled by Gentiles, whom the Moors call Cafers. These are brown men, who go bare, but covered from the waist downwards, with coloured stuffs, or skins of wild animals; and the persons most in honour among them wear some of the tails of the skin behind them, which go trailing on the ground for state and show....They carry swords in scabbards of wood bound with gold or other metals, and they wear them on the left hand side as we do, in sashes of coloured stuffs, which they make for this purpose with four or five knots, and their tassels hanging down, like gentlemen; and in their hands azagayes, and others carry bows and arrows: it must be mentioned that the bows are of middle size, and the iron points of the arrows are very large and well wrought. They are men of war, and some of them are merchants: their women go naked as long as they are girls, only covering their middles with cotton cloths, and when they are married and have children, they wear other cloths over their breasts.

ZINBAOCH

Leaving Sofala for the interior of the country, at xv days journey from it, there is a large town of Gentiles, which is called Zinbaoch; and it has houses of wood and straw, in which town the King of Benamatapa frequently dwells, and from there to the city of Benamatapa there are six days journey, and the road goes from Sofala, inland, towards the Cape of Good Hope. And in the said Benamatapa, which is a very large town, the king is used to make his longest residence; and it is thence that the merchants bring to Sofala the gold which they sell to the Moors without weighing it, for coloured stuffs and beads of Cambay, which are much used and valued amongst them; and the people of this city of Benamatapa say that this gold comes from still further off towards the Cape of Good Hope, from another kingdom subject to this king of Benamatapa, who is a great lord, and holds many other kings as his subjects, and many other lands, which extend far inland, both towards the Cape of Good Hope and towards Mozambich....

This king constantly takes with him into the field a captain, whom they call Sono, with a great quantity of men-at-arms, and amongst them they bring six thousand women, who also bear arms and fight. With these forces he goes about subduing and pacifying whatever kings rise up or desire to revolt. The said king of Benamatapa sends, each year, many honourable persons throughout his kingdoms to all the towns and lordships, to give them new regulations, so that all may do them obeisance....

ANGOY

After passing this river of Zuama, at XI leagues from it, there is a town of the Moors on the sea coast, which is called Angoy, and has a king, and the Moors who live there are all merchants, and deal in gold, ivory, silk, and cotton stuffs, and beads of Cambay, the same as do those of Sofala. And the Moors bring these goods from Quiloa, and Monbaza, and Melynde, in small vessels hidden from the Portuguese ships; and they carry from there a great quantity of ivory, and much gold. And in this town of Angos there are plenty of provisions of millet, rice, and some kinds of meat. These men are very brown and copper coloured; they go naked from the waist upwards, and from thence downwards, they wrap themselves with cloths of cotton and silk, and wear other cloths folded after the fashion of cloaks, and some wear caps and others hoods, worked with stuffs and silks; and they speak the language belonging to the country, which is that of the Pagans, and some of them speak Arabic. These people are sometimes in obedience to the king of Portugal, and at times they throw it off, for they are a long way off from the Portuguese forts.

MOZAMBIQUE ISLAND

Mozambique...has a very good port, and all the Moors touch there who are sailing to Sofala, Zuama, or Anguox. Amongst these Moors there is a sheriff, who governs them, and does justice. These are of the language and customs of the Moors of Anguox, in which island the King of Portugal now holds a fort, and keeps the said Moors under his orders and government. At this island the Portuguese ships provide themselves with water and wood, fish and other kinds of provisions; and at this place they refit those ships which stand in need of repair. And from this island likewise the Portuguese fort in Sofala draws its supplies, both of Portuguese goods and of the produce of India, on account of the road being longer by the mainland....

ISLAND OF QUILOA

There is another island close to the mainland, called Quiloa, in which there is a town of the Moors, built of handsome houses of stone and lime, and very lofty, with their windows like those of the Christians; in the same way it has streets, and these houses have got their terraces, and the wood worked in with the masonry, with plenty of gardens, in which there are many fruit trees and much water. This island has got a king over it, and from hence there is trade with Sofala with ships, which carry much gold, which is dispersed thence through all Arabia Felix, for henceforward all this country is thus named on account of the shore of the sea being peopled with many towns and cities of the Moors; and when the King of Portugal discovered this land, the Moors of Sofala, and Zuama, and Anguox, and Mozambique, were all under obedience to the King of Quiloa, who was a great king amongst them. And there is much gold in this town, because all the ships which go to Sofala touch at this island, both in going and coming back. These people are Moors, of a dusky colour, and some of them are black and some white; they are very well dressed with rich cloths of gold, and silk, and cotton, and the women also go very well dressed out with much gold and silver in chains and bracelets on their arms, and legs, and ears. The speech of these people is Arabic, and they have got books of the Alcoran, and honour greatly their prophet Muhamad. This King, for his great pride, and for not being willing to obey the King of Portugal, had this town taken from him by force, and in it they killed and captured many people, and the King fled from the island, in which the King of Portugal ordered a fortress to be built, and thus he holds under his command and government those who continued to dwell there.

ISLAND OF MOMBAZA

A city of the Moors, called Bombaza, [is] very large and beautiful, and built of high and handsome houses of stone and whitewash, and with very good streets, in the manner of those of Quiloa. And it also had a king over it. The people are of dusky white, and brown complexions, and likewise the women, who are much adorned with silk and gold stuffs. It is a town of great trade in goods, and has a good port, where there are always many ships, both of those that sail for Sofala and those that come from Cambay and Melinde, and others which sail to the islands of Zanzibar, Manfia, and Penda, which will be spoken of further on. This Monbaza is a country well supplied with plenty of provisions....The inhabitants at times are at war with the people of the continent, and at other times at peace, and trade with them, and obtain much honey and wax, and ivory. This King, for his pride and unwillingness to obey the King of Portugal, lost his city, and the Portuguese took it from him by force, and the King fled, and they killed and made captives many of his people, and the country was ravaged, and much plunder was carried off from it of gold and silver, copper, ivory, rich stuffs of gold and silk, and much other valuable merchandize.

MELINDE

This town has fine houses of stone and whitewash, of several stories, with their windows and terraces, and good streets. The inhabitants are dusky and black, and go naked from the waist upwards, and from that downwards they cover themselves with cloths of cotton and silk, and others wear wraps like cloaks, and handsome caps on their heads. The trade is great which they carry on in cloth, gold, ivory, copper, quicksilver, and much other merchandise, with both Moors and Gentiles of the kingdom of Cambay, who come to their port with ships laden with cloth, which they buy in exchange for gold, ivory, and wax. Both parties find great profit in this....This King and people have always been very friendly and obedient to the King of Portugal, and the Portuguese have always met with much friendship and good reception amongst them.

PENDA, MANFIA, AND ZANZIBAR

Between this island of San Lorenzo and the continent, not very far from it, are three islands, which are called one Manfia, another Zanzibar, and the other Penda; these are inhabited by Moors; they are very fertile islands, with plenty of provisions....They produce many sugar canes, but do not know how to make sugar. These islands have their kings. The inhabitants trade with the mainland with their provisions and fruits; they have small vessels, very loosely and badly made, without decks, and with a single mast; all their planks are sewn together with cords of reed or matting, and the sails are of palm mats. They are very feeble people, with very few and despicable weapons. In these islands they live in great luxury, and abundance; they dress in very good cloths of silk and cotton, which they buy in Mombaza of the merchants from Cambay, who reside there. Their wives adorn themselves with many jewels of gold from Sofala, and silver, in chains, ear-rings, bracelets, and ankle rings, and are dressed in silk stuffs: and they have many mosques, and hold the Alcoran of Mahomed.

DOCUMENT ANALYSIS

1. Based upon Barbosa's descriptions and comparisons, who might his audience have been?

2. Based upon Barbosa's descriptions, what can we discern about the lifestyles of the people of the east African coast? What are the similiarities and differences?

3. What role did Portugal play at this time in the areas Barbosa described?

Chapter Study Questions

1. What can we learn about people and cultures from studying their myths? What specifically can we learn about the Pima and the Iroquois by studying the myths presented in the first two selections?

2. Consider Duarte Barbosa's descriptions of the east African coast. How might his descriptions differ from those written by the people he observed? Why is it important to consider the perspective from which a person is writing as well as that person's intended audience?

3. What role do animals play in the Pima and Dekanawida selections? What is the role of magic?

4. Why would Barbosa include descriptions of people's styles of dress and housing? What might his readers have inferred from his descriptions?

Two

Europeans and Africans
Reach the Americas

W estern European monarchs were determined to find new sea routes to the East at the end of the fifteenth century. Inspired by the Portuguese voyages around Africa, the Spanish sponsored the voyage of Genoan mariner Christopher Columbus, who believed that sailing west would be a quicker and simpler way for Europeans to reach the markets of the East. Columbus's historic trip to the Caribbean was the advent of centuries of western colonization in the Americas. Columbus and subsequent Portuguese, Spanish, French, and English colonists arrived in a region very different from what they expected to find or what they had left at home across the Atlantic. Native Americans already populated much of the Americas, and for many of these peoples, the encounter with Europeans proved devastating. The documents in this chapter reveal some of the motivations and cultural biases of the European explorers and their countrymen.

Spain was the first European country to enjoy the political and economic power an expansive empire in the New World could provide. Undertaken under the banner of, "gold, glory and God," Spanish conquistadors in the sixteenth century conquered many of the richest regions of the New World and exploited natural wealth that would make Spain the greatest power in the world for almost three hundred years.

The first two selections in this chapter describe the reactions of Christopher Columbus and Alvar Núñez Cabeza de Vaca to the Americas and its inhabitants. They provide insight into the changing and varied treatment and perceptions of native peoples by early explorers. The third document, by the sixteenth-century cleric Bartolomé de Las Casas, is a brutal indictment of Spanish colonization which describes the indigenous peoples as "simple" and "delicate" and the conquistadors as "hungry wolves."

Father Jacques Marquette's account of his Mississippi expedition with Louis Joliet in 1673 provides a glimpse into the active French engagement in North America. Marquette's account also reflects the mix of imperial exploration and religious commitment that characterized much of European contact with what was, to them, a "new world."

The English came late to the game of colonization. Political and economic turmoil in the sixteenth century prevented England from focusing a national effort toward exploration. However, unlike in other western European nations, the drive for international expansion came from the private sector. Successful entrepreneurs, like the London merchant Thomas Mun, believed that the private and public sectors could jointly benefit from the wealth of the Americas. Excerpts from Thomas Mun's *England's Treasure by Foreign Trade* reveals some of the motivations for English settlement and some of the expectations and demands placed upon foreign trade.

Two.1

Christopher Columbus,
Letter to Luis de Sant' Angel
(1493)

In this letter to one of his leading supporters in the Spanish court, Christopher Columbus describes his reaction to the sights of the New World. He is describing the island of Hispaniola, present-day Haiti and the Dominican Republic. *

S^{ir},

As I know that you will have pleasure of the great victory which our Lord hath given me in my voyage, I write you this, by which you shall know that in [thirty-three] days I passed over the Indies with the fleet which the most illustrious King and Queen, our Lords, gave me: where I found very many islands peopled with inhabitants beyond number. And, of them all, I have taken possession for their Highnesses, with proclamation and the royal standard displayed; and I was not gainsaid. On the first which I found, I put the name Sant Salvador, in commemoration of His High Majesty, who marvelously hath given all this: the Indians call it [Guanhani]. The second I named the Island of Santa María de Concepción, the third Ferrandina, the fourth Fair Island, the fifth La Isla Juana; and so for each one a new name. When I reached Juana, I followed its coast westwardly, and found it so large that I thought it might be the mainland province of Cathay. And as I did not thus find any towns and villages on the seacoast, save small hamlets with the people whereof I could not get speech, because they all fled away forthwith, I went on further in the same direction, thinking I should not miss of great cities or towns. And at the end of many leagues, seeing that there was no change,…[I] turned back as far as a port agreed upon; from which I sent two men into the country to learn if there were a king, or any great cities. They traveled for three days, and found interminable small

---

* From Christopher Columbus's Letter to Luis de Sant' Angel, *Escribano de Racion of the Kingdom of Aragon*. Dated 15 February 1493. Reprinted in Facsimile, Translated and Edited from the Unique Copy of the Original Edition (London: 1891), 22–27.

villages and a numberless population, but nought of ruling authority; wherefore they returned.

I understood sufficiently from other Indians…that this land,…was an island; and so I followed its coast eastwardly for a hundred and seven leagues as far as where it terminated; from which headland I saw another island to the east [eighteen] leagues distant from this, to which I at once gave the name La Spanola. And I proceeded thither, and followed the northern coast, as with La Juana, eastwardly for a hundred and [eighty-eight] great leagues in a direct easterly course, as with La Juana.

The which, and all the others, are more [fertile] to an excessive degree, and this extremely so. In it, there are many havens on the seacoast, incomparable with any others that I know in Christendom, and plenty of rivers so good and great that it is a marvel. The lands thereof are high, and in it are very many ranges of hills, and most lofty mountains incomparably beyond the Island of [Tenerife]; all most beautiful in a thousand shapes, and all accessible, and full of trees of a thousand kinds, so lofty that they seem to reach the sky. And I am assured that they never lose their foliage; as may be imagined, since I saw them as green and as beautiful as they are in Spain during May.…

And the nightingale was singing, and other birds of a thousand sorts, in the month of November, round about the way I was going. There are palm trees of six or eight species, wondrous to see for their beautiful variety; but so are the other trees, and fruits, and plants therein. There are wonderful pine groves, and very large plains of verdure, and there is honey, and many kinds of birds, and many various fruits. In the earth there are many mines of metals; and there is a population of incalculable number. Spanola is a marvel; the mountains and hills, and plains, and fields, and land, so beautiful and rich for planting and sowing, for breeding cattle of all sorts, for building of towns and villages.

There could be no believing, without seeing, such harbors as are here, as well as the many and great rivers, and excellent waters, most of which contain gold. In the trees and fruits and plants, there are great differences from those of Juana. In [La Spanola], there are many spiceries, and great mines of gold and other metals.

The people of this island, and of all the others that I have found and seen, or not seen, all go naked, men and women, just as their mothers bring them forth; although some women cover a single place with the leaf of a plant, or a cotton something which they make for that purpose. They have no iron or steel, nor any weapons; nor are they fit thereunto; not be because they be not a well-formed people and of fair stature, but that they are most wondrously timorous. They have no other weapons than the stems of reeds in their seeding state, on the end of which they fix little sharpened stakes. Even these, they dare not use; for many times has it happened that I sent two or three men ashore to some village to parley, and countless numbers of them sallied forth, but as soon as they saw those approach, they fled away in such wise that even a father would not wait for his son. And this was not because any hurt had ever done to any of them:—but such they are, incurably timid. It is true that since they have become more assured, and are losing that terror, they are artless and generous with what they have, to such a degree as no one would believe but him who had seen it. Of anything they have, if it be asked for, they never say no, but do rather invite the person to accept it, and show as much lovingness as though they would give their hearts. And whether it be a thing of value, or one of little worth, they are straightways content with whatsoever trifle of whatsoever kind may be given them in return for it. I forbade that anything so worthless as fragments of broken platters, and pieces of broken glass, and strapbuckles, should be given them; although when they were able to get such things, they seemed to think they had the best jewel in the world....

And they knew no sect, nor idolatry; save that they all believe that power and goodness are in the sky, and they believed very firmly that I, with these ships and crew, came from the sky; and in such opinion, they received me at every place were I landed, after they had lost their terror. And this comes not because they are ignorant; on the contrary, they are men of very subtle wit, who navigate all those seas, and who give a marvellously good account of everything—but because they never saw men wearing clothes nor the like of our ships. And as soon as I arrived in the Indies, in the first island that I found, I took some of them by force to the intent that they should learn [our speech] and give me information of what there was in those parts. And so it was, that very soon they understood [us] and we them, what by speech or what by signs; and those [Indians] have been of much service...with loud cries of "Come! come to see the people from heaven!" Then, as soon as their minds were reassured about us, every one came, men as well as women, so that there remained none behind, big or little; and they all brought something to eat and drink, which they gave with wondrous lovingness....

It seems to me that in all those islands, the men are all content with a single wife; and to their chief or king they give as many as twenty. The women, it appears to me, do more work than the men. Nor have I been able to learn whether they held personal property, for it seemed to me that whatever one had, they all took share of, especially of eatable things. Down to the present, I have not found in those islands any monstrous men, as many expected, but on the contrary all the people are very comely; nor are they black like those in Guinea, but have flowing hair; and they are not begotten where there is an excessive violence of the rays of the sun....In those islands, where there are lofty mountains, the cold was very keen there, this winter; but they endured it by being accustomed thereto, and by the help of the meats which they eat with many and inordinately hot spices....

Since thus our Redeemer has given to our most illustrious King and Queen, and to their famous kingdoms, this victory in so high a matter, Christendom should take gladness therein and make great festivals, and give solemn thanks to the Holy Trinity for the great exaltation they shall have by the conversion of so many peoples to our holy faith; and next for the temporal benefit which will bring hither refreshment and profit, not only to Spain, to all Christians. This briefly, in accordance with the facts. Dated, on the caravel, off the Canary Islands, the 15 February of the year 1493.

DOCUMENT ANALYSIS

1. How does Columbus describe the reaction of the native peoples he encounters? Why do you think the native inhabitants of Hispaniola reacted to Columbus as they did?

2. Columbus writes that he has "taken possession" of these Caribbean islands. How

does this attitude contrast with the attitude toward ownership that Columbus found among the natives?

Álvar Núñez Cabeza de Vaca, "Indians of the Rio Grande" (1528–1536)

In 1528, half of the crew of the Spanish explorer Panfilo de Navarez was stranded in Florida. After sailing in makeshift vessels across the Gulf of Mexico, the crew was shipwrecked and enslaved by coastal peoples. After six years, Cabeza de Vaca, a black slave, Estevancio the Moor (referred to as "the negro" in this excerpt), and two others escaped and made the overland journey from Texas through the Southwest and south to Mexico City. In this selection from his journal, Cabeza de Vaca describes the native peoples and environment of what is now Texas and northern Mexico. *

They are so accustomed to running that, without resting or getting tired, they run from morning till night in pursuit of a deer, and kill a great many, because they follow until the game is worn out, sometimes catching it alive. Their huts are of matting placed over four arches. They carry them on their back and move every two or three days in quest of food; they plant nothing that would be of any use.

They are very merry people, and even when famished do not cease to dance and celebrate their feasts and ceremonials. Their best times are when "tunas" (prickly pears) are ripe, because then they have plenty to eat and spend the time in dancing and eating day and night. As long as these tunas last they squeeze and open them and set them to dry. When dried they are put in baskets like figs and kept to be eaten on the way. The peelings they grind and pulverize.

All over this country there are a great many deer, fowl and other animals which I have before enumerated. Here also they come up with cows; I have seen them thrice and have eaten their meat. They appear to me of the size of those in Spain. Their horns are small, like those of the Moorish cattle; the hair is very long, like fine wool and like a pea-

* From *The Journal of Álvar Núñez Cabeza de Vaca and His Companions from Florida to the Pacific*, 1528–1536, in *His Own Narrative*, ed. A. F. Bandelier (New York: A. S. Barnes & Company, 1905), 91, 94, 108, 143–145, 149–151, 167–168.

jacket; some are brownish and others black, and to my taste they have better and more meat than those from here. Of the small hides the Indians make blankets to cover themselves with, and of the taller ones they make shoes and targets. These cows come from the north, across the country further on, to the coast of Florida, and are found all over the land for over four hundred leagues. On this whole stretch, through the valleys by which they come, people who live there descend to subsist upon their flesh. And a great quantity of hides are met with inland.

We remained with the Avavares Indians for eight months, according to our reckoning of the moons. During that time they came for us from many places and said that verily we were children of the sun. Until then Donates and the negro had not made any cures, but we found ourselves so pressed by the Indians coming from all sides, that all of us had to become medicine men. I was the most daring and reckless of all in undertaking cures. We never treated anyone that did not afterwards say he was well, and they had such confidence in our skill as to believe that none of them would die as long as we were among them....

The women brought many mats, with which they built us houses, one for each of us and those attached to him. After this we would order them to boil all the game, and they did it quickly in ovens built by them for the purpose. We partook of everything a little, giving the rest to the principal man among those who had come with us for distribution among all. Every one then came with the share he had received for us to breathe on it and bless it, without which they left it untouched. Often we had with us three to four thousand persons. And it was very tiresome to have to breathe on and make the sign of the cross over every morsel they ate or drank. For many other things which they wanted to do they would come to ask our permission, so that it is easy to realize how greatly we were bothered. The women brought us tunas, spiders, worms, and whatever else they could find, for they would rather starve than partake of anything that had not first passed through our hands.

While traveling with those, we crossed a big river coming from the north and, traversing about thirty leagues of plains, met a number of people that came from afar to meet us on the trail, who treated us like the foregoing ones.

Thence on there was a change in the manner of reception, insofar as those who would meet us on the trail with gifts were no longer robbed by the Indians of our company, but after we had entered their homes they tendered us all they possessed, and the dwellings also. We turned over everything to the principals for distribution. Invariably those who had been deprived of their belongings would follow us, in order to repair their losses, so that our retinue became very large. They would tell them to be careful and not conceal anything of what they owned, as it could not be done without our knowledge, and then we would cause their death. So much did they frighten them that on the first few days after joining us they would be trembling all the time, and would not dare to speak or lift their eyes to Heaven.

Those guided us for more than fifty leagues through a desert of very rugged mountains, and so arid that there was no game. Consequently we suffered much from lack of food, and finally forded a very big river, with its water reaching to our chest. Thence on many of our people began to show the effects of the hunger and hardships they had undergone in those mountains, which were extremely barren and tiresome to travel.

The next morning all those who were strong enough came along, and at the end of three journeys we halted. Alonso del Castillo and Estevanico, the negro, left with the women as guides, and the woman who was a captive took them to a river that flows between mountains where there was a village in which her father lived, and these were the first adobes we saw that were like unto real houses. Castillo and Estevanico went to these and, after holding parley with the Indians, at the end of three days Castillo returned to where he had left us, bringing with him five or six of the Indians. He told how he had found permanent houses, inhabited, the people of which ate beans and squashes, and that he had also seen maize.

Of all things upon earth that caused us the greatest pleasure, and we gave endless thanks to our Lord for this news. Castillo also said that the negro was coming to meet us on the way, near by, with all the people of the houses. For that reason we started, and after going a league and a half met the negro and the people that came to receive us, who gave us beans and many squashes to eat, gourds to carry water in, robes of cowhide, and other things. As those people and the Indians of our company were enemies, and did not understand each other, we took leave of the latter, leaving them all that had been given to us, while we went on with the former and, six leagues beyond, when night was already approaching, reached their houses, where they received us with great ceremonies. Here we remained one day, and left on the next, taking them with us to other permanent houses, where they subsisted on the same food also, and thence on we found a new custom....

Having seen positive traces of Christians and become satisfied they were very near, we gave many thanks to our Lord for redeeming us from our sad and gloomy condition. Anyone can imagine our delight when he reflects how long we had been in that land, and how many dangers and hardships we had suffered. That night I entreated one of my companions to go after the Christians, who were moving through the part of the country pacified and quieted by us, and who were three days ahead of where we were. They did not like my suggestion, and excused themselves from going, on the ground of being tired and worn out, although any of them might have done it far better than I, being younger and stronger.

Seeing their reluctance, in the morning I took with me the negro and eleven Indians and, following the trail, went in search of the Christians. On that day we made ten leagues, passing three places where they slept. The next morning I came upon four Christians on horseback, who, seeing me in such a strange attire, and in company with Indians, were greatly startled. They stared at me for quite awhile, speechless; so great was their surprise that they could not find words to ask me anything. I spoke first, and told them to lead me to their captain, and we went together to Diego de Alcaraz, their commander.

DOCUMENT ANALYSIS

1. From what Cabeza de Vaca describes, how did the native peoples he encountered view the Catholic Church?

2. What kinds of foods does Cabeza de Vaca find popular among the native peoples he meets?

Two.3

Bartolomé de Las Casas, "Of the Island of Hispaniola" (1542)

This extract from Las Casas's Very Brief Account of the Destruction of the Indies *describes the island of Hispaniola (present-day Dominican Republic and Haiti), the island Columbus described in his letter to Luis de Sant' Angel. Las Casas wrote this gory and explosive account in 1542 to be read at a forum on Spanish colonization called by the Holy Roman Emperor Charles V. Widely translated, this account gave rise to a flood of anti-Spanish and anti-Catholic propaganda throughout Europe deriding the Spanish settlement of the Americas.** *

God has created all these numberless people to be quite the simplest, without malice or duplicity, most obedient, most faithful to their natural Lords, and to the Christians, whom they serve; the most humble, most patient, most peaceful and calm, without strife nor tumults; not wrangling, nor querulous, as free from uproar, hate and desire of revenge as any in the world....

Among these gentle sheep, gifted by their Maker with the above qualities, the Spaniards entered as soon as they knew them, like wolves, tiger and lions which had been starving for many days, and since forty years they have done nothing else; nor do they afflict, torment, and destroy them with strange and new, and divers kinds of cruelty, never before seen, nor heard of, nor read of....

The Christians, with their horses and swords and lances, began to slaughter and practice strange cruelty among them. They penetrated into the country and spared neither children nor the aged, nor pregnant women, nor those in child labour, all of whom they ran through the body and lacerated, as though they were assaulting so many lambs herded in their sheepfold.

They made bets as to who would slit a man in two, or cut off his head at one blow: or they opened up his bowels. They tore the babes from their mothers' breast by the feet,

---

* From Bartolomé de Las Casas, *Very Brief Account of the Destruction of the Indies*, in *Bartolomé de Las Casas*, trans. F. A. McNutt (Cleveland: Arthur H. Clark, 1909), 313–319.

and dashed their heads against the rocks. Others they seized by the shoulders and threw into the rivers, laughing and joking, and when they fell into the water they exclaimed: "boil body of so and so!" They spitted the bodies of other babes, together with their mothers and all who were before them, on their swords.

They made a gallows just high enough for the feet to nearly touch the ground, and by thirteens, in honour and reverence of our Redeemer and the twelve Apostles, they put wood underneath and, with fire, they burned the Indians alive.

They wrapped the bodies of others entirely in dry straw, binding them in it and setting fire to it; and so they burned them. They cut off the hands of all they wished to take alive, made them carry them fastened on to them, and said: "Go and carry letters": that is; take the news to those who have fled to the mountains.

They generally killed the lords and nobles in the following way. They made wooden gridirons of stakes, bound them upon them, and made a slow fire beneath; thus the victims gave up the spirit by degrees, emitting cries of despair in their torture....

Document Analysis

1. How do you account for the Spanish treatment of the native peoples that de Las Casas describes?

Jacques Marquette, from
The Mississippi Voyage of Joliet and Marquette (1673)

*Father Jacques Marquette, a Jesuit priest, and Louis Joliet, a seasoned French explorer, set out in 1673 to explore the Mississippi River. Joliet's journals were lost, but Father Marquette's account of their groundbreaking journey provides an upbeat and revealing account of the lands they visited and the natives they met along the way. In this excerpt from Marquette's journal, he describes their encounter with the Illinois.** *

On the 25th of June, we perceived on the water's edge some tracks of men, and a narrow and somewhat beaten path leading to a fine prairie….We silently followed the narrow path, and, after walking about two leagues, we discovered a village on the bank of a river, and two others on a hill distant about half a league from the first. Then we heartily commended ourselves to God, and, after imploring His aid, we went farther without being perceived, and approached so near that we could even hear the savages talking. We therefore decided that it was time to reveal ourselves. This we did by shouting with all our energy, and stopped, without advancing any farther. On hearing the shout, the savages quickly issued from their cabins, and having probably recognized us as Frenchmen, especially when they saw a black gown—or, at least, having no cause for distrust, as we were only two men, and had given them notice of our arrival—they deputed four old men to come and speak to us. Two of these bore tobacco-pipes, finely ornamented and adorned with various feathers. They walked slowly, and raised their pipes toward the sun, seemingly offering them to it to smoke, without, however, saying a word….Finally, when they had drawn near, they stopped to consider us attentively. I was reassured when I observed these ceremonies, which with them are performed only among friends; and much more so when I saw them clad in cloth, for I judged thereby that they were our allies. I therefore spoke to them first, and

* From R. G. Thwaites, Jesuit Relations and Allied Documents, LIX. Accessed from Wisconsin Historical Society Digital Library and Archives, www.wisconsinhistory.org.

asked them who they were. They replied that they were Ilinois; and, as a token of peace, they offered us their pipes to smoke....These pipes for smoking tobacco are called in this country *calumets*.

At the door of the cabin in which we were to be received was an old man, who await-ed us in a rather Surprising attitude, which constitutes a part of the ceremonial that they observe when they receive strangers. This man stood erect, and stark naked, with his hands extended and lifted toward the sun, as if he wished to protect himself from its rays, which nevertheless shone upon his face through his fingers. When we came near him, he paid us this compliment: "How beautiful the sun is, O Frenchman, when thou comest to visit us! All our village awaits thee, and thou shalt enter all our cabins in peace." Having said this, he made us enter his own, in which were a crowd of people; they devoured us with their eyes, but, nevertheless, observed profound silence....

After we had taken our places, the usual civility of the country was paid to us, which consisted in offering us the calumet. This must not be refused, unless one wishes to be considered an enemy, or at least uncivil; it suffices that one make a pretense of smoking. While all the elders smoked after us, in order to do us honor, we received an invitation on behalf of the great captain of all the Ilinois to proceed to his village where he wished to hold a council with us....

When we reached the village of the great captain, we saw him at the entrance of his cabin, between two old men, all three [upright] and naked, and holding their calumet turned toward the sun....He afterward offered us his calumet, and made us smoke while we entered his cabin, where we received all their usual kind attentions.

Seeing all assembled and silent, I spoke to them by four presents that I gave them. By the first, I told them that we were journeying peacefully to visit the nations dwelling on the river as far as the sea. By the second, I announced to them that God, who had cre-ated them, had pity on them, inasmuch as, after they had so long been ignorant of Him, He wished to make himself known to all the peoples; that I was sent by Him for that purpose; and that it was for them to acknowledge and obey Him. By the third, I said that the great captain of the French informed them that he it was who restored peace every-where; and that he had subdued the Iroquois. Finally, by the fourth, we begged them to give us all the information that they had about the sea, and about the nations through whom we must pass to reach it.

When I had finished my speech, the captain arose, and,...he spoke thus: "I thank thee, black gown, and thee, O Frenchman," addressing himself to Monsieur Jollyet, "for having taken so much trouble to come to visit us. Never has the earth been so beautiful, or the sun so bright, as to-day; never has our river been so calm, or so clear of rocks, which your canoes have removed in passing; never has our tobacco tasted so good, or our corn appeared so fine, as we now see them. Here is my son, whom I give thee to show thee my heart. I beg thee to have pity on me, and on all my nation. It is thou who knowest the great Spirit who has made us all. It is thou who speakest to Him, and who hearest His word. Beg Him to give me life and health, and to come and dwell with us, in order to make us know Him."

...When one speaks the word "Ilinois," it is as if one said in their language, "the men," as if the other savages were looked upon by them merely as animals. It must also be admitted that they have an air of humanity which we have not observed in the other nations that we have seen upon our route....

They are active and very skillful with bows and arrows. They also use guns, which they buy from our savage allies who trade with our French. They use them especially to inspire, through their noise and smoke, terror in their enemies; the latter do not use guns, and have never seen any, since they live too far toward the west. They are warlike, and make themselves dreaded by the distant tribes to the south and west, whither they go to procure slaves; these they barter, selling them at a high price to other nations, in exchange for other wares. Those very distant savages against whom they war have no knowledge of Europeans....

DOCUMENT ANALYSIS

1. How did the Illinois natives respond to the sudden arrival of Joliet and Marquette in their community? Did their reaction surprise you?

2. What role did religion play in Joliet and Marquette's expedition, and how did the Illinois respond to their religious message?

Thomas Mun, from
England's Treasure by Foreign Trade (1664)

Thomas Mun was a successful London merchant who served as one of the directors of the East India Company. In the late sixteenth and early seventeenth centuries most of the English ventures into the New World were capitalized by joint-stock companies like the East India Company. Mun's treatise, England's Treasure by Foreign Trade, *describes the idea merchant, the theory of mercantilism, and emphasizes the importance of a favorable balance of trade in order to enhance the wealth of a nation.**

The Qualities which are required in a perfect Merchant of Foreign Trade

The Love and service of our Country consisteth not so much in the knowledge of those duties which are to be performed by others, as in the skillful practice of that which is done by our selves; and therefore it is now fit that I say something of the Merchant...for the Merchant is worthily called the Steward of the Kingdoms Stock, by way of Commerce with other Nations; a work of no less Reputation than Trust, which ought to be performed with great skill and conscience, that so the private gain may ever accompany the publique good....I will briefly set down the excellent qualities which are required of a perfect Merchant.

1. He ought to be a good Penman, a good Arithmetician, and a good Accomptant, by that noble order of Debtor and Creditor, which is used only amongst Merchants; also to be expert in the order and form of Charter-parties, Bills of Lading, Invoyces, Contracts, Bills of Exchange, and Policies of Ensurance.

2. He ought to know the Measures, Weights, and Monies of all forraign Countries, especially where we have Trade, & the Monies not onely by their several denom-

---

* From Thomas Mun, *England's Treasure by Foreign Trade*, in *Early English Tracts on Commerce*, ed. J. R. McCulloch (Cambridge: University Press, 1954), 121–126, 134–141.

inations, but also by their intrinsique values in weight & fineness, compared with the Standard of this Kingdom, without which he cannot well direct his affaires.

3. He ought to know the Customs, Tools, Taxes, Impositions, Conducts and other charges upon all manner of Merchandize exported or imported to and from the said Forraign Countries.

4. He ought to know in what several commodities each Country abounds, and what be the wares which they want, and how and from whence they are furnished with the same.

5. He ought to understand, and to be a diligent observer of the rates of Exchanges by Bills, from one State to another, whereby he may the better direct his affairs, and remit over and receive home his Monies to the most advantage possible.

6. He ought to know what goods are prohibited to be exported or imported in the said forraign Countreys, lest otherwise he should incur great danger and loss in the ordering of his affairs.

7. He ought to know upon what rates and conditions to fraight his Ships, and ensure his adventures from one Countrey to another, and to be well acquainted with the laws, orders and customes of the Ensurance office both here and beyond the Seas, in the many accidents which may happen upon the damage or loss of Ships and goods, or both these.

8. He ought to have knowledge in the goodness and in the prices of all the several materials which are required for the building and repairing of Ships, and the divers workmanships of the same, as also for the Masts, Tackling, Cordage, Ordnance, Victuals, Munition, and Provisions of many kinds; together with the ordinary wages of Commanders, Officers, and Mariners, all which concern the Merchant as he is an Owner of Ships.

9. He ought (by the divers occasions which happen sometimes in the buying and selling of one commodity and sometimes in another) to have indifferent if not perfect knowledge in all manner of Merchandize or wares, which is to be as it were a man of all occupations and trades.

10. He ought by his voyaging on the Seas to become skilful in the Art of Navigation.

11. He ought, as he is a Traveller, and sometimes abiding in forraign Countreys, to attain to the speaking of divers Languages, and to be a diligent observer of the ordinary Revenues and expences of forraign Princes, together with their strength both by Sea and Land, their laws, customes, policies, manners, religions, arts, and the like; to be able to give account thereof in all occasions for the good of his Countrey.

12. Lastly, although there be no necessity that such a Merchant should be a great Scholar; yet it is (at least) required, that in his youth he learn the Latine tongue, which will the better enable him in all the rest of his endeavours.

The Means to Enrich this Kingdom, and to Encrease Our Treasure

The ordinary means therefore to increase our wealth and treasure is by Forraign Trade, wherein wee must ever observe this rule; to sell more to strangers yearly than wee consume of theirs in value. For suppose that when this Kingdom is plentifully served with the Cloth, Lead, Tinn, Iron, Fish and other native commodities, we doe yearly export the overplus to forraign Countreys to the value of twenty two hundred thousand pounds; by which means we are enable beyond the Seas to buy and bring in forraign wares for our use and Consumptions, to the value of twenty hundred thousand pounds.

The Exportation of our Moneys in Trade of Merchandize in a Means to Encrease our Treasure.

If we have such a quantity of wares as doth fully provide us of all things needful from beyond the seas: why should we then doubt that our monys sent out in trade, must not necessarily come back again in treasure; together with the great gains which it may procure in such manner as is before set down? And on the other side, if those Nations which send out their monies do it because they have but few wares of their own, how come they then to have so much Treasure as we ever see in those places which suffer it freely to be exported at all times and by whomsoever? I answer, Even by trading with their Moneys; for by what other means can they get it, having no Mines of Gold or Silver?

DOCUMENT ANALYSIS

1. Describe some of the key qualities Mun believes important for a trade merchant.
2. Based upon Mun's list of qualities, how difficult do you think it was to be a successful merchant of foreign trade?

Chapter Study Questions

1. Compare the Marquette, Cabeza de Vaca, and Columbus descriptions of the indigenous peoples they encountered. What do their descriptions reveal about their preconceptions of the New World and about the values of their own cultures?

2. Discuss the reactions of Columbus and Cabeza de Vaca to the physical environment of the New World. How did it compare to what they left behind in Europe?

3. Are Las Casas's descriptions of Native Americans more reliable than those of the early explorers? Could he be exploiting the sufferings of Native Americans for his own ends?

4. How did Native Americans approach the Europeans? How did they communicate?

5. What were the European expectations of the New World? Is there evidence that the goals of the French, the Spanish, and the English were different?

Three

Colonizing a Continent in the Seventeenth Century

Within a hundred years of the first settlement in Virginia, England had established colonies along much of the North American coastline. As seen in your text, these settlements fostered the transplantation of immigrants, whose colonial societies were shaped by their European traditions and the environment of the New World. Many came voluntarily, motivated by hopes and dreams of political, social, and economic opportunities. Others came forcibly: enslaved Africans were brought to the Americas from the countries of western Africa to fill the labor needs of the southern colonies.

Captain John Smith's history of Virginia describes the "starving times" in the colony's early history. By 1676, Virginia had developed a distinct lifestyle, a prominent feature of which was the ownership of the best land by a small group of planters. Under the leadership of Governor William Berkeley, these planters dominated the political and economic life of the colony. Later arrivals to the colony were forced to settle further inland in a more hostile and less fertile environment. Realizing the inequity of their situation and believing that they had little support from the colonial government, their frustrations came to a head in an attempt to take control of the colony. The Declaration from Bacon's Rebellion details these settlers' specific grievances and challenges to the authority of colonial rule. It is an important example of the tensions that developed throughout the colonies between the frontier and coastal regions.

Massachusetts was intended to be, in John Winthrop's words, "a city upon a hill." Winthrop envisioned a perfect Christian community that could serve as a model society for the rest of the world. Some who came to Massachusetts, however, had such ardent religious opinions that they challenged the peace of the colony. One of those was Anne Hutchinson, who was put on trial and banished for being a "dangerous" presence in the community. The economic success of the colony all but doomed its religious mission: the colony's growth and prosperity made it difficult for citizens to focus on maintaining a closed Christian community, a situation exacerbated by an influx of non-Puritans, which diverted attention from religion to money.

The next few documents contrast voluntary and involuntary servitude in the colonies. In the seventeenth century, indentured servants were considered the best way to meet labor demands in the southern colonies. These young men and women were generally landless Europeans who agreed to work for a set period (usually five to seven years) in return for their transportation to America. The first Africans were brought to the Virginia colony in 1619 but it wasn't until later in the seventeenth century that black African slaves began to replace white indentured servants as field labor. By the 1660s, though, slavery had become institutionalized in Virginia and Maryland, and in the South, slaves had largely replaced indentured servants by the eighteenth century.

Life was difficult for indentured servants, who were often badly treated by their masters. In *Journey to Pennsylvania in the Year 1750 and Return to Germany in the Year 1754*, Gottlieb Mittelberger narrates the horror of the trans-Atlantic trip and how the end of the journey brought further terror as servants were auctioned off. Elizabeth Sprigs describes her own experiences in her letter home. Sprigs conveys the dreadful loneliness and physical hardships endured by indentured servants.

But difficult as life was for indentured servants, they lived with the knowledge that their bondage was not permanent and that, eventually, freedom could be achieved. This was not the case for African slaves. *The Interesting Narrative of the Life of Olaudah Equiano* describes the horrors of the "middle passage" and enslavement from the points of view of an Ibo child who later bought himself out of slavery.

Three.1

John Smith, "The Starving Time" (1624)

Early colonists endured hard times indeed. Captain John Smith had an extraordinary career as a soldier of fortune, adventurer, and explorer, and within a short time after colonists arrived in Virginia, he became their acknowledged leader. In 1624, he wrote a history of Virginia. This document is from a section called "The Starving Time," which relates the period just after Smith returned to England in 1609. Smith refers to himself in the third person in this account. Note the reference to Pocahontas. *

It might well be thought, a Countrie so faire (as Virginia is) and a people so tractable, would long ere this have beene quietly possessed to the satisfaction of the adventurers, & the eternizing of the memory of those that effected it. But because all the world doe see a defailement; this following Treatise shall give satisfaction to all indifferent Readers, how the businesse hath bin carried; where no doubt they will easily understand and answer to their question, how it came to passe there was no better speed and successe in those proceedings....

The day before Captain Smith returned for England with the ships, Captain Davis arrived in a small Pinace, with some sixteene proper men more...for the Salvages no sooner understood Smith was gone, but they all revolted, and did spoile and murther all they incountered. Now wee were all constrained to live onely on that Smith had onely for his owne Companie, for the rest had consumed their proportions...Sicklemore upon the confidence of Powhatan, with about thirtie others as carelesse as himselfe, were all slaine, onely Jeffrey Shortridge escaped, and Pokahontas the Kings daughter saved a boy called Henry Spilman, that lived many yeeres after, by her meanes, amongst the Patawomekes....Now we all found the losse of Captain Smith, yea his greatest maligners could now curse his losse: as for corne, provision and contribution from the Salvages,

* From John Smith, *The Generall Historie of Virginia, New England and the Summer Isles*, vol. I (Glasgow: James MacLehoge and Sons, 1907).

we had nothing but mortall wounds, with clubs and arrowes; as for our Hogs, Hens, Goats, Sheepe, Horse, or what lived, our commanders, officers & Salvages daily consumed them, some small proportions sometimes we tasted, till all was devoured; then swords, armes, pieces, or any thing, wee traded with the Salvages, whose cruell fingers were so oft imbrewed in our blouds, that what by their crueltie, our Governours indiscretion, and the losse of our ships, of five hundred within six moneths after Captain Smiths departure, there remained not past sixtie men, women and children, most miserable and poore creatures; and those were preserved for the most part, by roots, herbes, acornes, walnuts, berries, now and then a little fish: they that had startch in these extremities, made no small use of it; yea, even the very skinnes of our horses. Nay, so great was our famine, that a Salvage we slew, and buried, the poorer sort tooke him up againe and eat him, and so did divers one another boyled and stewed with roots and herbs: And one amongst the rest did kill his wife, powdered [salted] her, and had eaten part of her before it was knowne, for which hee was executed, as hee well deserved; now whether shee was better roasted, boyled or carbonado'd [grilled], I know not, but of such a dish as powdered wife I never heard of. This was that time, which still to this day we called the starving time; it were too vile to say, and scarce to be beleeved, what we endured.

DOCUMENT ANALYSIS

1. How does this vivid account by Smith compare with your previous sense of early life in colonial Virginia?

2. Who or what do you think was to blame for the severity of the conditions endured by Virginia colonists during the so-called "starving time"?

Three.2

Bacon's Rebellion: The Declaration (1676)

In 1676, tobacco planters in western Virginia, considered by the authorities in Jamestown to be a backward bunch, requested permission to lead an expedition—a thinly disguised land grab— against the Susquehannock Indians, who had been sporadically attacking settlements nearby. The autocratic royal governor, Sir William Berkeley, who had led Virginia for over thirty years, refused. In response, the frontiersmen, led by Nathaniel Bacon, raised a force of five hundred and marched against not only the Susquehannock but also Governor Berkeley. After burning Jamestown and slaughtering many Indians, Bacon became ill and died in October 1676. Shortly after, British troops arrived and order was restored in the colony. In this declaration, note the broad range of grievances the frontierspeople have and how they appeal in the name of the king in England to justify their actions. *

1. For having, upon specious pretenses of public works, raised great unjust taxes upon the commonalty for the advancement of private favorites and other sinister ends, but no visible effects in any measure adequate; for not having, during this long time of his government, in any measure advanced this hopeful colony either by fortifications, towns, or trade.

2. For having abused and rendered contemptible the magistrates of justice by advancing to places of judicature scandalous and ignorant favorites.

3. For having wronged his Majesty's prerogative and interest by assuming monopoly of the beaver trade and for having in it unjust gain betrayed and sold his Majesty's country and the lives of his loyal subjects to the barbarous heathen.

4. For having protected, favored, and emboldened the Indians against his Majesty's

* From "Declaration of Nathaniel Bacon in the Name of the People of Virginia, July 30, 1676," in *Foundations of Colonial America: A Documentary History, Southern Colonies*, ed. Keith Kavenagh (New York: Chelsea House Publishers, 1973), 1783–1784.

loyal subjects, never contriving, requiring, or appointing any due or proper means of satisfaction for their many invasions, robberies, and murders committed upon us.

5. For having, when the army of English was just upon the track of those Indians, who now in all places burn, spoil, murder and when we might with ease have destroyed them who then were in open hostility, for then having expressly countermanded and sent back our army by passing his word for the peaceable demeanor of the said Indians, who immediately prosecuted their evil intentions, committing horrid murders and robberies in all places, being protected by the said engagement and word past of him the said Sir William Berkeley, having ruined and laid desolate a great part of his Majesty's country, and have now drawn themselves into such obscure and remote places and are by their success so emboldened and confirmed by their confederacy so strengthened that the cries of blood are in all places, and the terror and consternation of the people so great, are now become not only difficult but a very formidable enemy who might at first with ease have been destroyed.

6. And lately, when, upon the loud outcries of blood, the assembly had, with all care, raised and framed an army for the preventing of further mischief and safeguard of this his Majesty's colony.

7. For having, with only the privacy of some few favorites without acquainting the people, only by the alteration of a figure, forged a commission, by we know not what hand, not only without but even against the consent of the people, for the raising and effecting civil war and destruction, which being happily and without bloodshed prevented; for having the second time attempted the same, thereby calling down our forces from the defense of the frontiers and most weakly exposed places.

8. For the prevention of civil mischief and ruin amongst ourselves while the barbarous enemy in all places did invade, murder, and spoil us, his Majesty's most faithful subjects.

Of this and the aforesaid articles we accuse Sir William Berkeley as guilty of each and every one of the same, and as one who has traitorously attempted, violated, and injured his Majesty's interest here by a loss of a great part of this his colony and many of his faithful loyal subjects by him betrayed and in a barbarous and shameful manner exposed to the incursions and murder of the heathen. And we do further declare these the ensuing persons in this list to have been his wicked and pernicious councilors, confederates, aiders, and assisters against the commonalty in these our civil commotions.

Sir Henry Chichley	Richard Whitacre
Lt. Col. Christopher Wormeley	Nicholas Spencer
Phillip Ludwell	Joseph Bridger
Robt. Beverley	William Claiburne, Jr.
Ri. Lee	Thomas Hawkins
Thomas Ballard	William Sherwood
William Cole	John Page Clerke
	John Clauffe Clerk

John West, Hubert Farrell, Thomas Reade, Math. Kempe

And we do further demand that the said Sir William Berkeley with all the persons in this list be forthwith delivered up or surrender themselves within four days after the notice hereof, or otherwise we declare as follows.

That in whatsoever place, house, or ship, any of the said persons shall reside, be hid, or protected, we declare the owners, masters, or inhabitants of the said places to be confederates and traitors to the people and the estates of them is also of all the aforesaid persons to be confiscated. And this we, the commons of Virginia, do declare, desiring a firm union amongst ourselves that we may jointly and with one accord defend ourselves against the common enemy. And let not the faults of the guilty be the reproach of the innocent, or the faults or crimes of the oppressors divide and separate us who have suffered by their oppressions.

These are, therefore, in his Majesty's name, to command you forthwith to seize the persons abovementioned as traitors to the King and country and them to bring to Middle Plantation and there to secure them until further order, and, in case of opposition, if you want any further assistance you are forthwith to demand it in the name of the people in all the counties of Virginia.

Nathaniel Bacon

General by Consent of the people.
William Sherwood

DOCUMENT ANALYSIS

1. Does the list of grievances described here seem sufficient to justify a colonial revolt?

2. How do you think Governor Berkeley might have dismissed each of these charges?

Three.3

John Winthrop,
"A Model of Christian Charity"
(1630)

John Winthrop, a Cambridge-trained lawyer, was the leader of the group of about a thousand Puritans who settled Massachusetts Bay in 1630. Unlike the Virginians, or perhaps learning from their experience, the Massachusetts settlers arrived with structures of government and social order already established. They founded what became a successful and growing colony. This famous document is a sermon written on board the Arabella *and delivered to the Puritans on the eve of their settlement of Massachusetts Bay.* *

God almighty in His most holy and wise providence hath so disposed of the condition of mankind, as in all times some must be rich, some poor, some high and eminent in power and dignity, others mean and in subjection.

Reason: First, to hold conformity with the rest of His works, being delighted to show forth the glory of His wisdom in the variety and difference of the creatures and the glory of His power, in ordering all these differences for the preservation and good of the whole.

Reason: Secondly, that He might have the more occasion to manifest the work of His spirit. First, upon the wicked in moderating and restraining them, so that the rich and mighty should not eat up the poor, nor the poor and despised rise up against their superiors and shake off their yoke. Secondly, in the regenerate in exercising His graces in them, as in the great ones, their love, mercy, gentleness, temperance, etc., in the poor and inferior sort, their faith, patience, obedience, etc.

Reason: Thirdly, that every man might have need of other, and from hence they might all be knit more nearly together in the bond of brotherly affection. From hence it appears plainly that no man is made more honorable than another, or more wealthy, etc., out of any particular and singular respect to himself, but for the glory of his creator and the common good of the creature, man.

* From *Winthrop Papers: Volume 11, 1623–1630* (The Massachusetts Historical Society, 1931).

Thus stands the cause between God and us. We are entered into covenant with Him for this work, we have taken out a commission, the Lord hath given us leave to draw our own articles we have professed to enterprise these actions upon these and these ends, we have hereupon besought Him of favor and blessing. Now if the Lord shall please to hear us, and bring us in peace to the place we desire, then hath He ratified this covenant and sealed our commission, [and] will expect a strict performance of the articles contained in it, but if we shall neglect the observations of these articles which are the ends we have propounded, and dissembling with our God, shall fall to embrace this present world and prosecute our carnal intentions seeking great things for ourselves and our posterity, the Lord will surely break out in wrath against us, be revenged of such a perjured people, and make us know the price of the breach of such a covenant.

Now the only way to avoid this shipwreck and to provide for our posterity is to follow the counsel of Micah, to do justly, to love mercy, to walk humbly with our God. For this end we must be knit together in this work as one man, we must entertain each other in brotherly affection, we must be willing to abridge ourselves of our superfluities for the supply of others' necessities, we must uphold a familiar commerce together in all meekness, gentleness, patience, and liberality, we must delight in each other, make others' conditions our own, rejoice together, mourn together, labor and suffer together, always having before our eyes our commission and community in the work, our community as members of the same body. So shall we keep the unity of the spirit in the bond of peace. The Lord will be our God and delight in all our ways, so that we shall see much more of His wisdom, power, goodness, and truth than formerly we have been acquainted with. We shall find that the God of Israel is among us, when ten of us shall be able to resist a thousand of our enemies, when He shall make us a praise and glory, that men shall say of succeeding plantations, the Lord make it like that of New England. For we must consider that we shall be as a city upon a hill, the eyes of all people are upon us. So that if we shall deal falsely with our God in this work we have undertaken and so cause Him to withdraw His present help from us, we shall be made a story and byword throughout the world, we shall open the mouths of enemies to speak evil of the ways of God and all professors for God's sake, we shall shame the faces of many of God's worthy servants, and cause their prayers to be turned into curses upon us till we be consumed out of the good land whither we are going. And to shut up this discourse with that exhortation of Moses, that faithful servant of the Lord in His last farewell to Israel, Deut. 30., Beloved there is now set before us life and good, death and evil, in that we are commanded this day to love the Lord our God, and to love one another, to walk in His ways and to keep His commandments and His ordinance, and His laws, and the articles of our covenant with Him that we may live and be multiplied, and that the Lord our God my bless us in the land whither we go to possess it. But if our hearts shall turn away so that we will not obey, but shall be seduced and worship other Gods, our pleasures, our profits, and serve them, it is propounded unto us this day we shall surely perish out of the good land whither we pass over this vast sea to possess it. Therefore let us choose life, that we, and our seed, may live, and by obeying His voice, and cleaving to Him, for He is our life and our prosperity.

DOCUMENT ANALYSIS

1. What does Winthrop imply would be the consequences should these early Puritans fail to lead devout lives in the new Massachusetts Bay Colony?

2. Does the notion of creating a "city upon a hill" appeal to you? Why, or why not?

Excerpt from the Trial of Anne Hutchinson (1637)

One of the challenges faced by the Puritan authorities in Massachusetts Bay Colony was how, as dissenters themselves from the Church of England, they should handle dissenters within their theocratic community. In the 1630s, Governor John Winthrop and Puritan leaders chose to banish outspoken Separatist Roger Williams (who then founded Rhode Island), and also banished the devout Anne Hutchinson, who challenged local religious authorities and did not accept a secondary social role as a woman. Hutchinson led religious discussions in her home, publicly condemned some of Boston's most famous clergymen as deficient, and, at her banishment trial, claimed that she received direct revelation from God.*

Gov. John Winthrop: Mrs. Hutchinson, you are called here as one of those that have troubled the peace of the commonwealth and the churches here; you are known to be a woman that hath had a great share in the promoting and divulging of those opinions that are the cause of this trouble, and to be nearly joined not only in affinity and affection with some of those the court had taken notice of and passed censure upon, but you have spoken divers things, as we have been informed, very prejudicial to the honour of the churches and ministers thereof, and you have maintained a meeting and an assembly in your house that hath been condemned by the general assembly as a thing not tolerable nor comely in the sight of God nor fitting for your sex, and notwithstanding that was cried down you have continued the same. Therefore we have thought good to send for you to understand how things are, that if you be in an erroneous way we may reduce you that so you may become a profitable member here among us. Otherwise if you be obstinate in your course that then the court may take such course that you may trouble us no further. Therefore I would intreat you to express whether you do assent and hold in practice to those opinions and factions that have been handled in court already, that is to say, whether you do not justify Mr. Wheelwright's

* From Transcript of Trial at Court at Newton, 1637, online at www.annehutchinson.com.

sermon and the petition....Why do you keep such a meeting at your house as you do every week upon a set day?

Mrs. Anne Hutchinson: It is lawful for me to do so, as it is all your practices, and can you find a warrant for yourself and condemn me for the same thing? The ground of my taking it up was, when I first came to this land because I did not go to such meetings as those were, it was presently reported that I did not allow of such meetings but held them unlawful and therefore in that regard they said I was proud and did despise all ordinances. Upon that a friend came unto me and told me of it and I to prevent such aspersions took it up, but it was in practice before I came. Therefore I was not the first.

Gov. John Winthrop: ...By what warrant do you continue such a course?

Mrs. Anne Hutchinson: I conceive there lies a clear rule in Titus that the elder women should instruct the younger and then I must have a time wherein I must do it....

If you please to give me leave I shall give you the ground of what I know to be true. Being much troubled to see the falseness of the constitution of the Church of England, I had like to have turned Separatist. Whereupon I kept a day of solemn humiliation and pondering of the thing; this scripture was brought unto me—he that denies Jesus Christ to be come in the flesh is antichrist. This I considered of and in considering found that the papists did not deny him to be come in the flesh, nor we did not deny him—who then was antichrist? Was the Turk antichrist only? The Lord knows that I could not open scripture; he must by his prophetical office open it unto me. So after that being unsatisfied in the thing, the Lord was pleased to bring this scripture out of the Hebrews. He that denies the testament denies the testator, and in this did open unto me and give me to see that those which did not teach the new covenant had the spirit of antichrist, and upon this he did discover the ministry unto me; and ever since, I bless the Lord, he hath let me see which was the clear ministry and which the wrong.

Since that time I confess I have been more choice and he hath left me to distinguish between the voice of my beloved and the voice of Moses, the voice of John the Baptist and the voice of antichrist, for all those voices are spoken of in scripture. Now if you do condemn me for speaking what in my conscience I know to be truth I must commit myself unto the Lord.

Mr. Nowel (assistant to the Court): How do you know that was the spirit?

Mrs. Anne Hutchinson: How did Abraham know that it was God that bid him offer his son, being a breach of the sixth commandment?

Dep. Gov. Thomas Dudley: By an immediate voice.

Mrs. Anne Hutchinson: So to me by an immediate revelation.

Dep. Gov. Thomas Dudley: How! an immediate revelation.

Mrs. Anne Hutchinson: By the voice of his own spirit to my soul. I will give you another scripture, Jeremiah 46: 27–28—out of which the Lord showed me what he would do for me and the rest of his servants. But after he was pleased to reveal himself to me I did presently, like Abraham, run to Hagar. And after that he did let me see the atheism of my own heart, for which I begged of the Lord that it might not remain in my heart, and being thus, he did show me this (a twelvemonth after) which I told you of before....

Therefore, I desire you to look to it, for you see this scripture fulfilled this day and therefore I desire you as you tender the Lord and the church and commonwealth to consider and look what you do.

You have power over my body but the Lord Jesus hath power over my body and soul; and assure yourselves thus much, you do as much as in you lies to put the Lord Jesus Christ from you, and if you go on in this course you begin, you will bring a curse upon you and your posterity, and the mouth of the Lord hath spoken it....

Gov. John Winthrop: I am persuaded that the revelation she brings forth is delusion...

The court hath already declared themselves satisfied concerning the things you hear, and concerning the troublesomeness of her spirit and the danger of her course amongst us, which is not to be suffered....

Mrs. Hutchinson, the sentence of the court you hear is that you are banished from out of our jurisdiction as being a woman not fit for our society, and are to be imprisoned till the court shall send you away.

Mrs. Anne Hutchinson: I desire to know wherefore I am banished?

Gov. John Winthrop: Say no more. The court knows wherefore and is satisfied.

DOCUMENT ANALYSIS

1. What sense do you get of Anne Hutchinson's religious zeal from this transcript excerpt? Why do you think such zeal was considered "dangerous" by Winthrop and others on the court?

2. When, after sentencing, Hutchinson asks why she is being banished, what does this query suggest about her attitude toward Governor Winthrop and the court?

Gottlieb Mittelberger,
The Passage of Indentured Servants
(1750)

*Gottlieb Mittelberger was an indentured servant from Germany who worked in Pennsylvania, where he served as a schoolmaster and organist. After only four years, he returned to Germany. The following is a detailed and graphic account of the trans-Atlantic journey and the fate that awaited indentured servants upon arrival in North America.**

Both in Rotterdam and in Amsterdam the people are packed densely, like herrings so to say, in the large sea-vessels. One person receives a place of scarcely 2 feet width and 6 feet length in the bedstead, while many a ship carries four to six hundred souls; not to mention the innumerable implements, tools, provisions, water-barrels and other things which likewise occupy such space.

On account of contrary winds it takes the ships sometimes 2, 3, and 4 weeks to make the trip from Holland to…England. But when the wind is good, they get there in 8 days or even sooner. Everything is examined there and the custom-duties paid, whence it comes that the ships ride there 8, 10 or 14 days and even longer at anchor, till they have taken in their full cargoes. During that time every one is compelled to spend his last remaining money and to consume his little stock of provisions which had been reserved for the sea; so that most passengers, finding themselves on the ocean where they would be in greater need of them, must greatly suffer from hunger and want. Many suffer want already on the water between Holland and Old England.

When the ships have for the last time weighed their anchors near the city of Kaupp [Cowes] in Old England, the real misery begins with the long voyage. For from there the ships, unless they have good wind, must often sail 8, 9, 10 to 12 weeks before they reach Philadelphia. But even with the best wind the voyage lasts 7 weeks.

But during the voyage there is on board these ships terrible misery, stench, fumes, hor-

* From Gottlieb Mittelberger, *Journey to Pennsylvania in the Year 1750 and Return to Germany in the Year 1754*, trans. Carl Theo Eben (Philadelphia: John Jos. McVey, n.d.).

ror, vomiting, many kinds of sea-sickness, fever, dysentery, headache, heat, constipation, boils, scurvy, cancer, mouth rot, and the like, all of which come from old and sharply salted food and meat, also from very bad and foul water, so that many die miserably.

Add to this want of provisions, hunger, thirst, frost, heat, dampness, anxiety, want, afflictions and lamentations, together with other trouble, as…the lice abound so frightfully, especially on sick people, that they can be scraped off the body. The misery reaches the climax when a gale rages for 2 or 3 nights and days, so that every one believes that the ship will go to the bottom with all human beings on board. In such a visitation the people cry and pray most piteously.

Children from 1 to 7 years rarely survive the voyage. I witnessed…misery in no less than 32 children in our ship, all of whom were thrown into the sea. The parents grieve all the more since their children find no resting-place in the earth, but are devoured by the monsters of the sea.

That most of the people get sick is not surprising, because, in addition to all other trials and hardships, warm food is served only three times a week, the rations being very poor and very little. Such meals can hardly be eaten, on account of being so unclean. The water which is served out of the ships is often very black, thick and full of worms, so that one cannot drink it without loathing, even with the greatest thirst. Toward the end we were compelled to eat the ship's biscuit which had been spoiled long ago; though in a whole biscuit there was scarcely a piece the size of a dollar that had not been full of red worms and spiders' nests.…

At length, when, after a long and tedious voyage, the ships come in sight of land, so that the promontories can be seen, which the people were so eager and anxious to see, all creep from below on deck to see the land from afar, and they weep for joy, and pray and sing, thanking and praising God. The sight of the land makes the people on board the ship, especially the sick and the half dead, alive again, so that their hearts leap within them; they shout and rejoice, and are content to bear their misery in patience, in the hope that they may soon reach the land in safety. But alas!

When the ships have landed at Philadelphia after their long voyage, no one is permitted to leave them except those who pay for their passage or can give good security; the others, who cannot pay, must remain on board the ships till they are purchased, and are released from the ships by their purchasers. The sick always fare the worst, for the healthy are naturally preferred and purchased first; and so the sick and wretched must often remain on board in front of the city for 2 or 3 weeks, and frequently die, whereas many a one, if he could pay his debt and were permitted to leave the ship immediately, might recover and remain alive.

The sale of human beings in the market on board the ship is carried out thus: Every day Englishmen, Dutchmen and High-German people come from the city of Philadelphia and other places, in part from a great distance, say 20, 30, or 40 hours away, and go on board the newly arrived ship that has brought and offers for sale passengers from Europe, and select among the healthy persons such as they deem suitable for their business, and bargain with them how long they will serve for their passage money, which most of them are still in debt for. When they have come to an agreement, it happens that adult persons bind themselves in writing to serve 3, 4, 5 or 6 years for the amount due by them, according to their age and strength. But very young people, from 10 to 15 years, must serve till they are 21 years old.

Many parents must sell and trade away their children like so many head of cattle; for if their children take the debt upon themselves, the parents can leave the ship free and unrestrained; but as the parents often do not know where and to what people their children are going, it often happens that such parents and children, after leaving the ship, do not see each other again for many years, perhaps no more in all their lives....

It often happens that whole families, husband, wife and children, are separated by being sold to different purchasers, especially when they have not paid any part of their passage money.

When a husband or wife has died a sea, when the ship has made more than half of her trip, the survivor must pay or serve not only for himself or herself but also for the deceased.

When both parents have died over half-way at sea, their children, especially when they are young and have nothing to pawn or pay, must stand for their own and their parents' passage, and serve till they are 21 years old. When one has served his or her term, he or she is entitled to a new suit of clothes at parting; and if it has been so stipulated, a man gets in addition a horse, a woman, a cow. When a serf has an opportunity to marry in this country, he or she must pay for each year which he or she would have yet to serve, 5 or 6 pounds.

DOCUMENT ANALYSIS

1. Describe the conditions aboard ship described by Mittelberger.

2. For those who arrived safely in America as indentured servants, what awaited them?

Elizabeth Sprigs, Letter to Her Father (1756)

This letter was written by Elizabeth Sprigs, an indentured servant in Maryland, to her father in England. It is clear that conditions for indentured servants had not improved much in the more than 100 years since Richard Freethorne wrote from Virginia to his parents. Note how Sprigs compares her treatment to that of "Negroes."*

Maryland, Sept'r 22'd 1756

Honred Father

My being for ever banished from your sight, will I hope pardon the Boldness I now take of troubling you with these, my long silence has been purely owning to my undutifullness to you, and well knowing I had offended in the highest Degree, put a tie to my tongue and pen, for fear I should be extinct from your good Graces and add a further Trouble to you, but too well knowing your care and tenderness for me so long as I retain'd my Duty to you, induced me once again to endeavor if possible, to kindle up that flame again. O Dear Father, believe what I am going to relate the words of truth and sincerity, and Balance my former bad Conduct my sufferings here, and then I am sure you'll pity your Destress Daughter, What we unfortunate English People suffer here is beyond the probability of you in England to Conceive, let it suffice that I one of the unhappy Number, am toiling almost Day and Night, and very often in the Horses drudgery, with only this comfort that you Bitch you do not halfe enough, and then tied up and whipp'd to that Degree that you'd not serve an Animal, scarce any thing but Indian Corn and Salt to eat and that even begrudged nay many Negroes are better

* From Elizabeth Sprigs, "Letter to Mr. John Sprigs in White Cross Street near Cripple Gate, London," September 22, 1756. Reprinted by permission of the Connecticut Chapter of the National Society of Colonial Dames of America.

used, almost naked no shoes nor stockings to wear, and the comfort after slaving during Masters pleasure, what rest we can get is to rap ourselves up in a Blanket and ly upon the Ground, this is the deplorable Condition your poor Betty endures, and now I beg if you have any Bowels of Compassion left show it by sending me some Relief, Clothing is the principal thing wanting, which if you should condiscend to, may easily send them to me by any of the ships bound to Baltimore Town Patapsco River Maryland, and give me leave to conclude in Duty to you and Uncles and Aunts, and Respect to all Friends

Honored Father

Your undutifull and Disobedient Child
Elizabeth Sprigs

DOCUMENT ANALYSIS

1. What complaints does Elizabeth Sprigs make to her father about her condition as an indentured servant in Maryland?

Three.7

Olaudah Equiano, The Middle Passage (1788)

This is a selection from the autobiography of Olaudah Equiano (or Gustavus Vassa), who was brought to Barbados, Virginia, and, later, England from his home West Africa in the early eighteenth century. He was able to purchase his freedom in England and became an abolitionist. His autobiography was written to describe the inhumanity of slavery as part of his abolitionist activities. These passages describe the middle passage and Equiano's experiences as a slave in Virginia. *

. . . The first object which saluted my eyes when I arrived on the coast was the sea, and a slave ship, which was then riding at anchor, and waiting for its cargo. These filled me with astonishment, which was soon converted into terror when I was carried on board. I was immediately handled and tossed up to see if I were sound by some of the crew; and I was now persuaded that I had gotten into a world of bad spirits, and that they were going to kill me. Their complexions too differing so much from ours, their long hair, and the language they spoke, (which was very different from any I had ever heard) united to confirm me in this belief. Indeed such were the horrors of my views and fears at the moment, that, if ten thousand worlds had been my own, I would have freely parted with them all to have exchanged my condition with that of the meanest slave in my own country. When I looked round the ship too and saw a large furnace of copper boiling, and a multitude of black people of every description chained together, every one of their countenances expressing dejection and sorrow, I no longer doubted of my fate; and, quite overpowered with horror and anguish, I fell motionless on the deck and fainted. When I recovered a little I found some black people about me, who I believe were some of those who brought me on board, and had been receiving their pay; they talked to me in order to cheer me, but all in vain. I asked them if we were not to be

* From *The Interesting Narrative of the Life of Olaudah Equiano, or Gustavus Vassa the African: Written by Himself* (New York, 1791).

eaten by those white men with horrible looks, red faces, and loose hair. They told me I was not; and one of the crew brought me a small portion of spirituous liquor in a wine glass; but, being afraid of him, I would not take it out of his hand. One of the blacks therefore took it from him and gave it to me, and I took a little down my palate, which, instead of reviving me, as they thought it would, threw me into the greatest consternation at the strange feeling it produced, having never tasted any such liquor before. Soon after this the blacks who brought me on board went off, and left me abandoned to despair. I now saw myself deprived of all chance or returning to my native country or even the least glimpse of hope of gaining the shore, which I now considered as friendly; and I even wished for my former slavery in preference to my present situation, which was filled with horrors of every kind, still heightened by my ignorance of what I was to undergo. I was not long suffered to indulge my grief; I was soon put down under the decks, and there I received such a salutation in my nostrils as I had never experienced in my life: so that, with the loathsomeness of the stench, and crying together, I became so sick and low that I was not able to eat, nor had I the least desire to taste anything. I now wished for the last friend, death, to relieve me; but soon, to my grief, two of the white men offered me eatables; and, on my refusing to eat, one of them held me fast by the hands, and laid me across I think the windlass, and tied my feet, while the other flogged me severely. I had never experienced anything of this kind before; and although, not being used to the water, I naturally feared that element the first time I saw it, yet nevertheless, could I have got over the nettings, I would have jumped over the side, but I could not; and, besides, the crew used to watch us very closely who were not chained down to the decks, lest we should leap into the water: and I have seen some of these poor African prisoners most severely cut for attempting to do so, and hourly whipped for not eating. This indeed was often the case with myself. In a little time after, amongst the poor chained men, I found some of my own nation, which in a small degree gave ease to my mind. I inquired of these what was to be done with us; they gave me to understand we were to be carried to these white people's country to work for them. I then was a little revived, and thought, if it were no worse than working, my situation was not so desperate: but still I feared I should be put to death, the white people looked and acted, as I thought, in so savage a manner; for I had never seen among any people such instances of brutal cruellty; and this not only shewn towards us blacks, but also to some of the whites themselves. One white man in particular I saw when we were permitted to be on deck, flogged so unmercifully with a large rope near the foremast, that he died in consequence of it; and they tossed him over the side as they would have done a brute. This made me fear these people the more; and I expected nothing less than to be treated in the same manner. I could not help expressing my fears and apprehensions to some of my countrymen: I asked them if these people had no country, but lived in this hollow place (the ship): they told me they did not, but came from a distant one. "Then," said I, "how comes it in all our country we never heard of them?" They told me because they lived so very far off. I then asked where were their women? had they any like themselves? "and why," said I, "do we not see them?" they answered, because they were left behind....

The stench of the hold while we were on the coast was so intolerably loathsome, that it was dangerous to remain there for any time, and some of us had been permitted to stay on the deck for the fresh air; but now that the whole ship's cargo were confined together, it became absolutely pestilential. The closeness of the place, and the heat of the climate, added to the number in the ship, which was so crowded that each had scarcely room to turn himself, almost suffocated us. This produced copious perspirations, so that the air soon became unfit for respiration, from a variety of loathsome smells, and brought on a sickness among the slaves, of which many died, thus falling victims to the improvident avarice, as I may call it, of their purchasers. This wretched situation was again aggravated by the galling of the chains, now become insupportable; and the filth of the necessary tubs, into which the children often fell, and were almost suffocated. The shrieks of the women, and the groans of the dying, rendered the whole a scene of horror almost inconceivable. Happily perhaps for myself I was soon reduced so low here that it was thought necessary to keep me almost always on deck; and from my extreme youth I was not put in fetters. In this situation I expected every hour to share the fate of my companions, some of whom were almost daily brought upon deck at the point of death, which I began to hope would soon put an end to my miseries. Often did I think many of the inhabitants of the deep much more happy than myself. I envied them the freedom they enjoyed, and as often wished I could change my condition for theirs. Every circumstance I met with served only to render my state more painful, and heighten my apprehensions, and my opinion of the cruelty of the whites. One day they had taken a number of fishes; and when they had killed and satisfied themselves with as many as they thought fit, to our astonishment who were on the deck, rather than give any of them to us to eat as we expected, they tossed the remaining fish into the sea again, although we begged and prayed for some as well as we could, but in vain; and some of my countrymen, being pressed by hunger, took an opportunity, when they thought no one saw them, of trying to get a little privately; but they were discovered, and the attempt procured them some very severe floggings....

...I and some few more slaves, that were not saleable amongst the rest, from very much fretting, were shipped off in a sloop for North America....While I was in this plantation [in Virginia] the gentleman, to whom I suppose the estate belonged, being unwell, I was one day sent for to his dwelling house to fan him; when I came into the room where he was I was very much affrighted at some things I saw, and the more so as I had seen a black woman slave as I came through the house, who was cooking the dinner, and the poor creature was cruelly loaded with various kinds of iron machines; she had one particularly on her head, which locked her mouth so fast that she could scarcely speak; and could not eat nor drink. I was much astonished and shocked at this contrivance, which I afterwards learned was called the iron muzzle...

DOCUMENT ANALYSIS

1. How does Equiano react when placed aboard the slave ship? Why does he not commit suicide by jumping overboard into the ocean?

2. What were the conditions aboard the slave ship? How do you account for the behavior of the ship's crew as described by Equiano?

Chapter Study Questions

1. Many Virginians came to the colony after reading extravagant claims about the opportunities and virtues of life there. How might this have affected their adjustment to life in the colonies?

2. In what ways was life in Virginia different from life in the Massachusetts Bay Colony?

3. Is there anything in Winthrop's sermon that might foreshadow Anne Hutchinson's banishment from Massachusetts?

4. Compare the treatment of indentured servants and slaves on the passage to the New World.

5. What effect did indentured servitude and slavery have on families?

6. What does Elizabeth Sprigs's letter reveal about the growing institutionalization of slavery and racism in North America?

Four

The Maturing
of Colonial Society

The interaction of European people and culture with the wilderness of the Americas produced a new culture and a new people, which we identify as American. Your text shows that this transformation was not always easy. In a vast land with few people, forced lifetime servitude of African slaves had its financial benefits, but it also had its drawbacks. In colonial South Carolina, an early uprising known as the Stono Rebellion made it clear that many African slaves would not accept their situation, but could and would resort to violence to attain their freedom. This contributed to the character of the southern colonies and later states. William Byrd, II, a member of the Virginia gentry, reveals his desperate attempt to become an English gentleman in his diary while Michel-Guillaume-Jean de Crèvecoeur, a French immigrant who settled in New York State, embraced his lot as a new "American." Taken together, Byrd and Crèvecoeur illustrate how individuals grappled with leaving their Old World cultures behind and accepting the new cultures and customs of the New World.

The religious revivals of the early eighteenth century also served to shaped American society. The Great Awakening not only rekindled religious enthusiasm in the colonies, it served as a common and unifying experience for Americans. Three documents in this section describe the religious revivalism that swept the East. Benjamin Franklin describes the preaching of the famous English evangelist George Whitefield. American Jonathan Edwards' famous sermon "Sinners in the Hands of an Angry God" is an example of this fantastic jeremiad genre.

On the Statue of Liberty, erected in 1886, the words of the poet Emma Lazarus ("Give me your tired, your poor, your huddled masses...") celebrate the United States as the refuge for the world's dispossessed. An early attempt to provide such a refuge here was the establishment of the colony of Georgia in 1732, the brainchild of a British social reformer, James Oglethorpe. In Oglethorpe's vision, Georgia would provide great benefits to those who settled there as well as to England itself.

Four.1

William Bull, Report on the Stono Rebellion (1739)

By the early 1700s, African slaves made up a majority of the population of colonial South Carolina. These slaves provided valuable labor, especially on sugar and rice plantations. But such a majority meant great potential risk of a slave revolt, and the Stono Rebellion of 1739 showed the lurking danger of this forced servitude. Here, Lieutenant Governor William Bull reports back to England on the Stono Rebellion and how it was put down.*

M y Lords,

I beg leave to lay before your Lordships an account of our Affairs, first in regard to the Desertion of our Negroes....On the 9th of September last at Night a great Number of Negroes Arose in Rebellion, broke open a Store where they got arms, killed twenty one White Persons, and were marching the next morning in a Daring manner out of the Province, killing all they met and burning several Houses as they passed along the Road. I was returning from Granville County with four Gentlemen and met these Rebels at eleven o'clock in the forenoon and fortunately deserned the approaching danger time enough to avoid it, and to give notice to the Militia who on the Occasion behaved with so much expedition and bravery, as by four a'Clock the same day to come up with them and killed and took so many as put a stop to any further mischief at that time, forty four of them have been killed and Executed; some few yet remain concealed in the Woods expecting the same fate, seem desperate....

It was the Opinion of His Majesty's Council with several other Gentlemen that one of the most effectual means that could be used at present to prevent such desertion of our Negroes is to encourage some Indians by a suitable reward to pursue and if possible to

* From UK Crown Copyright: Public Record Office; accessed online at
www.pbs.org/wgbh/aia/part1/1h311t.html.

bring back the Deserters, and while the Indians are thus employed they would be in the way ready to intercept others that might attempt to follow and I have sent for the Chiefs of the Chickasaws living at New Windsor and the Catawbaw Indians for that purpose....

My Lords,
Your Lordships Most Obedient and Most Humble Servant
Wm Bull

DOCUMENT ANALYSIS

1. Based upon Bull's account, what happened during the Stono Rebellion?
2. How were nearby Indian tribes to be brought into service in the attempt to keep slaves from escaping in the future?

William Byrd II, Diary
(1709)

William Byrd II of Westover, Virginia was a prime example of a "new American." Byrd was a member of the American gentry, but spent his life in a desperate attempt to live up to his own conception of an English gentleman. He compulsively ordered his life in an attempt to reflect the lifestyle of the English gentry he had only read about. He had to fashion himself a gentleman literally by the book. Naturally, this produced a somewhat skewed image of what it meant to be a British gentleman. Moreover, the realities of life in the colonies were far different from those in England, guaranteeing Byrd's quest to be quixotic at best. In fact, unknown to himself, he represented something entirely new—an American gentleman.*

7. I rose at 5 o'clock and read a chapter in Hebrew and some Greek in Josephus. I said my prayers and ate milk for breakfast. I danced my dance, and settled my accounts. I read some Latin. It was extremely hot. I ate stewed mutton for dinner. In the afternoon it began to rain and blow very violently so that it blew down my fence. It likewise thundered. In all the time I have been in Virginia I never heard it blow harder. I read Latin again and Greek in Homer. In the evening we took a walk in the garden. I said my prayers and had good health, good humor, and good thoughts, thanks be to God Almighty.

8. I rose at 5 o'clock and read a chapter in Hebrew and some Greek in Josephus. I said my prayers and ate milk for breakfast. I danced my dance. I read some Latin. Tom returned from Williamsburg and brought me a letter from Mr. Bland which told me the wine came out very well. I ate nothing but pudding for dinner. In the afternoon I read some more Latin and Greek in Homer. Then I took a walk about the plantation. I said my prayers and had good health, good thoughts, and good humor, thanks be to God Almighty.

* From William Byrd, *The Secret Diary of William Byrd of Westover*, 1709–1712, eds. Louis B. Wright and Marion Tinling (Richmond, VA: Dietz Press, 1941).

9. I rose at 5 o'clock and read two chapters in Hebrew and some Greek in Josephus. I said my prayers and ate milk and apples for breakfast with Captain Wilcox who called here this morning. I danced my dance. I wrote a letter to England and read some Latin. I ate roast chicken for dinner. In the afternoon I saluted my wife and took a nap. I read more Latin and Greek in Homer. Then I took a walk about the plantation. I neglected to say my prayers. I had good health, good thoughts, and good humor, thanks be to God Almighty.

DOCUMENT ANALYSIS

1. Why would it have been virtually impossible for an indentured servant in Virginia to have written diary entries similar to those of Byrd's?

2. Based on these diary entries, what, if anything, impresses you about Byrd's approach to life?

Michel-Guillaume-Jean de Crèvecoeur, from
Letters from an American Farmer
(1782)

Michel-Guillaume-Jean de Crèvecoeur (1735–1813) was born in Caen, Normandy. In 1755, he migrated to French Canada, where he served with the French in the French and Indian War against the British. While serving under Montcalm in the defense of Quebec, Crèvecoeur was wounded and hospitalized. He made his way to New York, where he worked as an Indian trader and surveyor. Eventually, he married and began a new life as a farmer in Orange County, New York, where he lived as "an American farmer" from 1769 to 1780. His American is a mixture of European cultures, changed by contact with the wilderness. *

He [an "enlightened Englishman" on first seeing America] is arrived on a new continent; a modern society offers itself to his contemplation, different from what he had hitherto seen. It is not composed, as in Europe, of great lords who possess everything, and of a herd of people who have nothing. Here are no aristocratical families, no courts, no kings, no bishops, no ecclesiastical dominion, no invisible power giving to a few a very visible one, no great manufacturers employing thousands, no great refinements of luxury. The rich and the poor are not so far removed from each other as they are in Europe....

The next wish of this traveller will be to know whence came all these people? They are a mixture of English, Scotch, Irish, French, Dutch, Germans, and Swedes. From this promiscuous breed, that race now called Americans have arisen....

What then is the American, this new man? He is either an European, or the descendant of an European, hence that strange mixture of blood, which you will find in no other country. I could point out to you a family whose grandfather was an Englishman, whose wife was Dutch, whose son married a French woman, and whose present four sons have now four wives of different nations. He is an American, who, leaving behind him all his ancient prejudices and manners, receives new ones from the new mode of life

---

* From Michel-Guillaume-Jean de Crèvecoeur, *Letters from an American Farmer* (New York, 1782).

he has embraced, the new government he obeys, and the new rank he holds....The Americans were once scattered all over Europe; here they are incorporated into one of the finest systems of population which has ever appeared, and which will hereafter become distinct by the power of the different climates they inhabit....

But to return to our back settlers. I must tell you, that there is something in the proximity of the woods, which is very singular. It is with men as it is with the plants and animals that grow and live in the forests; they are entirely different from those that live in the plains....By living in or near the woods, their actions are regulated by the wildness of the neighbourhood....

DOCUMENT ANALYSIS

1. What specific examples does Crèvecoeur provide to contrast an American from a European?

2. Does Crèvecoeur's definition of an American still ring true in the early twenty-first century?

Four.4

Benjamin Franklin,
"Upon Hearing George Whitefield Preach"
(1771)

Benjamin Franklin wrote and rewrote his autobiography in the years between 1771 and his death in 1790. In it, he recalled the impact of hearing George Whitefield preach in 1739. As Franklin was recalling an incident that took place many years earlier, this excerpt may be colored by the time that passed.*

In 1739 arriv'd among us from England the Rev. Mr. Whitefield, who had made himself remarkable there as an itinerant preacher....The Multitudes of all Sects and Denominations that attended his Sermons were enormous, and it was matter of Speculation to me who was one of the Number, to observe the extraordinary Influence of his Oratory on his Hearers, and how much they admir'd & respected him, notwithstanding his common Abuse of them, by assuring them they were naturally half Beasts and half Devils. It was wonderful to see the Change soon made in the Manners of our Inhabitants; from being thoughtless or indifferent about Religion, it seem'd as if all the World were growing Religious; so that one could not walk thro' the Town in an Evening without Hearing Psalms sung in different Families of every Street....Mr. Whitefield, in leaving us, went preaching all the Way thro' the Colonies to Georgia. The Settlement of that Province had lately been begun; but instead of being made with hardy industrious Husbandmen accustomed to Labor, the only People fit for such an Enterprise, it was with Families of broken Shopkeepers and other insolvent Debtors, many of indolent & idle habits, taken out of the Gaols, who being set down in the Woods, unqualified for clearing Land, & unable to endure the Hardships of a new Settlement, perished in Numbers, leaving many helpless Children unprovided for. The Sight of their miserable Situation inspired the benevolent Heart of Mr. Whitefield with the idea of building an Orphan House there....Returning northward he preached up this Charity, & made large Collections; for his Eloquence had a wonderful Power over the Hearts and Purses

* From Benjamin Franklin, *The Autobiography of Benjamin Franklin* (New York: Penguin, 1986).

of his Hearers, of which I myself was an Instance. I did not disapprove of the Design, but as Georgia was then destitute of Materials & Workmen, and it was propos'd to send them from Philadelphia at a great Expense, I thought it would have been better to have built the House here & Brought the Children to it. This I advis'd, but he was resolute in his first Project, and rejected my Counsel, and I thereupon refus'd to contribute. I happened soon after on one of his Sermons, in the Course of which I perceived he intended to finish with a Collection, & I silently resolved he should get nothing from me. I had in my Pocket a Handful of Copper Money, three or four silver Dollars, and five Pistoles in gold. As he proceeded I began to soften, and concluded to give the Coppers. Another Stroke of his Oratory made me asham'd of that, and determin'd me to give the Silver & he finished so admirably, that I empty'd my Pocket wholly into the Collector's Dish, Gold and all. At this Sermon there was also one of our Club, who being of my Sentiments respecting the Building in Georgia, and suspecting a Collection might be intended, had by Precaution emptied his Pockets before he came from home; towards the Conclusion of the Discourse, however, he felt a strong Desire to give, and apply'd to a Neighbor who stood near him to borrow some Money for the Purpose.

DOCUMENT ANALYSIS

1. What does this excerpt from Franklin's autobiography suggest about the persuasive powers of George Whitefield?

2. What sense do you get of Franklin himself from his account of Whitefield's preaching?

Jonathan Edwards, from
"Sinners in the Hands of an Angry God"
(1741)

Jonathan Edwards was the greatest American-born revivalist preacher. "Sinners in the Hands of an Angry God," delivered first at Northampton, Massachusetts, in 1741, was his most famous sermon. No record was kept of the sermon's impact the first time Edwards delivered it, but Reverend Stephen Williams of Longmeadow noted in his diary that when Edwards preached later in Enfield, Connecticut, "the shrieks and cries were piercing and amazing." The emotionalism of the sermon and its description of the moment of tension as man dangles over the fire produced the sermon's impact. In Edwards's sermon, God finally tires of protecting unworthy man from the flames, revealing its most disturbing part: its message of the insecurity of temporary protection by an all-powerful and infinitely angry God.*

. . . This that you have heard is the case of every one of you that are out of Christ. That world of misery, that lake of burning brimstone, is extended abroad under you. There is the dreadful pit of the glowing flames of the wrath of God; there is hell's wide gaping mouth open; and you have nothing to stand upon, nor any thing to take hold of; there is nothing between you and hell but the air; 'tis only the power and mere pleasure of God that holds you up.

You probably are not sensible of this; you find you are kept out of hell, but don't see the hand of God in it, but look at other things, as the good state of your bodily constitution, your care of your own life, and the means you use for your own preservation. But indeed these things are nothing; if God should withdraw his hand, they would avail no more to keep you from falling, than the thin air to hold up a person that is suspended in it.

Your wickedness makes you as it were heavy as lead, and to tend downwards with great weight and pressure towards hell; and, if God should let you go, you would immediately sink, and swiftly descend and plunge into the bottomless gulf; and your healthy

* From Jonathan Edwards, "Sinners in the Hands of an Angry God (1741)," in *The Great Awakening*, eds. Alan Heimert and Perry Miller (Indianpolis: Bobbs-Merrill, 1969).

constitution, and your own care and prudence, and best contrivance, and all your right-eousness, would have no more influence to uphold you and keep you out of hell, than a spider's web would have to stop a falling rock....

The God that holds you over the pit of hell, much as one holds a spider or some loathsome insect over the fire, abhors you, and is dreadfully provoked. His wrath towards you burns like fire; he looks upon you as worthy of nothing else but to be cast into the fire. He is of purer eyes than to bear you in his sight; you are ten thousand times as abominable in his eyes as the most hateful, venomous serpent is in ours. You have offended him infinitely more than ever a stubborn rebel did his prince, and yet 'tis nothing but his hand that holds you from falling into the fire every moment....

O sinner! Consider the fearful danger you are in! 'Tis a great furnace of wrath, a wide and bottomless pit, full of fire and of wrath that you are held over in the hand of that God whose wrath is provoked and incensed as much against you as against many of the damned in hell. You hang by a slender thread, with the flames of Divine wrath flashing about it, and ready every moment to singe it and burn it asunder....

It would be dreadful to suffer this fierceness and wrath of Almighty God one moment; but you must suffer it to all eternity. There will be no end to this exquisite, horrible, misery....

How dreadful is the state of those that are daily and hourly in danger of this great wrath and infinite misery! But this is the dismal case of every soul in this congregation that has not been born again, however moral and strict, sober and religious, they may otherwise be. Oh! that you would consider it, whether you be young or old!

Document Analysis

1. According to Edwards, what fate is in store for upright moral churchgoers who haven't been "born again"?

Four.6

James Oglethorpe, Establishing the Colony of Georgia (1733)

The last of the original thirteen colonies established was Georgia, chartered by King George II in 1732. Georgia was set up to be a refuge for debtors and other "worthy poor" from England, the humanitarian project of an English social reformer, James Oglethorpe. As lead trustee, Oglethorpe led Georgia in its early years, frustrated that his early vision was not adequately funded by England, and often finding his young colony threatened by the Spanish in neighboring Florida.*

In America there are fertile lands sufficient to subsist all the useless Poor in *England*, and distressed Protestants in Europe; yet Thousands starve for want of mere sustenance. The distance makes it difficult to act thither. The same want that renders men useless here, prevents their paying their passage; and if others pay it for them, they become servants, or rather slaves for years to those who have defrayed the expense. Therefore, money for passage, is necessary, but is not the only want; for if people were set down in America, and the land before them, they must cut down trees, build houses, fortify towns, dig and sow the land before they can get in a harvest; and till then, they must be provided with food, and kept together, that they may be assistant to each other for their natural support and protection....

FROM THE CHARTER.— His Majesty having taken into his consideration, the miserable circumstances of many of his own poor subjects, ready to perish for want: as likewise the distresses of many poor foreigners, who would take refuge here from persecution; and having a Princely regard to the great danger the southern frontiers of South Carolina are exposed to, by reason of the small number of white inhabitants there, hath, out of his Fatherly compassion towards his subjects, been graciously pleased

---

* From James Oglethorpe, "Some Account of the Designs of the Trustees for Establishing the Colony of Georgia," 1733, accessible online at http://wps.ablongman.com/wps/media/objects/1676/1716309/documents/doc_d02d12.html.

to grant a charter for incorporating a number of gentlemen by the name of *The Trustees for establishing the Colony of Georgia in America*. They are impowered to collect benefactions; and lay them out in cloathing, arming, sending over, and supporting colonies of the poor, whether subjects or foreigners, in Georgia. And his Majesty farther grants all his lands between the rivers *Savannah and Alatamaha*, which lie erects into a Province by the name of *GEORGIA*, unto the Trustees, in trust for the poor, and for the better, support of the Colony....

The Trustees intend to relieve such unfortunate persons as cannot subsist here, and establish them in an orderly manner, so as to form a well regulated town. As far as their fund goes, they will defray the charge of their passage to Georgia; give them necessaries, cattle, land, and subsistence, till such time as they can build their houses and clear some of their land. They rely for success, first on the goodness of Providence, next on the compassionate disposition of the people of England; and, they doubt not, that much will be spared from luxury, and superfluous expenses, by generous tempers, when such an opportunity is offered them by the giving of £20 to provide for a man or woman, or £10 to a child for ever.

By such a Colony, many families, who would otherwise starve, will be provided for, and made masters of houses and lands; the people in Great Britain to whom these necessitous families were a burthen, will be relieved; numbers of manufacturers will be here employed, for supplying them with clothes, working tools, and other necessaries; and by giving refuge to the distressed Saltzburghers, and other persecuted Protestants, the power of Britain, as a reward for its hospitality, will be encreased by the addition of so many religious and industrious subjects....

As towns are established and grow populous along the rivers Savannah and Alatamaha, they will make such a barrier as will render the southern frontier of the British Colonies on the Continent of America, safe from Indian and other enemies.

All human affairs are so subject to chance, that there in no answering for events; yet from reason and the nature of things, it may be concluded, that the riches and also the number of the inhabitants in *Great Britain* will be increased, by importing at a cheap rate from this new Colony, the materials requisite for carrying on in Britain several manufactures. For our Manufacturers will be encouraged to marry and multiply, when they find themselves in circumstances to provide for their families, which must necessarily be the happy effect of the increase and cheapness of our materials of those Manufactures, which at present we purchase with our money from foreign countries, at dear rates; and also many people will find employment here, on account such farther demands by the people of this Colony, for those manufactures which are made for the produce of our own country; and, as has been justly observed, the people will always abound where there is full employment for them.

DOCUMENT ANALYSIS

1. What benefits does Oglethorpe claim will come to England because of the establishment of Georgia? Do these seem legitimately likely results, or merely utopian promises?

Chapter Study Questions

1. Why was it so difficult for Byrd to accept being an American gentleman? Did his embrace of things English make him less "American"?

2. How does Crèvecoeur's description of an American apply to Byrd?

3. In what ways does Franklin's account betray a certain provincialism? How does he regard the settlers of Georgia? How does Franklin's portrayal of Georgia contrast with Oglethorpe's description of the original ideal for Georgia?

4. Franklin was impressed with the immediate impact of Whitefield's sermon. Would Edwards's sermon have the same kind of impact? What were the key ingredients Edwards used to sway his audience?

Five

The Strains of Empire

I t is difficult to discern the exact moment in which the path of the American colonies and the British government diverged. Perhaps it was inevitable, given the changes within the colonies as they developed an American identity. As seen in your text, the British imperial government made a number of attempts to assert greater control over the economic and political arrangements it had with the colonies prior to 1756. However, turmoil within its own political system made it difficult to achieve these objectives. It was only after the French and Indian War that a new, coherent imperial policy calling for tighter restrictions over the colonies developed.

Within ten years, differences between England and its colonies blossomed into an ideological and political dispute that drove them apart. This set of documents centers on the major political debates of the period, following the path of the American colonists as they considered independence and what the promise of a new nation held for Americans.

Americans were divided about their relationship with Britain, and some of the most vociferous among them were radicalized by the taxes and duties imposed on the colonies in the 1760s. John Dickinson, a Philadelphian, typified many Americans; he was loyal to Great Britain but nonetheless opposed the imposition of taxes on the colonists by Parliament. Some Americans, however, still believed that the British government had the right to tax them, as demonstrated by the 1774 letter from colonial loyalists to North Carolina Governor Josiah Martin. Expressing a contrary sentiment, Patrick Henry's famous speech, "Give Me Liberty or Give Me Death," is from the meeting of the Virginia Convention in 1775. It is probably the best-known statement of the opinion that the colonists had no choice other than to break with Britain.

John Dickinson, from
Letters from a Farmer in Pennsylvania
(1768)

John Dickinson's Letters from a Pennsylvania Farmer, *were written in protest to the passage of the Townshend Duties in 1767. Dickinson was not really a farmer; he was one of the wealthiest lawyers in Philadelphia and considered himself a loyal subject of the British crown. Nonetheless, he believed that Parliament had no right to tax the colonies. The following is an excerpt from his defense of the legal fights of free-born Englishmen.* *

There is [a] late act of Parliament, which seems to me to be…destructive to the liberty of these colonies,…that is the act for granting duties on paper, glass, etc. It appears to me to be unconstitutional.

The Parliament unquestionably possesses a legal authority to regulate the trade of Great Britain and all its colonies. Such an authority is essential to the relation between a mother country and its colonies and necessary for the common good of all. He who considers these provinces as states distinct from the British Empire has very slender notions of justice or of their interests. We are but parts of a whole; and therefore there must exist a power somewhere to preside, and preserve the connection in due order. This power is lodged in the Parliament, and we are as much dependent on Great Britain as a perfectly free people can be on another.

I have looked over every statute relating to these colonies, from their first settlement to this time; and I find every one of them founded on this principle till the Stamp Act administration. All before are calculated to preserve or promote a mutually beneficial intercourse between the several constituent parts of the Empire. And though many of them imposed duties on trade, yet those duties were always imposed with design to restrain the commerce of one part that was injurious to another, and thus to promote the general welfare.…Never did the British Parliament, till the period abovementioned,

* From John Dickinson, *Letters from a Farmer in Pennsylvania to the Inhabitants of the British Colonies* (Boston: John Mein, 1768), 5–35.

think of imposing duties in American for the purpose of raising a revenue.…This I call an innovation, and a most dangerous innovation.

That we may be legally bound to pay any general duties on these commodities, relative to the regulation of trade, is granted. But we being obliged by her laws to take them from Great Britain, any special duties imposed on their exportation to us only, with intention to raise a revenue from us only, are as much taxes upon us as those imposed by the Stamp Act.…It is nothing but the edition of a former book with a new title page,…and will be attended with the very same consequences to American liberty.

Sorry I am to learn that there are some few persons, [who] shake their heads with solemn motion, and pretend to wonder what can be the meaning of these letters.…I will now tell the gentlemen.…The meaning of them is to convince the people of these colonies that they are at this moment exposed to the most imminent dangers, and persuade them immediately, vigorously, and unanimously to exert themselves, in the most firm, but most peaceable manner for obtaining relief. The cause of liberty is a cause of too much dignity to be sullied by turbulence and tumult. It ought to be maintained in a manner suitable to her nature.…I hope, my dear countrymen, that you will in every colony be upon your guard against those who may at any time endeavour to stir you up, under pretences of patriotism, to any measures disrespectful to our sovereign and our mother country. Hot, rash, disorderly proceedings injure the reputation of a people as to wisdom, valour and virtue, without procuring them the least benefit.…

Every government, at some time or other, falls into wrong measures. They may proceed from mistake or passion. But every such measure does not dissolve the obligation between the governors and the governed. The mistake may be corrected, the passion may pass over. It is the duty of the governed to endeavour to rectify the mistake and appease the passion. They have not at first any other right than to represent their grievances and to pray for redress.…

DOCUMENT ANALYSIS

1. How does Dickinson contrast earlier British statutes and duties impacting the colonies with the effects of the Stamp Act and Townshend duties?

2. What does Dickinson fear would happen if the Townshend duties were collected?

Address of the Inhabitants of Anson County to Governor Martin (1774)

Many Americans remained loyal to England before, during, and after the Revolutionary War. Loyalists were particularly strong where British government was stable (like around New York City) and where colonists relied on the British for protection (like on the Carolina frontiers). This is a letter sent by colonial Loyalists from Anson County, North Carolina, to their governor, pledging their loyalty and asking, in part, for protection. *

To His Excellency, Josiah Martin Esquire, Captain General, Governor, &c,

Most Excellent Governor:

Permit us, in behalf of ourselves, and many others of His Majesty's most dutiful and loyal subjects within the County of Anson, to take the earliest opportunity of addressing your Excellency, and expressing our abomination of the many outrageous attempts now forming on this side of the Atlantick, against the peace and tranquillity His Majesty's Dominions in North America, and to witness to your Excellency, by this our Protest, a disapprobation and abhorence of the many lawless combinations and unwarrantable practices actually carrying on by a gross tribe of infatuated anti-Monarchists in the several Colonies in these Dominions; the baneful consequence of whose audacious contrivance can, *in fine*, only tend to extirpate the fundamental principles of all Government, and illegally to shake off their obedience to, and dependence upon, the imperial Crown and Parliament of Great Britain; the infection of whose pernicious example being already extended to this particular County, of which we now bear the fullest testimony.

It is with the deepest concern (though with infinite indignation) that we see in all

* From *The Colonial Records of North Carolina, Volume IX, 1771 to 1775*, ed. William I. Saunders (Raleigh: North Carolina Printers, 1890), 1161–1164.

public places and papers disagreeable votes, speeches and resolutions, said to be entered into by our sister Colonies, in the highest contempt and derogation of the superintending power of the legislative authority of Great Britain. And we further, with sorrow, behold their wanton endeavors to vilify and arraign the honour and integrity of His Majesty's most honourable Ministry and Council, tending to sow the seed of discord and sedition, in open violation of their duty and allegiance....

...We are truly invigorated with the warmest zeal and attachment in favour of the British Parliament, Constitution and Laws, which our forefathers gloriously struggled to establish, and which are now become the noblest birthright and inheritance of all Britannia's Sons....

We are truly sensible that those invaluable blessings which we have hitherto enjoyed under His Majesty's auspicious Government, can only be secured to us by the stability of his Throne, supported and defended by the British Parliament, the only grand bulwark and guardian of our civil and religious liberties.

Duty and affection oblige us further to express our grateful acknowledgements for the inestimate blessings flowing from such a Constitution. And we do assure your Excellency that we are determined, by the assistance of Almighty God, in our respective stations, steadfastly to continue His Majesty's loyal Subjects, and to contribute all in our power for the preservation of the publick peace; so, that, by our unanimous example, we hope to discourage the desperate endeavours of a deluded multitude, and to see a mis-led people turn again from their atrocious offences to a proper exercise of their obedience and duty.

And we do furthermore assure your Excellency, that we shall endeavor to cultivate such sentiments in all those under our care, and to warm their breasts with a true zeal for His Majesty, and affection for his illustrious family. And may the Almighty God be pleased to direct his Councils, his Parliament, and all those in authority under him, that their endeavors may be for the advancement of piety, and the safety, honour and welfare of our Sovereign and his Kingdoms, that the malice of his enemies may be assuaged, and their evil designs confounded and defeated; so that all the world may be convinced that his sacred person, his Royal family, his Parliament, and our Country, are the special objects of Divine dispensation and Providence.

[Signed by two hundred twenty-seven of the inhabitants of Anson County.]

DOCUMENT ANALYSIS

1. How do those who signed this letter regard the colonial critics of the British empire in the 1770s?

Patrick Henry,
"Give Me Liberty or Give Me Death"
(1775)

There are few Americans who are not familiar with Patrick Henry's cry "give me liberty or give me death." This fiery speech is popular not only as a document of the revolutionary struggle but as one of the great speeches of all time. Patrick Henry served in the French and Indian Wars and first attracted attention as the leader of the objections to the Stamp Act in the Virginia House of Burgesses. In this speech, he argues that the colonists have no other choice after exhausting all the avenues for reconciliation with Britain. **

M<small>r.</small> President:

It is natural to man to indulge in the illusions of hope. We are apt to shut our eyes against a painful truth, and listen to the song of the siren till she transforms us into beasts. Is this the part of wise men, engaged in a great and arduous struggle for liberty? Are we disposed to be of the number of those who having eyes see not, and having ears hear not, the things which so nearly concern their temporal salvation? For my part, whatever anguish of spirit it may cost, I am willing to know the whole truth; to know the worst and to provide for it.

I have but one lamp by which my feet are guided; and that is the lamp of experience. I know of no way of judging of the future but by the past. And judging by the past, I wish to know what there has been in the conduct of the British ministry for the last ten years, to justify those hopes with which gentlemen have been pleased to solace themselves and the house? Is it that insidious smile with which our petition has been lately received? Trust it not, sir: It will prove a snare to your feet. Suffer not yourselves to be betrayed with a kiss. Ask yourselves how this gracious reception of our petition comports

* From Patrick Henry, "Speech in the Virginia Convention, March 23, 1775," In *Library of the World's Best Literature, Ancient and Modern*, vol. XII, ed. Charles D. Warner (New York: R. S. Peale and J. A. Hill, 1897), 7242–7244.

with those warlike preparations which cover our waters and darken our land. Are fleets and armies necessary to a work of love and reconciliation? Have we shown ourselves so unwilling to be reconciled that force must be called in to win back our love? Let us not deceive ourselves, sir. These are the implements of war and subjugation—the last arguments to which kings resort. I ask gentlemen, sir, what means this martial array, if its purpose be not to force us to submission? Can gentlemen assign any other possible motive for it? Has Britain any enemy in this quarter of the world, to call for all this accumulation of navies and armies? No, sir, she has none. They are meant for us; they can be meant for no other. They are sent over to bind and rivet upon us those chains which the British ministry have been so long forging. And what have we to oppose them? Shall we try argument? Sir, we have been trying that for the last ten years. Have we anything new to offer upon the subject? Nothing. We have held the subject up in every light of which it is capable; but it has been all in vain. Shall we resort to entreaty and humble supplication? What terms shall we find which have not been already exhausted? Let us not, I beseech you, sir, deceive ourselves longer.

Sir, we have done everything that could be done to avert the storm which is now coming on. We have petitioned, we have remonstrated, we have supplicated, we have prostrated ourselves before the throne, and have implored its interposition to arrest the tyrannical hands of the ministry and Parliament. Our petitions have been slighted; our remonstrances have produced additional violence and insult; our supplications have been disregarded; and we have been spurned with contempt from the foot of the throne. In vain, after these things, may we indulge the fond hope of peace and reconciliation. There is no longer any room for hope. If we wish to be free, if we mean to preserve inviolate those inestimable privileges for which we have been so long contending, if we mean not basely to abandon the noble struggle in which we have been so long engaged, and which we have pledged ourselves never to abandon until the glorious object of our contest shall be obtained—we must fight! I repeat, sir, we must fight! An appeal to arms and to the God of Hosts is all that is left us!

They tell us, sir, that we are weak—unable to cope with so formidable an adversary. But when shall we be stronger? Will it be the next week, or the next year? Will it be when we are totally disarmed, and when a British guard shall be stationed in every house? Shall we gather strength by irresolution and inaction? Shall we acquire the means of effectual resistance by lying supinely on our backs, and hugging the delusive phantom of hope until our enemies shall have bound us hand and foot? Sir, we are not weak, if we make a proper use of those means which the God of nature hath placed in our power. Three millions of people, armed in the holy cause of liberty, and in such a country as that which we possess, are invincible by any force which our enemy can send against us. Besides, sir, we shall not fight our battles alone. There is a just God who presides over the destinies of nations; and who will raise up friends to fight our battles for us. The battle, sir, is not to the strong alone; it is to the vigilant, the active, the brave. Besides, sir, we have no election. If we were base enough to desire it, it is not too late to retire from the contest. There is no retreat but in submission and slavery! Our chains are forged; their clanking may be heard on the plains of Boston! The war is inevitable—and let it come! I repeat it, sir, let it come!

It is in vain, sir, to extenuate the matter. Gentlemen may cry, Peace, peace; but there is no peace. The war is actually begun. The next gale that sweeps from the north will bring to our ears the clash of resounding arms. Our brethren are already in the field. Why stand we here idle? What is it that gentlemen wish? What would they have? If life so dear, or peace sweet, as to be purchased at the price of chains and slavery? Forbid it Almighty God—I know not what course others may take; but as for me, give me liberty or give me death!

DOCUMENT ANALYSIS

1. How compelling do you find Henry's argument here? Is it aimed predominantly at reason or the emotions?

2. Why do you think Henry's rhetoric, particularly the "give me liberty or give me death" line, became so widely popular during and after the American Revolution?

Chapter Study Questions

1. Dickinson strongly challenges Britain's decision to raise revenue in the colonies through the Stamp Act and the Townshend duties. What motivated Britain to seek such revenue?

2. Compare Patrick Henry and the North Carolina Loyalists on their attitudes toward the role of the English government.

3. How do taxes in the United States today compare to those imposed by Britain on the colonies?

PART TWO

A REVOLUTIONARY PEOPLE, 1775–1828

Six

A People in Revolution

As the American Revolution drew to a close, the new nation took its first shaky steps toward unity. Many Americans hoped that the sacrifices of war meant a better future for them and the nation. Unfortunately, many met frustration and disappointment. As seen in the text, many Americans, particularly women and African Americans, found less liberty after the Revolution than they anticipated.

The documents in this chapter expose the limits of revolutionary freedom and liberal promises. The writer Judith Sargent Murray issued a call in 1790 for equality for women, imploring that the Declaration of Independence's promise that "all men are created equal," apply to all mankind and not just all men.

The Revolution's rhetoric also inspired women and free blacks to aspire to equal treatment and education. The years after the Revolution witnessed a great expansion of educational opportunity, based on the belief that a republic required a well-educated citizenry to function properly. Women's education received a boost from this idea. The ideal republican woman was a patriot, a virtuous wife, and the mother and teacher of good citizens of the republic.

Nevertheless, women's education lagged far behind that of men. Blacks enjoyed even less opportunity. Molly Wallace's valedictory oration from the Young Ladies Academy in Philadelphia and the petition of Massachusetts blacks for inclusion in the state's system of public education are examples of how eager diverse Americans were to be well-educated members of the republic.

Judith Sargent Murray, "On the Equality of the Sexes" (1790)

Judith Sargent Murray was a writer and publisher from Massachusetts who provided an early argument for gender equality in the new republic. This excerpt is from an essay she published in 1790, a year many decades before any woman in the United States could vote. *

Yes, ye lordly, ye haughty sex, our souls are by nature equal to yours; the same breath of God animates, enlivens, and invigorates us; and that we are not fallen lower than yourselves, let those witness who have greatly towered above the various discouragements by which they have been so heavily oppressed; and though I am unacquainted with the list of celebrated characters on either side, yet from the observations I have made in the contracted circle in which I have moved, I dare confidently believe, that form the commencement of time to the present day, there hath been as many females, as males, who, by the mere force of natural powers, have merited the crown of applause; who thus unassisted, have seized the wreath of fame.

I know there are those who assert, that as the animal powers of the one sex are superiour, of course their mental faculties must also be stronger; thus attributing strength of mind to the transient organization of this earth born tenement. But if this reasoning is just, man must be content to yield the palm to many of the brute creation, since by not a few of his brethren of the field, he is far surpassed in bodily strength. Moreover, was this argument admitted, it would prove too much, for ocular demonstration evinceth, that there are many robust masculine ladies, and effeminate gentlemen....Besides, were we to grant that animal strength proved anything, taking into consideration the accustomed impartiality of nature, we should be induced to imagine, that she had invested the female mind with superiour strength as an equivalent for the bodily powers of man. But waiving this however palpable advantage, for equality only, we wish to contend.

---

* From Judith Sargent Murray, "On the Equality of the Sexes," *Massachusetts Magazine*, 1790, available online at http://personal.pitnet.net/primarysources/judithmurray.html.

DOCUMENT ANALYSIS

1. How would you describe the tone of Murray's argument? How persuasive is it?

Molly Wallace, Valedictory Oration
(1792)

Molly Wallace delivered this valedictory oration to the Young Ladies' Academy in Philadelphia, which offered girls a curriculum similar to that offered in schools for boys. Men founded and taught in the school and, although the education was similar to that available to boys, the young ladies were expected to apply their education within the home. *

The silent and solemn attention of a respectable audience, has often, at the beginning of discourses intimidated, even veterans, in the art of public elocution. What then must my situation be, when my sex, my youth and inexperience all conspire to make me tremble at the talk which I have undertaken?…With some, however, it has been made a question, whether we ought ever to appear in so public a manner. Our natural timidity, the domestic situation to which by nature and custom we seem destined, are, urged as arguments against what I have now undertaken: Many sarcastical observations have been handed out against female oratory: But to what do they amount? Do they not plainly inform us, that, because we are females, we ought therefore to be deprived of what is perhaps the most effectual means of acquiring a just, natural and graceful delivery? No one will pretend to deny, that we should be taught to read in the best manner. And if to read, why not to speak?…But yet it might be asked, what, has a female character to do with declamation? That she should harangue at the head of an Army, in the Senate, or before a popular Assembly, is not pretended, neither is it requested that she ought to be an adept in the stormy and contentious eloquence of the bar, or in the abstract and subtle reasoning of the Senate;—we look not for a female Pitt, Cicero, or Demosthenes.

There are more humble and milder scenes than those which I have mentioned, in which a woman may display her elocution. There are numerous topics, on which she

---

* From Molly Wallace, *The Rise and Progress of the Young Ladies' Academy of Philadelphia* (Philadelphia: Stewart and Cochran, 1794), 212–213.

may discourse without impropriety, in the discussion of which, she may instruct and please others, and in which she may exercise and improve her own understanding. After all, we do not expect women should become perfect orators. Why then should they be taught to speak in public? This question may possibly be answered by asking several others.

Why is a boy diligently and carefully taught the Latin, the Greek, or the Hebrew language, in which he will seldom have occasion, either to write or to converse? Why is he taught to demonstrate the propositions of Euclid, when during his whole life, he will not perhaps make use of one of them? Are we taught to dance merely for the sake of becoming dancers? No, certainly. These things are commonly studied, more on account of the habits, which the learning of them establishes, than on account of any important advantages which the mere knowledge of them can afford. So a young lady, from the exercise of speaking before a properly selected audience, may acquire some valuable habits, which, otherwise she can obtain from no examples, and that no precept can give. But, this exercise can with propriety be performed only before a select audience: a promiscuous and indiscriminate one, for obvious reasons, would be absolutely unsuitable, and should always be carefully avoided....

DOCUMENT ANALYSIS

1. Why does Wallace argue that women should be allowed to speak in public?

"Petition for Access to Education" (1787)

After the Revolution, African Americans arrived in northern cities (like Boston, Philadelphia, and New York) in greater numbers, developing new community institutions which sometimes were granted equal treatment as those of whites. This is a petition to the Massachusetts legislature protesting the exclusion of blacks from public education; one of the movement's organizers was Prince Hall, the founder of the Negro Masonic Order.*

To the Honorable the Senate and House of Representatives of the Commonwealth of Massachusetts Bay, in General Court assembled.

The petition of a great number of blacks, freemen of this Commonwealth, humbly sheweth, that your petitioners are held in common with other freemen of this town and Commonwealth and have never been backward in paying our proportionate part of the burdens under which they have, or may labor under; and as we are willing to pay our equal part of these burdens, we are of the humble opinion that we have the right to enjoy the privileges of free men. But that we do not will appear in many instances, and we beg leave to mention one out of many, and that is of the education of our children which now receive no benefit from the free schools in the town of Boston, which we think is a great grievance, as by woeful experience we now feel the want of a common education. We, therefore, must fear for our rising offspring to see them in ignorance in a land of gospel light when there is provision made for them as well as others and yet can't enjoy them, and for no other reason can be given than they are black...

We therefore pray your Honors that you would in your wisdom make some provision...for the education of our dear children. And in duty bound shall ever pray.

---

* From "Petition for Equal Education," 1787, in *A Documentary History of the Negro People in the United States*, ed. Herbert Aptheker (Secaucus, NJ: Carol Publishing Group, 1951). Copyright © 1951 by Carol Publishing Group. A Citadel Press Book.

DOCUMENT ANALYSIS

1. On what basis does the petition appeal to the state of Massachusetts to provide equal public education to blacks?

Chapter Study Questions

1. How does Judith Sargent Murray reflect the inspiration of the American Revolution in making their claims for equality? Why did such claims largely go unheeded in the United States for several generations?

2. What connections can be drawn between the ideology of the Revolution, the arguments for women's education, and the African-American petition for access to public schools?

Seven

Consolidating the Revolution

A s the country learned the difficulties of self-government during and after the Revolutionary War, Americans would spend the decade searching to create national and local governments that could provide stability and unity and protect their liberties. As your text demonstrates, it became evident during the American Revolution that the central government was in a financial dilemma. Determined to maintain a level of solvency, it had withheld the pay of the soldiers and officers in the early 1780s. In 1783, future president George Washington appealed to the army for their loyalty in the Newburgh Address—revealing how precarious the unity and existence of the new nation was.

The first national government, under the Articles of Confederation, was unable to solve the economic problems of the postwar period. A lack of a national currency, runaway inflation, interstate tariffs, and little foreign trade combined to drive the nation into a depression by the mid-1780s. With a restricted marketplace and mounting debts, many American farmers were driven to economic ruin. In western Massachusetts, believing they had no other recourse, a group of farmers led by Daniel Shays marched on the state government offices to force it to address their problems.

In 1787 there was little doubt that the national government was no longer able to govern as it was then configured. Delegates from twelve states met in Philadelphia in May to revise the Articles of Confederation. The newly written Constitution made a powerful argument for a republican government rooted in a strong central government. Ratification was not easy, given the vivid memories of life under the rule of the British government. George Mason's piece below shows some of the arguments against the new Constitution.

What have become known as the *Federalist Papers* sought to win Americans over. In 85 pamphlets and newspaper articles, "Publius" (Alexander Hamilton, John Jay, and James Madison) argued the strengths of this new government.

James Madison's *Federalist Paper #10* is one of the most well-known of these documents and provides one of the clearest analyses of American federalism. Critics of the Constitution, known as anti-Federalists, were especially critical of the lack of a bill of rights in the original Constitution.

Seven.1

George Washington, The Newburgh Address (1783)

A number of officers met in Newburgh, New York, in 1783 to discuss ways to address their grievances after the central government had withheld their pay for many months. As they debated a course of action, Washington appeared and spoke to them. In his address, he acknowledges the hardships under which they won the war and appeals to them to find "greater strength not to succumb" to their anger. This speech forestalled further actions by the officers. *

To the Officers of the Army

Gentlemen—A fellow soldier, whose interest and affections bind him strongly to you, whose past sufferings have been as great, and whose future fortune may be as desperate as yours—would beg leave to address you.

Age has its claims, and rank is not without its pretensions to advise: but, though unsupported by both, he flatters himself, that the plain language of sincerity and experience will neither be unheard nor unregarded.

Like many of you, he loved private life, and left it with regret. He left it, determined to retire from the field, with the necessity that called him to it, and not till then—not till the enemies of his country, the slaves of power, and the hirelings of injustice, were compelled to abandon their schemes, and acknowledge America as terrible in arms as she had been humble in remonstrance. With this object in view, he has long shared in your toils and mingled in your dangers. He has felt the cold hand of poverty without a murmur, and has seen the insolence of wealth without a sigh. But, too much under the direction of his wishes, and sometimes weak enough to mistake desire for opinion, he has till lately—very lately—believed in the justice of his country. He hoped that, as the clouds

* From *Journals of the Continental Congress*, 34 vols., eds. W. C. Ford, et al., (Washington D.C., 1904–1937), xxiv, 295–297.

of adversity scattered, and as the sunshine of peace and better fortune broke in upon us, the coldness and severity of government would relax, and that, more than justice, that gratitude would blaze forth upon those hands, which had upheld her, in the darkest stages of her passage, from impending servitude to acknowledged independence. But faith has its limits as well as temper, and there are points beyond which neither can be stretched, without sinking into cowardice or plunging into credulity.—This, my friends, I conceive to be your situation.—Hurried to the very verge of both, another step would ruin you forever.—To be tame and unprovoked when injuries press hard upon you, is more than weakness; but to look up for kinder usage, without one manly effort of your own, would fix your character, and shew the world how richly you deserve those chains you broke. To guard against this evil, let us take a review of the ground upon which we now stand, and from thence carry our thoughts forward for a moment, into the unexplored field of expedient.

After a pursuit of seven long years, the object for which we set out is at length brought within our reach. Yes, my friends, that suffering courage of yours was active once—it has conducted the United States of America through a doubtful and a bloody war. It has placed her in the chair of independency, and peace returns again to bless— whom? A country willing to redress your wrongs, cherish your worth and reward your services, a country courting your return to private life, with tears of gratitude and smiles of admiration, longing to divide with you that independency which your gallantry has given, and those riches which your wounds have preserved? Is this the case? Or is it rather a country that tramples upon your rights, disdains your cries and insults your distresses? Have you not, more than once, suggested your wishes, and made known your wants to Congress? Wants and wishes which gratitude and policy should have anticipated, rather than evaded. And have you not lately, in the meek language of entreating memorials, begged from their justice, what you would no longer expect from their favour? How have you been answered? Let the letter which you are called to consider to-morrow make reply.

If this, then, be your treatment, while the swords you wear are necessary for the defence of America, what have you to expect from peace, when your voice shall sink, and your strength dissipate by division? When those very swords, the instruments and companions of your glory, shall be taken from your sides, and no remaining mark of military distinction left but your wants, infirmities and scars? Can you then consent to be the only sufferers by this revolution, and retiring from the field, grow old in poverty, wretchedness and contempt? Can you consent to wade through the vile mire of dependency, and owe the miserable remnant of that life to charity, which has hitherto been spent in honor? If you can—GO—and carry with you the jest of tories and scorn of whigs—the ridicule, and what is worse, the pity of the world. Go, starve, and be forgotten! But, if your spirit should revolt at this; if you have sense enough to discover, and spirit enough to oppose tyranny under whatever garb it may assume; whether it be the plain coat of republicanism, or the splendid robe of royalty; if you have yet learned to discriminate between a people and a cause, between men and principles—awake; attend to your situation and redress yourselves. If the present moment be lost, every future effort is in vain; and your threats then, will be as empty as your entreaties now.

I would advise you, therefore, to come to some final opinion upon what you can bear, and what you will suffer. If your determination be in any proportion to your wrongs, carry your appeal from the justice to the fears of government. Change the milk-and-water style of your last memorial; assume a bolder tone—decent, but lively, spirited and determined, and suspect the man who would advise to more moderation and longer forbearance. Let two or three men, who can feel as well as write, be appointed to draw up your last remonstrance; for, I would no longer give it the sueing, soft, unsuccessful epithet of memorial. Let it be represented in language that will neither dishonor you by its rudeness, nor betray you by its fears, what has been promised by Congress, and what has been performed, how long and how patiently you have suffered, how little you have asked, and how much of that little has been denied. Tell them that, though you were the first, and would wish to be the last to encounter danger: though despair itself can never drive you into dishonor, it may drive you from the field: that the wound often irritated, and never healed, may at length become incurable; and that the slightest mark of indignity from Congress now, must operate like the grave, and part you forever: that in any political event, the army has its alternative. If peace, that nothing shall separate them from your arms but death: if war, that courting the auspices, and inviting the direction of your illustrious leader, you will retire to some unsettled country, smile in your turn, and "mock when their fear cometh on." But let it represent also, that should they comply with the request of your late memorial, it would make you more happy and them more respectable. That while war should continue, you would follow their standard into the field, and when it came to an end, you would withdraw into the shade of private life, and give the world another subject of wonder and applause; an army victorious over its enemies—victorious over itself.

DOCUMENT ANALYSIS

1. What fear did Washington express regarding the threatened actions of the army?

Publius (James Madison), *Federalist Paper #10* (1788)

The Federalist Papers, of which this is one of the best known, were published in support of ratification of the Constitution by James Madison, Alexander Hamilton, and John Jay under the pseudonym Publius. This document rebuts the Anti-Federalists' argument that a republic would soon crumble under the pressure of factional divisions. Madison outlined how a republican government could balance the needs of the minority and majority while preserving liberty and diversity.*

. . . [I]t may be concluded that a pure democracy, by which I mean a society, consisting of a small number of citizens, who assemble and administer the government in person, can admit of no cure for the mischiefs of faction. A common passion or interest will, in almost every case, be felt by a majority of the whole; a communication and concert results from the form of government itself; and there is nothing to check the inducements to sacrifice the weaker party, or an obnoxious individual. Hence it is, that such democracies have ever been spectacles of turbulence and contention; have ever been found incompatible with personal security, or the rights of property; and have in general been short in their lives, as they have been violent in their deaths. Theoretic politicians, who have patronized this species of government, have erroneously supposed, that by reducing mankind to a perfect equality in their political rights, they would, at the same time, be perfectly equalized, and assimilated in their possessions, their opinions, and their passions.

A republic, by which I mean a government in which the scheme of representation takes place, opens a different prospect, and promises the cure for which we are seeking. Let us examine the points in which it varies from pure democracy, and we shall compre-

* From James Madison, *The Federalist, #10*, November 22, 1787, in *The Papers of James Madison, Volume 10, May 27, 1783–March 3, 1788*, eds. Robert Rutland et al. (Chicago: University of Chicago Press, 1977), 267–270.

hend both the nature of the cure, and the efficacy which it must derive from the union.

The two great points of difference between a democracy and a republic, are first, the delegation of the government, in the latter, to a small number of citizens elected by the rest; secondly, the greater number of citizens, and greater sphere of country, over which the latter may be extended.

The effect of the first difference is, on the one hand, to refine and enlarge the public views, by passing them through the medium of a chosen body of citizens, whose wisdom may best discern the true interest of their country, and whose patriotism and love of justice, will be least likely to sacrifice it to temporary or partial considerations. Under such a regulation, it may well happen that the public voice pronounced by the representatives of the people, will be more consonant to the public good, than if pronounced by the people themselves convened for the purpose. On the other hand, the effect may be inverted. Men of factious tempers, of local prejudices, or of sinister designs, may by intrigue, by corruption, or by other means, first obtain the suffrages, and then betray the interests of the people. The question resulting is, whether small or extensive republics are most favourable to the election of proper guardians of the public wealth; and it is clearly decided in favour of the latter by two obvious considerations.

In the first place it is to be remarked, that however small the republic may be, the representatives must be raised to a certain number, in order to guard against the cabals of a few; and that however large it may be, they must be limited to a certain number, in order to guard against the confusion of a multitude. Hence the number of representatives in the two cases not being in proportion to that of the constituents, and being proportionally greatest in the small republic, it follows, that if the proportion of fit characters be not less in the large than in the small republic, the former will present a greater opinion, and consequently a greater probability of a fit choice.

In the next place, as each representative will be chosen by a greater number of citizens in the large than in the small republic, it will be more difficult for unworthy candidates to practise with success the vicious arts, by which elections are too often carried; and the suffrages of the people being more free, will be more likely to centre on men who possess the most attractive merit, and the most diffusive and established characters.

It must be confessed, that in this, as in most other cases, there is a mean, on both sides of which inconveniences will be found to lie. By enlarging too much the number of electors, you render the representative too little acquainted with all their local circumstances and lesser interests; as by reducing it too much, you render him unduly attached to these, and too little fit to comprehend and pursue great and national objects. The federal constitution forms a happy combination in this respect; the great and aggregate interests being referred to the national, the local and particular to the state legislatures.

The other point of difference is, the greater number of citizens and extent of territory which may be brought within the compass of republican, than of democratic government; and it is this circumstance principally which renders factious combinations less to be dreaded in the former, than in the latter. The smaller the society the fewer probably will be the distinct parties and interests composing it; the fewer the distinct parties and interests, the more frequently will a majority be found of the same party; and the smaller the number of individuals composing a majority, and the smaller the compass within which they are placed, the more easily will they concert and execute their plans of oppression. Extend the sphere, and you take in a greater variety of parties and interests; you make it less probable that a majority of the whole will have a common motive to invade the rights of other citizens; or if such a common motive exists, it will be more difficult for all who feel it to discover their own strength, and to act in unison with each other. Besides other impediments, it may be remarked, that where there is a consciousness of unjust dishonourable purposes, communication is always checked by distrust, in proportion to the number whose concurrence is necessary.

Hence it clearly appears, that the same advantage, which a republic has over a democracy, in controlling the effects of faction, is enjoyed by a large over a small republic—is enjoyed by the union over the states composing it. Does this advantage consist in the substitution of representatives, whose enlightened views and virtuous sentiments render them superior to local prejudices and to schemes of injustice? It will not be denied, that the representation of the union will be most likely to possess these requisite endowments. Does it consist in the greater security afforded by a greater variety of parties, against the event of any one party being able to outnumber or oppress the rest? In an equal degree does the encreased variety of parties, comprised within the union, encrease this security. Does it, *in fine*, consist in the greater obstacles opposed to the concert and accomplishment of the secret wishes of an unjust and interested majority? Here, again, the extent of the union gives it the most palpable advantage.

The influence of factious leaders may kindle a flame within their particular states, but will be unable to spread a general conflagration through the other states: A religious sect, may degenerate into a political faction in a part of the confederacy; but the variety of sects dispersed over the entire face of it, must secure the national councils against any danger from that source: A range of paper money, for an abolition of debts, for an equal division of property, or for any other improper or wicked project, will be less apt to pervade the whole body of the union, than a particular member of it; in the sample proportion as such a malady is more likely to taint a particular county or district, than an entire sate.

In the extent an proper structure of the union, therefore, we behold a republican remedy for the diseases most incident to republican government. And according to the degree of pleasure and pride, we feel in being republicans, ought to be our zeal in cherishing the spirit, and supporting the character of federalists.

Publius.

DOCUMENT ANALYSIS

1. What attitude does Madison express toward direct democracy?

Seven.3

George Mason, "Objections to This Constitution of Government" (1787)

George Mason played a prominent role in Virginia politics before, during, and after the American Revolution. His groundbreaking Virginia Declaration of Rights would find echoes in Thomas Jefferson's Declaration of Independence, and he was widely respected for his political skills. At the Constitutional Convention in Philadelphia in 1787, Mason was an active participant in the debates. When it came time to sign the final document, however, Mason withheld his support, fearing that the new government created under the Constitution would lead to the same abuse of power that had been charged against England. *

There is no Declaration of Rights, and the Laws of the general Government being paramount to the Laws & Constitutions of the several States, the Declarations of Rights in the separate States are no Security. Nor are the People secured even in the Enjoyment of the Benefits of the common Law.

In the House of Representatives, there is not the Substance, but the Shadow only of Representation; which can never produce proper Information in the Legislature, or inspire Confidence in the People; the Laws will therefore be generally made by men little concern'd in, and unacquainted with their Effects and Consequences.

The Senate have the Power of altering all money Bills, and of originating appropriations of money, & the Sallerys of the Officers of their own Appointment, in Conjunction with the president of the United States; altho' they are not the Representatives of the People, or amenable to them.

These, with their other great Powers (viz: their Power in the Appointment of Ambassadors and all public Officers, in making Treaties, and in trying all Impeachments) their Influence upon & Connection with the supreme Executive from these Causes, their Duration of Office, and their being a constant existing Body, almost continually sit-

* From George Mason, "Objections to This Constitution of Government," Manuscript written on the verso of the Committee of Style draft of the U.S. Constitution, Chapin Library, Williams College.

ting, joined with their being one compleat Branch of the Legislature will destroy any Ballance in the Government, & enable them to accomplish what Usurpations they please upon the Rights and Liberty of the People.

The Judiciary of the United States is so constructed & extended, as to absorb and destroy the Judiciarys of the several States; thereby rendering Law as tedious intricate and expensive, & Justice as unattainable, by a great Part of the Community, as in England, and enabling the Rich to oppress & ruin the Poor.

The President of the United States has no constitutional Council (a thing unknown in any safe & regular Government) he will therefore be unsupported by proper information and Advice; and will generally be directed by Minions and Favourites. Or he will become a Tool to the Senate—or a Council of State will grow out of the principal Officers of the great Departments; the worst & most dangerous of all Ingredients for such a Council, in a free country.

From this fatal Defect has arisen the improper Power of the Senate in the appointment of public Officers, and the alarming Dependence & Connection between that Branch of the Legislature and the supreme Executive.

Hence also sprung that unnecessary Officer, the Vice-President; who for want of other Employment, is made President of the Senate; thereby dangerously blending the executive and legislative Powers; besides always giving to some one of the States an unnecessary and unjust pre-eminence over the others....

Under their own Construction of the general Clause, at the End of the enumerated Powers, the Congress may grant Monopolies in Trade & Commerce, constitute new Crimes, inflict unusual and severe Punishments, & extend their Powers as far as they shall think proper; so that the state Legislatures have no Security for their Powers now presumed to remain to them, or the People for their Rights.

There is no Declaration of any kind, for preserving the Liberty of the Press, or the Tryal by Jury in Civil Causes; nor against the Danger of standing Armys in time of Peace....

This Government will set out a moderate Aristocracy: it is at present impossible to foresee whether it will, in its operation, produce a Monarchy, or a corrupt tyrannical Aristocracy; it will most probably vibrate some years between the two, and then terminate in the one or the other.

Document Analysis

1. Why is Mason so opposed to the newly drafted Constitution? Do his concerns seem valid?

2. Why does Mason find the constitutional powers given to the U.S. Senate especially disturbing?

Chapter Study Questions

1. What did Washington mean when he told the officers, "give the world another subject of wonder…an army victorious over its enemies—victorious over itself"?

2. According to James Madison, how would the new constitution balance the "cabals of a few" with the "confusion of the multitude"? What objections might George Mason make to Madison's *Federalist Paper #10*?

Eight

Creating a Nation

The writers of the Constitution provided a framework for a government for the new nation. As seen in your text, it would be left to the first four presidential administrations, of Washington, Adams, Jefferson, and Madison, to prove that it was a workable compact. Their task was a difficult one, as policies, programs, and procedures had to be developed for the nation and divisions quickly appeared within the leadership over which policies and programs would be the most effective for the nation and how to implement them. These differences led to the rise of political parties, something that the framers of the Constitution had hoped to avoid. But despite these obstacles, by the end of the War of 1812, the country had settled into its institutional structures and learned that politics could be a natural part of the political process, while at the same time it almost doubled in size, withstood a war with a major European power, and re-established independence from Europe.

This chapter begins with Benjamin Banneker's letter to Thomas Jefferson which reminds us (and the then secretary of state) that the Declaration of Independence's promise that "all men are created equal," as well as the new government under the Constitution, did not apply to slaves.

George Washington's melancholy farewell address is an argument for national unity by a man who personified the nation. As he left office, Washington was disheartened by the disputes between Republicans and Federalists, believed in strong economic development, and argued for an America independent in foreign affairs.

The deep divide between the parties could be seen in the Alien and Sedition Acts, enacted by the Federalists in 1798, during the so-called "Quasi War" with France. Not only did these laws reveal a deep suspicion of foreign radicals threatening America, they made it criminal for any American to criticize the actions of the federal government. After serving one term as John Adams's vice president, Thomas Jefferson, a Democratic-Republican, became the third president of the United States in 1801.

When Jefferson took office, the Republicans detested the judiciary. Not a single Republican judge had been appointed to the federal judiciary in the 1790s, and Republican newspaper editors were regularly hauled before federal courts under the Sedition Act. As soon as it met, the Republican Congress repealed the Federal Judiciary Act of 1801, which had created new courts, packed by John Adams with Federalists.

One of Adam's appointees, William Marbury, petitioned the Supreme Court for a writ of mandamus, or order, to restore his commission as a justice of the peace for Washington, D.C. John Marshall, the chief justice of the Supreme Court, ruled in *Marbury v. Madison* that the Supreme Court's right of mandamus was unconstitutional and incorrectly based on a clause in the Judiciary Act of 1789. He thereby established the Court's right to review and reverse federal state court decisions that conflicted with federal law or the Constitution. This is known as the principle of judicial review. Judicial review was not explicitly mentioned in the Constitution, although Alexander Hamilton asserted it in *Federalist Paper #78*, and future cases codified and strengthened it.

At the same time as it fleshed out the scope and limits of its governing and judicial institutions, the nation also experienced significant territorial growth under Jefferson. The Louisiana Purchase is considered one of the greatest accomplishments of the Jefferson administration. With one act, Jefferson doubled the size of the nation and laid the foundation for one of the largest territorial expansions undertaken by any country in history. He asked his private secretary, Meriwether Lewis, to lead an expedition to explore and map the newly purchased land. Led by Lewis and his partner, William Clark, the party trekked for over two years, reaching the Pacific in 1805. Included in this chapter is a series of selections from the journals they kept during their journey. Despite the enormity of the Louisiana Purchase, in the first decades of the 1800s settlement of the "west" still meant the region immediately beyond the Appalachians, including what are now the states of Alabama, Indiana, and Missouri.

Eight.1

Benjamin Banneker,
Letter to Thomas Jefferson
(1791)

Benjamin Banneker was a free black mathematician and surveyor living in Maryland who helped lay out Washington, D.C. He also published an astronomical almanac which was sold throughout the Middle Atlantic states. This is an excerpt from his letter to the then secretary of state Thomas Jefferson, inspired by Banneker's reading of Jefferson's Notes on the State of Virginia. *

Sir, I am fully sensible of the greatness of that freedom which I take with you on the present occasion; a liberty which Seemed to me Scarcely allowable, when I reflected on that distinguished, and dignifying station in which you Stand; and the almost general prejudice and prepossession which is so previlent in the world against those of my complexion....

Sir I freely and Chearfully acknoweldge, that I am of the African race, and, in that colour which is natural to them of the deepest dye:[†] and it is under a Sense of the most profound gratitude to the Supreme Ruler of the universe, that I do now confess to you, that I am not under that State of tyrannical thralldom, and inhuman captivity, to which too many of my bretheren are doomed; but that I have abundantly tasted of the fruition of those blessings which proceed from that free and unequalled liberty with which you are favoured and which I hope you will willingly allow you have received from the immediate Hand of that Being from whom proceedeth every good and perfect gift.

Sir, Suffer me to recall to your mind that time in which the Arms and tyranny of the British Crown were exerted with powerful effort, in order to reduce you to a State of Servitude; look back I entreat you on the variety of dangers to which you were exposed, reflect on that time in which every human aid appeared unavailable, and in which even hope and fortitude wore the greatful Sense of your miraculous and providential preser-

---

* From Silvio A. Bedini, *The Life of Benjamin Banneker* (New York: Landmark Enterprises, 1984), 152–159.

[†] My Father was Brought here a Slave from Africa.

vation; You cannot but acknowledge, that the present freedom and tranquility which you enjoy you have mercifully received, and that it is the peculiar blessing of Heaven.

This, Sir, was a time in which you clearly saw into the injustice of a State of Slavery, and in which you have Just apprehension of the horrors of its condition, it was now Sir, that you abhorrence thereof was so excited, that you publickly held forth this true and invaluable doctrine, which is worthy to be recorded and remembered in all Succeeding ages. "We hold these truths to be Self evident, that all men are created equal, and that they are endowed by their creator with certain inalienable rights, that amongst them are life, liberty, and the persuit of happiness."…

Sir, I suppose that your knowledge of the situation of my brethren is too extensive to need a recital here; neither shall I presume to prescribe methods by which they may be relieved, otherwise than by recommending to you, and all others, to wean yourselves from those narrow prejudices which you have imbibed with respect to them, and as Job proposed to his friends, "Put your Souls in their Souls' stead," thus shall your hearts be enlarged with kindness and benevolence towards them, and thus shall you need neither the direction of myself or others in what manner to proceed herein.

And now, Sir, altho my Sympathy and affection for my brethren hath caused my enlargement thus far, I ardently hope that your candour and generosity will plead with you in my behalf, when I make known to you, that it was not originally my design; but that having taken up my pen in order to direct to you as a present, a copy of an Almanack which I have calculated for the Succeeding year, I was unexpectedly and unavoidably led thereto.…

DOCUMENT ANALYSIS

1. What is Banneker's attitude toward slavery, and what evidence does he offer to suggest that, while he is a free man, he takes slavery very personally?

Eight.2

George Washington, Farewell Address (1796)

George Washington delivered his farewell address in September 1796, stating that he would not accept a third term as president. He was 64 years old and disheartened: the patriot, war hero, president, and national symbol had been unable to stay above the fray of political argument. In his address, he argues for a nation united rather than divided by parties, economic policies, and foreign affairs.*

Observe good faith and justice toward all nations. Cultivate peace and harmony with all. Religion and morality enjoin this conduct. And can it be that good policy does not equally enjoin it? It will be worthy of a free, enlightened, and, at no distant period, a great nation to give to mankind the magnanimous and too novel example of a people always guided by an exalted justice and benevolence....

In the execution of such a plan nothing is more essential than that permanent, inveterate antipathies against particular nations and passionate attachments for others should be excluded, and that, in place of them just and amicable feelings toward all should be cultivated. The nation which indulges toward another an habitual hatred or an habitual fondness is in some degree a slave. It is a slave to its animosity or to its affection either of which is sufficient to lead it astray from its duty and its interest....

The nation prompted by ill will and resentment sometimes impels to war the government, contrary to the best calculations of policy. The government sometimes participates in the national propensity, and adopts through passion what reason would reject....

So, likewise, a passionate attachment of one nation for another produces a variety of evils. Sympathy for the favorite nation, facilitating the illusion of an imaginary common interest in cases where no real common interest exists, and infusing into one the enmi-

* From *Messages and Papers of the Presidents*, ed. J. D. Richardson, National Archives and Records Administration, (1986) 1, 221–223.

ties of the other, betrays the former into a participation in the quarrels and wars of the latter without adequate inducement or justification....

As avenues to foreign influence in innumerable ways, such attachments are particularly alarming to the truly enlightened and independent patriot. How many opportunities do they afford to tamper with domestic factions to practice the arts of seduction, to mislead public opinion, to influence or awe the public councils! Such an attachment of a small or weak toward a great and powerful nation dooms the former to be the satellite of the latter.

Against the insidious wiles of foreign influence (I conjure you to believe me, fellow citizens) the jealousy of a free people ought to be constantly awake, since history and experience prove that foreign influence is one of the most baneful foes of republican government....

The great rule of conduct for us in regard to foreign nations is, in extending our commercial relations, to have with them as little political connection as possible. So far as we have already formed engagements, let them be fulfilled with perfect good faith. Here let us stop.

Europe has a set of primary interests which to us have no, or a very remote, relation. Hence she must be engaged in frequent controversies, the causes of which are essentially foreign to our concerns. Hence, therefore, it must be unwise in us to implicate ourselves by artificial ties in the ordinary vicissitudes of her politics, or the ordinary combinations and collisions of her friendships and enmities.

Our detached and distant situation invites and enables us to pursue a different course. If we remain one people, under an efficient government, the period is not far off when we may defy material injury from external annoyance; when we may take such as attitude as well cause the neutrality we may at any time resolve upon to be scrupulously respected; when belligerent nations, under the impossibility of making acquisitions upon us, will not lightly hazard the giving us provocation; when we may choose peace or war, as our interest, guided by justice, shall counsel.

Why forego the advantages of so peculiar a situation? Why quit our own to stand upon foreign ground? Why, by interweaving our destiny with that of any part of Europe, entangle our peace and prosperity in the toils of European ambition, rivalship, interest, humor, or caprice?

It is our true policy to steer clear of permanent alliances with any portion of the foreign world, so far, I mean, as we are now at liberty to do it. For let me not be understood as capable of patronizing infidelity to existing engagements. I hold the maxim of less applicable to public than to private affairs that honesty is always the best policy. I repeat, therefore, let those engagements be observed in their genuine sense. But in my opinion it is unnecessary and would be unwise to extend them.

Taking care always to keep ourselves by suitable establishments on a respectable defensive posture, we may safely trust to temporary alliances for extraordinary emergencies.

Harmony, liberal intercourse with all nations, are recommended by policy, humanity, and interest. But even our commercial policy should hold an equal and impartial hand, neither seeking nor granting exclusive favors or preference;...constantly keeping in view that it is folly in one nation to look for disinterested favors from another; that it must pay with a portion of its independence for whatever it may accept under that character; that by such acceptance it may place itself in the condition of having given equivalents for nominal favor, and yet of being reproached with ingratitude for not giving more. There can be no greater error than to expect or calculate upon real favors from nation to nation. It is an illusion which experience must cure, which a just pride ought to discard.

DOCUMENT ANALYSIS

1. What did Washington mean in his statement, "the jealousy of a free people ought to be consistently awake"?
2. How does Washington contrast the United States to Europe?

The Alien and Sedition Acts
(1798)

During the 1790s, many in the United States were understandably disturbed by the violent excesses of the French Revolution, and the United States and France entered a hostile period for a few years. Federalists, who controlled Congress, were especially suspicious about the pro-France sympathies of Thomas Jefferson and his Republican friends. In 1798, Federalists passed the Alien and Sedition Acts, which were used to silence opposition to their policies. These acts made the political climate of this era all the more heated, and the legislatures of Virginia and Kentucky passed resolutions seeking to nullify these laws as unconstitutional. When Jefferson and the Republicans came to power after the election of 1800, they repealed the Alien and Sedition Acts.*

An Act respecting alien enemies.

SECTION 1.

Be it enacted by the Senate and House of Representatives of the United States of America, in Congress assembled, That whenever there shall be a declared war between the United States and any foreign nation or government, or any invasion or predatory incursion shall be perpetrated, attempted, or threatened against the territory of the United States, by any foreign nation or government, and the President of the United States shall make public proclamation of the event, all natives, citizens, denizens, or subjects of the hostile nation or government, being males of the age of fourteen years and upwards, who shall be within the United States, and not actually naturalized, shall be liable to be apprehended, restrained, secured and removed, as alien enemies....

---

* From Pearson Online, accessible at http://wps.ablongman.com/wps/media/objects/1676/1716309/documents/doc_d07d06.html.

Sedition Act (1798)

SEC. 1

Be it enacted by the Senate and House of Representatives of the United States of America, in Congress assembled, That if any persons shall unlawfully combine or conspire together, with intent to oppose any measure or measures of the government of the United States, which are or shall be directed by proper authority, or to impede the operation of any law of the United States, or to intimidate or prevent any person holding a place or office in or under the government of the United States, from undertaking, performing or executing his trust or duty; and if any person or persons, with intent as aforesaid, shall counsel, advise or attempt to procure any insurrection, riot, unlawful assembly, or combination, whether such conspiracy, threatening, counsel, advice, or attempt shall have the proposed effect or not, he or they shall be deemed guilty of a high misdemeanor, and on conviction, before any court of the United States having jurisdiction thereof, shall be punished by a fine not exceeding five thousand dollars, and by imprisonment during a term not less than six months nor exceeding five years; and further, at the discretion of the court may be holden to find sureties for his good behaviour in such sum, and for such time, as the said court may direct.

SEC. 2

And be it further enacted, That if any person shall write, print, utter or publish, or shall cause or procure to be written, printed, uttered or publishing, or shall knowingly and willingly assist or aid in writing, printing, uttering or publishing any false, scandalous and malicious writing or writings against the government of the United States, or either house of the Congress of the United States, or the President of the United States, with intent to defame the said government, or either house of the said Congress, or the said President, or to bring them, or either of them, into contempt or disrepute; or to excite against them, or either or any of them, the hatred of the good people of the United States, or to excite any unlawful combinations therein, for opposing or resisting any law of the United States, or any act of the President of the United States, done in pursuance of any such law, or of the powers in him vested by the constitution of the United States, or to resist, oppose, or defeat any such law or act, or to aid, encourage or abet any hostile designs of any foreign nation against the United States, their people or government, then such person, being thereof convicted before any court of the United States having jurisdiction thereof, shall be punished by a fine not exceeding two thousand dollars, and by imprisonment not exceeding two years.

DOCUMENT ANALYSIS

1. Which parts of the Alien and Sedition Acts do you find reasonable, and which parts do you find most unreasonable? Explain.

2. In what ways did the Alien and Sedition Acts run contrary to the nation's founding principles, and the Bill of Rights?

Eight.4

Marbury v. Madison
(1803)

In Marbury v. Madison, John Marshall, the Federalist chief justice, deflected much of the Republican hostility directed at the Supreme Court and laid the foundation for the Court's eventual independence from purely political interests. Just as important, he established the principle of judicial review and the supremacy of the national government over the states. Among the tactics Marshall used was the device of having one justice's opinion (in this case, and often elsewhere, his own) speak for the whole Court. By making his claim cautiously and tentatively, Marshall deflected possible opposition while establishing an important precedent. *

[**C**hief Justice Marshall delivered the opinion of the Court.]

In the order in which the Court has viewed this subject, the following questions have been considered and decided: 1st. Has the applicant a right to the commission he demands? 2d. If he has a right, and that right has been violated, do the laws of this country afford him a remedy? 3d. If they do afford him a remedy, is it a mandamus issuing from this court?...

It is...the opinion of the Court: 1st. That by signing the commission of Mr. Marbury, the President of the United States appointed him a justice of the peace for the county of Washington, in the District of Columbia; and that the seal of the United States, affixed thereto by the secretary of state, is conclusive testimony of the verity of the signature, and of the completion of the appointment; and that the appointment conferred on him a legal right to the office of the space of five years. 2d. That, having this legal title to the office, he has a consequent right to the commission; a refusal to deliver which is a plain violation of that right, for which the laws of his country afford him a remedy. 3d. It remains to be inquired whether he is entitled to the remedy for which he applies?...

* From Citations: 5 U.S. (1 Cranch) 137; 2 L. Ed. 60; 1803 U.S. LEXIS 352.

This...is a plain case of a mandamus, either to deliver the commission, or a copy of it from the record; and it only remains to be inquired, whether it can issue from this court?

The act to establish the judicial courts of the United States authorizes the Supreme Court, "to issue writs of mandamus, in cases warranted by the principles and usages of law, to any courts appointed or persons holding office, under the authority of the United States." The secretary of state, being a person holding an office under the authority of the United States, is precisely within the letter of this description; and if this court is not authorized to issue a writ of mandamus to such an officer, it must be because the law is unconstitutional...

The Constitution vests the whole judicial power of the United States in one Supreme Court, and such inferior courts as Congress shall, from time to time, ordain and establish...

In the distribution of this power, it is declared that "the Supreme Court shall have original jurisdiction in all cases affecting ambassadors, other public ministers and consuls, and those in which a state shall be a party. In all other cases, the Supreme Court shall have appellate jurisdiction."...

If it had been intended to leave it in the discretion of the legislature to apportion the judicial power between the supreme and inferior courts according to the will of that body, it would certainly have been useless to have proceeded further than to have defined the judicial power, and the tribunals in which is should be vested. The subsequent part of the section is mere surplusage, is entirely without meaning,...

It cannot be presumed that any clause in the Constitution is intended to be without effect...

To enable this court, then, to issue a mandamus, it must be shown to be an exercise of appellate jurisdiction...

The authority, therefore, given to the Supreme Court, by the Act establishing the judicial courts of the United States, to issue writs of mandamus to public officers, appears not to be warranted by the Constitution...

DOCUMENT ANALYSIS

1. What does Marshall mean in his ruling when he states that the law in question "appears not to be warranted by the Constitution"?

Eight.5

Meriwether Lewis, Journal (1805)

Meriwether Lewis, Jefferson's personal secretary, and Lewis's friend William Clark had both served in the West in the army. In 1803 they were sent on a mission by President Jefferson to gather scientific information, explore the Louisiana Purchase territory, establish formal relationships with the Native American groups, and evaluate the fur trade. Lewis and Clark, with a party of almost fifty experienced men, left from St. Louis and traveled to the Pacific along the Missouri, Yellowstone, and Columbia Rivers with the help of a Shoshone guide, Sacajawea, and her French-Canadian husband, Toussaint Charbonneau. Their journals expanded interest in and disseminated information about the West.*

Saturday August 17th 1805

we made them [the Indians] sensible of their dependance on the will of our government for every species of merchandize as well for their defence & comfort; and apprized them of the strength of our government and its friendly dispositions toward them. we also gave them as a reason why we wished to pe[ne]trate the country as far as the ocean to the west of them was to examine and find out a more direct way to bring merchandize to them. that as no trade could by carryed on with them before our return to our homes that it was mutually advantageous to them as well as to ourselves that they should render us such aids as they had in their power to furnish in order to haisten our voyage and of course our return home. that such were their horses to transport our baggage without which we could not subsist, and that a pilot to conduct us through the mountains was also necessary if we could not decend the river by water. but that we did not ask either their horses or their services without giving a satisfactory compensation in return.

* From *The Journals of Lewis and Clark*, ed., Barnard De Voto (Boston: Houghton Mifflin, 1981), 202–206, 207–211, 213–214. Copyright © 1953 by Barnard De Voto. Copyright © renewed 1981 by Avis Devoto. Reprinted by permission of Houghton Mifflin Company.

that at present we wished them to collect as many horses as were necessary to transport our baggage to their village on the Columbia where we would then trade with them at our leasure for such horses as they could spare us.

the chief thanked us for friendship towards himself and nation & declared his wish to serve us in every rispect. that he was sorry to find that it must yet be some time before they could be furnished with firearms but said they could live as they had done heretofore until we brought them as we had promised. he said they had not horses enough with them at present to remove our baggage to their village over the mountain, but that he would return tomorrow and encourage his people to come over with their horses and that he would bring his own and assist us. this was complying with all we wished at present.

Sunday August 18th 1805

this morning while Capt. Clark was busily engaged in preparing for his rout, I exposed some articles to barter with the Indians for horses as I wished a few at this moment to releive the men who were going with Capt. Clark from the labour of carrying their baggage, and also one to keep here in order to pack the meat to camp which the hunters might kill. i soon obtained three very good horses for which I gave an uniform coat, a pair of legings, a few handkerchiefs, three knives and some other small article the whole of which did not cost more than about 20$ in the U'States. the Indians seemed quite as well pleased with their bargin as I was. the men also purchased one for an old checked shirt a pair of old legings and a knife. two of those I purchased Capt. C. took on him. At 10 a.m. Capt. Clark departed with his detachment and all the Indians except 2 men and 2 women who remained with us.

Tuesday August 20th 1805

i now prevailed on the Chief to instruct me with rispect to the geography of his country. This he undertook very cheerfully, by delineating the rivers on the ground. but I soon found that his information fell far short of my expectation or wishes. He drew the river on which we now are [the Lemhi] to which he placed two branches just above us, which he shewed me from the openings on the mountains were in view; he next made it discharge itself into a large river which flowed from the S.W. about ten miles below us [the Salmon], then continued this joint stream in the same direction of this valley or N.W. for one days march and then enclined to the West for 2 more days march. here we placed a number of heaps of sand on each side which he informed me represented the vast mountains of rock eternally covered with snow through which the river passed. that the perpendicular and even juting rocks so closely hemmed in the river that there was no possibil[it]y of passing along the shore; that the bed of the river was obstructed by sharp pointed rocks and the rapidity of the stream such that the whole surface of the river was beat into perfect foam as far as the eye could reach. that the mountains were also inaccessible to man or horse. he said that this being the state of the country in that direction that himself nor none of his nation had ever been further down the river than these mountains.

in this manner I spend the day smoking with them and acquiring what information I could with respect to their country. they informed me that they could pass the Spaniards by the way of the yellowstone river in 10 days. I can discover that these people are by no means friendly to the Spaniards. their complaint is, that the Spaniards will not let them have fire arms and ammunition, that they put them off by telling them that if they suffer them to have guns they will kill each other, thus leaving them defenceless and an easy prey to their bloodthirsty neighbours to the East of them who being in possession of fire arms hunt them up and murder them without rispect to sex or age and plunder them of their horses on all occasions. they told me that to avoid their enemies who were eternally harrassing them that they were obliged to remain in the interior of these mountains at least two thirds of the year where the[y] suffered as we then saw great hardships for the want of food sometimes living for weeks without meat and only a little fish roots and berries. but this added Cameahwait, with his ferce eyes and lank jaws grown meager for the want of food, would not be the case if we had guns, we could then live in the country of buffaloe and eat as our enimies do and not be compelled to hide ourselves in these mountains and live on roots and berries as the bear do. whitemen would come to them with an abundance of guns and every other article necessary to their defence and comfort, and that they would be enabled to supply themselves with these articles on reasonable terms in exchange for the skins of the beaver Otter and Ermin so abundant in their country. they expressed great pleasure at this information and said they had been long anxious to see the whitemen that traded guns; and that we might rest assured of their friendship and that they would do whatever we wished them.

Document Analysis

1. How did the Lewis and Clark expedition relate to Native Americans? How does Lewis describe the Native American reaction to their expedition?

Chapter Study Questions

1. How does Benjamin Banneker reflect the inspiration of the American Revolution in making his claims for equality? Why did such claims largely go unheeded in the United States for several generations?

2. Was it realistic in 1796 to expect the nation, as Washington urged, to "steer clear of permanent alliances"? Is it realistic in the early twenty-first century? Why or why not?

3. What accounts for the bitter hatred between the early Federalists and Republicans in the 1790s, and the suspicion evident in the Alien and Sedition Acts?

4. Why is the *Marbury v. Madison* ruling so significant in the nation's early history?

Nine

Society and Politics in the Early Republic

In the early nineteenth century, America consisted of several distinctive regions, loosely joined by transportation and communication. In the Northeast, farmers struggled to rest a living from long-cultivated land. To the South, cotton was beginning to emerge as the dominant staple crop. As it did, the region's sagging economy, together with its system of slave labor, began a fateful expansion. West of the Appalachian Mountains, as whites continued to settle in lands that had been held by natives for generations, frequent conflicts erupted. In 1810, the Shawnee chief, Tecumseh, appealed to Indiana territorial governor William Henry Harrison for protection against what he felt was the illegal purchase of his tribal lands. Tecumseh's appeal was not heeded, and he would die in the War of 1812, fighting on the side of the British.

The "opening" of American society was driven by an expanding market economy with its relentless discipline of supply and demand, pursuit of individual profit, and impersonal, contractual relationships. As the market expanded it weakened long-standing commitments to a "just price" and other values of an earlier "moral economy."

In addition, the wave of religious revivalism known as the Second Great Awakening swept through American society beginning about 1800 and strengthened belief in individualism and equality. But not all Americans benefited equally from these changes. Doctrines of equality, opportunity, and individual autonomy resonated far more powerfully in the lives of white men than of white women. In the south, African Americans found their lives harshly constrained by a revitalized system of slavery, while in the North, free blacks faced an increasingly racialized society. Questions about the spread of slavery, described in the Missouri Enabling Act, were becoming more prominent.

Patterns of change appeared in the political arena as well, where democratic forces were promoted by a new generation of political leaders eager to claim their place in shaping the nation's future. A diplomatic revolution of major importance followed the War of 1812 when the American people broke free of their centuries-old dependence on

Europe and turned their energies toward exploiting the vast North American continent. As evidenced by the Monroe Doctrine, the United States asserted a bold new role among the emerging nations of Latin America as those nations also threw off the yoke of European colonialism.

Tecumseh,
Letter to Governor William Henry Harrison
(1810)

When the Shawnee Chief, Tecumseh, was away from his people in August 1810, several members of his tribe, without authorization, sold off significant lands along the Wabash River to the whites. Tecumseh considered these sales illegal, and appealed to the Indiana territorial governor, William Henry Harrison, to fix this injustice. Harrison refused, and would later go on to win fame as a fighter of Indians in the Battle of Tippecanoe. Tecumseh would join the side of the British in the War of 1812, and die in the fighting.*

August 12, 1810

Tecumseh

It is true I am a Shawnee. My forefathers were warriors. Their son is a warrior. From them I take only my existence; from my tribe I take nothing. I am the maker of my own fortune; and oh! that I could make of my own fortune; and oh! that I could make that of my red people, and of my country, as great as the conceptions of my mind, when I think of the Spirit that rules the universe. I would not then come to Governor Harrison to ask him to tear the treaty and to obliterate the landmark; but I would say to him: "Sir, you have liberty to return to your own country."

The being within, communing with past ages, tells me that once, nor until lately, there was no white man on this continent; that it then all belonged to red men, children of the same parents, placed on it by the Great Spirit that made them, to keep it, to traverse it, to enjoy its productions, and to fill it with the same race, once a happy race, since made miserable by the white people, who are never contented but always encroaching. The way, and the only way, to check and to stop this evil, is for all the red men to unite in claiming a common and equal right in the land, as it was at first, and

* From James Madison Center.

should be yet; for it never was divided, but belongs to all for the use of each. For no part has a right to sell, even to each other, much less to strangers—those who want all, and will not do with less.

The white people have no right to take the land from the Indians, because they had it first; it is theirs. They may sell, but all must join. Any sale not made by all is not valid. The late sale is bad. It was made by a part only. Part do not know how to sell. All red men have equal rights to the unoccupied land. The right of occupancy is as good in one place as in another. There can not be two occupations in the same place. The first excludes all others. It is not so in hunting or traveling; for there the same ground will serve many, as they may follow each other all day; but the camp is stationary, and that is occupancy. It belongs to the first who sits down on his blanket or skins which he has thrown upon the ground; and till he leaves it no other has a right.

DOCUMENT ANALYSIS

1. How does Tecumseh's plea to Governor Harrison reflect how most Native Americans regarded their tribal land?

2. What is Tecumseh's attitude toward the white settlers?

Nine.2

Missouri Enabling Act
(1820)

In 1817 the Territory of Missouri applied for statehood. When the question came before the U.S. Congress in 1819, an intense debate ensued concerning the status of slavery in Missouri. At that time there were an equal number of slave and free states, and both sides feared the consequences of becoming outnumbered by the other. The issue was resolved when Maine—then a part of Massachusetts—also applied for statehood. The Missouri Compromise of February 1820 admitted Maine as a free state and Missouri as a slave state. The following month the Missouri Enabling Act officially authorized Missouri to draft a constitution and organize a state government.

An Act to authorize the people of the Missouri territory to form a constitution and state government, and for the admission of such state into the Union on an equal footing with the original states, and to prohibit slavery in certain territories.

Be it enacted… That the inhabitants of that portion of the Missouri territory included within the boundaries hereinafter designated, be, and they are hereby, authorized to form for themselves a constitution and state government, and to assume such name as they shall deem proper; and the said state, when formed, shall be admitted into the Union, upon an equal footing with the original states, in all respects whatsoever.

SEC. 2. That the said state shall consist of all the territory included within the following boundaries, to wit: Beginning in the middle of the Mississippi river, on the parallel of thirty-six degrees of north latitude; thence west, along that parallel of latitude, to the St. Francois river; thence up, and following the course of that river, in the middle of the main channel thereof, to the parallel of latitude of thirty-six degrees and thirty minutes; thence west, along the same, to a point where the said parallel is intersected by a meridian line passing through the middle of the mouth of the Kansas river, where the same empties into the Missouri river, thence, from the point aforesaid north, along the said meridian line, to the intersection of the parallel of latitude which passes through the rapids of the river Des Moines, making the said line to correspond with the Indian boundary line; thence east, from the point of intersection last aforesaid, along the said parallel of latitude, to the middle of the channel of the main fork of the said river Des Moines; thence down and along the middle of the main channel of the said river Des Moines, to the mouth of the same, where it empties into the Mississippi river; thence, due east, to the middle of the main channel of the Mississippi river; thence down, and following the course of the Mississippi river, in the middle of the main channel thereof, to the place of beginning:...

SEC. 3. That all free white male citizens of the United States, who shall have arrived at the age of twenty-one years, and have resided in said territory three months previous to the day of election, and all other persons qualified to vote for representatives to the general assembly of the said territory, shall be qualified to be elected, and they are hereby qualified and authorized to vote, and choose representatives to form a convention....

SEC. 8. That in all that territory ceded by France to the United States, under the name of Louisiana, which lies north of thirty-six degrees and thirty minutes north latitude, not included within the limits of the state, contemplated by this act, slavery and involuntary servitude, otherwise than in the punishment of crimes, whereof the parties shall have been duly convicted, shall be, and is hereby, forever prohibited: Provided always, That any person escaping into the same, from whom labour or service is lawfully claimed, in any state or territory of the United States, such fugitive may be lawfully reclaimed and conveyed to the person claiming his or her labour or service as aforesaid.

DOCUMENT ANALYSIS

1. To which groups of people did the Enabling Act extend the right to vote? Which groups were denied this right?

2. What provisions pertaining to slavery were incorporated into the Enabling Act?

The Monroe Doctrine
(1823)

President James Monroe presented this doctrine as part of his annual message to Congress in December 1823. He proposed it at a time when the Old World powers were losing their colonial interests in the New World. The United States had recognized the former colonies of Argentina, Chile, Peru, Mexico, and Colombia as independent nations in 1822. Monroe was in the unenviable position of trying to maintain a strong stance with the European powers, who were struggling over a balance of world power. When the British suggested that the United States should ally with them in order to impede French and Spanish interference in the Americas, Monroe had to make a decision. Greatly influenced by Secretary of State John Quincy Adams, Monroe chose to announce the new policy, which basically stated that the United States would not interfere in European matters and it would view any interference in the Americas as endangering "our peace and happiness."

The Monroe Doctrine set a precedent in U.S. foreign relations. When European policymakers heard it, they thought it "arrogant" and "blustering," but it became important as a declaration of principles later in the nineteenth century, as the economic and military power of the United States caught up with the Monroe vision. One reaction to the doctrine below is an editorial from the Baltimore Chronicle. *It is typical of some of the patriotic acclaim that the statement by Monroe received.**

In the discussion to which this interest [Russia's on the northwest coast] has given rise, the occasion has been judged proper for asserting, as a principle in which the rights and interests of the United States are involved, that the American continents, by the free and independent condition which they have assumed and maintain, are henceforth not to be considered as subjects for the future colonization by any European powers....

* From *Messages and Papers of the Presidents*, ed. J. D. Richardson, National Archives and Records Administration, (1896), II, 209, 218–219.

The political system of the Allied Powers [Holy Alliance] is essentially different …from that of America. This difference proceeds from that which exists in their prospective [monarchical] governments; and to the defence of our own…this whole nation is devoted. We owe it, therefore, to candor and to the amicable relations existing between the United States and those powers to declare that we should consider any attempt on their part to extend their system to any portion of this hemisphere as dangerous to our peace and safety.

With the existing colonies or dependencies of any European power, we have not interfered and shall not interfere. But with the governments [of Spanish America] who have declared their independence and maintained it, and whose independence we have, on great consideration and on just principles, acknowledged, we could not view any interposition for the purpose of oppressing them, or controlling in any other light than as the manifestation of an unfriendly disposition toward the United States.…

Our policy in regard to Europe, which was adopted at an early stage of the wars which have so long agitated that quarter of the globe, nevertheless remains the same, which is, not to interfere in the internal concerns of any of its powers; to consider the government *de facto* as the legitimate government for us; to cultivate friendly relations with it, and to preserve those relations by a frank, firm, and manly policy, meeting in all instances the just claims of every power, submitting to injuries from none.

But in regard to those [American] continents, circumstances are eminently and conspicuously different. It is impossible that the Allied Powers should extend their political system to a portion of either continent without endangering our peace and happiness. Nor can anyone believe that our southern brethren, if left to themselves, would adopt it of their own accord. It is equally impossible, therefore, that we should behold such interposition in any form with indifference.

Baltimore Chronicle, Editorial

We can tell…further that this high-toned, independent, and dignified message will not be read by the crowned heads of Europe without a revolting stare of astonishment. The conquerors of Bonaparte, with their laurels still green and blooming on their brows, and their disciplined animal machines, called armies, at their backs, could not have anticipated that their united force would so soon be defied by a young republic, whose existence, as yet, cannot be measured with the ordinary life of man.

This message itself constitutes an era in American history, worthy of commemoration.…We are confident that, on this occasion, we speak the great body of American sentiment, such as exulting millions are ready to re-echo.…We are very far from being confident that, if Congress occupy the high and elevated ground taken in the Message, it may not, under the smiles of Divine Providence, be the means of breaking up the Holy Alliance.

Of this we are positively sure: that all timidity, wavering imbecility, an backwardness on our part will confirm these detested tyrants in their confederacy; paralyze the exertions of freedom in every country; accelerate the fall of those young sister republics whom we have recently recognized; and, perhaps, eventually destroy our own at the feet of absolute monarchy.

DOCUMENT ANALYSIS

1. Restate the first two paragraphs of the Monroe Doctrine in simple terms. Which area is Monroe describing? What action does the Doctrine disallow?

2. How did Monroe describe relations between the U.S. and Europe? Does it differ significantly with U.S.–European relations today?

3. For what reasons is the editorial so positive in its review of the Monroe Doctrine? What would happen without the Monroe Doctrine?

Chapter Study Questions

1. In what ways did the documents presented here affect the lives of Native Americans and African Americans?

2. Compare the Monroe Doctrine with the Missouri Enabling Act. Both aim to protect certain rights. What are those rights? How would they be protected?

3. What hints to these documents offer for understanding American values in the Early Republic? What kinds of language and imagery are used to describe America and Americans?

PART THREE

AN EXPANDING PEOPLE, 1820–1877

Ten

Economic Transformations
in the Northeast
and the Old Northwest

By 1850 America was on the verge of becoming a modern society. As described in this chapter, the North and the West were undergoing revolutions in their economics. These changes would draw them closer together as they began to reap the benefits of technological advances that would revolutionize every segment of their societies. As depicted in the *Albany Daily Advertiser*, the Erie Canal was one of the engines of economic change that sparked a canal boom throughout the nation, including in the South. The South generally, however, did not industrialize but instead maintained its traditional agriculturally based economy. It found itself increasingly isolated from the rest of country.

Many Americans were moving away from rural areas into rapidly industrializing cities and towns such as Lowell, Massachusetts, and Cincinnati, Ohio. Lowell, founded in 1823 by a group of Boston entrepreneurs led by Francis Cabot Lowell, was considered the birthplace of the American factory system and the prototype for the soon-widespread employment of young rural women in the production of textiles.

Textile corporations built boardinghouses around their mills to accommodate the recent migrants and established paternalistic regulations governing these women. Regulations required that women workers be in their boardinghouses by ten o'clock each evening and that operators of the boardinghouses report violations to the mill's management. At least in the early years, the women were required to attend church. Such controls were designed to "protect" the workers and to assure Yankee parents that their daughters might leave home to work in the mills without injury to their persons or their reputations. In the mid-1830s, the women earned about $3.25 for a 73-hour week; room and board in a company boardinghouse cost about $1.25 per week. These earnings compared favorably with incomes from other areas open to women, like teaching, domestic service, or sewing. *The Harbinger* report on textile mills and the letters of Mary Paul, a worker, provide contrasting pictures of the textile factories of Lowell.

Albany Daily Advertiser on the Erie Canal (1819)

The Erie Canal was not completed until 1825, but the middle section, which ran from Utica to Rome, was completed in 1819. That opening is recounted in the excerpt below. The impact of the canal was immense. When completed, it traversed New York State and linked New York Harbor to the Great Lakes. It provided commercial transportation, encouraged westward expansion, and was the engineering marvel of its age. Cities and towns along its banks prospered, and New York City became the nation's shipping center.

The last two days have presented in this village, a scene of the liveliest interest; and I consider it among the privileges of my life to have been present to witness it. On Friday afternoon I walked to the head of the grand canal, the eastern extremity of which reaches within a very short distance of the village, and from one of the slight and airy bridges which crossed it, I had a sight that could not but exhilarate and elevate the mind. The waters were rushing in from the westward, and coming down their untried channel towards the sea. Their course, owing to the absorption of the new banks of the canal, and the distance they had to run from where the stream entered it, was much slower than I had anticipated; they continued gradually to steal along from bridge to bridge, and at first only spreading over the bed of the canal, imperceptibly rose and washed its sides with a gentle wave. It was dark before they reached the eastern extremity; but at sunrise next morning, they were on a level, two feet and a half deep throughout the whole distance of thirteen miles. The interest manifested by the whole country, as this new internal river rolled its first waves through the state, cannot be described. You might see the people running across the fields, climbing on trees and fences, and crowding the bank of the canal to gaze upon the welcome sight. A boat had been prepared at Rome, and as the waters came down the canal, you might mark their progress by that of this new Argo, which floated triumphantly along the Hellespont of the west, accompanied by the shouts of the peasantry, and having on her deck a military band. At nine the next morning, the bells began a merry peal, and the commissioners in carriages, proceeded from Bagg's hotel, to the place of embarkation.

The governor, accompanied by Gen. Van Rensselaer, Rev. Mr. Stansbury, of Albany, Rev. Dr. Blatchford, of Lansingburgh, Judge Miller, of Utica, Mr. Holly, Mr. Seymour, Judge Wright, Col. Lansing, Mr. Childs, Mr. Clark, Mr. Bunner, and a large company of their friends, embarked, at a quarter past nine, and were received with the roll of the drum, and the shouts of a large multitude of spectators. The boat, which received them, is built for passengers;—is sixty-one feet in length, and seven and an half feet in width;—having two rising cabins, of fourteen feet each, with a flat deck between them. In forty minutes the company reached Whitesborough, a distance of two miles and three quarters; the boat being drawn by a single horse, which walked on the towing path, attached to a tow rope, of about sixty feet long. The horse travelled, apparently, with the utmost ease. The boat, though literally loaded with passengers, drew but fourteen inches water. A military band played patriotic airs. From bridge to bridge, from village to village, the procession was saluted with cannon, and every bell whose sound could reach the canal, swung, as with instinctive life, as it passed by. At Whitesborough, a number of ladies embarked, and heightened, by their smiles, a scene which wanted but this to make it complete.

Document Analysis

1. How far did the boat travel on the canal in 40 minutes? How does this performance compare to modern means of transportation?

2. Why was the canal such an innovation? How had goods and people been transported prior to its opening?

3. Which transportation modes eventually replaced the canal system? Why?

The Harbinger, Female Workers of Lowell (1836)

The following is a selection from a magazine report investigating the textile mills of New England. Textile mills formed the backbone of the rapidly industrializing north while other industrial operations expanding during the period included paper mills (primarily in Philadelphia), iron and metalworking, refineries, and shoemaking (again, like textiles, primarily in New England). In 1836 Lowell had 17,000 inhabitants, and women composed nearly 70 percent of the laboring population. In addition to providing relatively cheap and dependable labor, it was hoped that the young unmarried women would keep the factories clean, Christian, and productive.*

We have lately visited the cities of Lowell [Mass.] and Manchester [N.H.] and have had an opportunity of examining the factory system more closely than before. We had distrusted the accounts which we had heard from persons engaged in the labor reform now beginning to agitate New England. We could scarcely credit the statements made in relation to the exhausting nature of the labor in the mills, and to the manner in which the young women—the operatives—lived in their boardinghouses, six sleeping in a room, poorly ventilated.

We went through many of the mills, talked particularly to a large number of the operatives, and ate at their boardinghouses, on purpose to ascertain by personal inspection the facts of the case. We assure our readers that very little information is possessed, and no correct judgments formed, by the public at large, of our factory system, which is the first germ of the industrial or commercial feudalism that is to spread over our land....

In Lowell live between seven and eight thousand young women, who are generally daughters of farmers of the different states of New England. Some of them are members of families that were rich in the generation before....

* From *The Harbinger*, Nov. 14, 1836.

The operatives work thirteen hours a day in the summer time, and from daylight to dark in the winter. At half past four in the morning the factory bell rings, and at five the girls must be in the mills. A clerk, placed as a watch, observes those who are a few minutes behind the time, and effectual means are taken to stimulate to punctuality. This is the morning commencement of the industrial discipline (should we not rather say industrial tyranny?) which is established in these associations of this moral and Christian community.

At seven the girls are allowed thirty minutes for breakfast, and at noon thirty minutes more for dinner, except during the first quarter of the year, when the time is extended to forty-five minutes. But within this time they must hurry to their boardinghouses and return to the factory, and that through the hot sun or the rain or the cold. A meal eaten under such circumstances must be quite unfavorable to digestion and health, as any medical man will inform us. After seven o'clock in the evening the factory bell sounds the close of the day's work.

Thus thirteen hours per day of close attention and monotonous labor are extracted from the young women in these manufactories....So fatigued—we should say, exhausted and worn out, but we wish to speak of the system in the simplest language —are numbers of girls that they go to bed soon after their evening meal, and endeavor by a comparatively long sleep to resuscitate their weakened frames for the toil of the coming day.

When capital has got thirteen hours of labor daily out of a being, it can get nothing more. It would be a poor speculation in an industrial point of view to own the operative; for the trouble and expense of providing for times of sickness and old age would more than counterbalance the difference between the price of wages and the expenses of board and clothing. The far greater number of fortunes accumulated by the North in comparison with the South shows that hireling labor is more profitable for capital than slave labor.

Now let us examine the nature of the labor itself, and the conditions under which it is performed. Enter with us into the large rooms, when the looms are at work. The largest that we saw is in the Amoskeag Mills at Manchester....The din and clatter of these five hundred looms, under full operation, struck us on first entering as something frightful and infernal, for it seemed such an atrocious violation of one of the faculties of the human soul, the sense of hearing. After a while we became somewhat used to it, and by speaking quite close to the ear of an operative and quite loud, we could hold a conversation and make the inquiries we wished.

The girls attended upon an average three looms; many attended four, but this requires a very active person, and the most unremitting care. However, a great many do it. Attention to two is as much as should be demanded of an operative. This gives us some idea of the application required during the thirteen hours of daily labor. The atmosphere of such a room cannot of course be pure; on the contrary, it is charged with cotton filaments and dust, which, we are told, are very injurious to the lungs.

On entering the room, although the day was warm, we remarked that the windows were down. We asked the reason, and a young woman answered very naively, and without seeming to be in the least aware that this privation of fresh air was anything else than perfectly natural, that "when the wind blew, the threads did not work well." After we had been in the room for fifteen or twenty minutes, we found ourselves, as did the persons who accompanied us, in quite a perspiration, produced by a certain moisture which we observed in the air, as well as by the heat....

The young women sleep upon an average six in a room, three beds to a room. There is no privacy, no retirement, here. It is almost impossible to read or write alone, as the parlor is full and so many sleep in the same chamber. A young woman remarked to us that if she had a letter to write, she did it on the head of a bandbox, sitting on a trunk, as there was no space for a table.

So live and toil the young women of our country in the boardinghouses and manufactories which the rich and influential of our land have built for them.

Document Analysis

1. Why did industrialists prefer to hire unmarried women for work in factories and mills like those in Lowell?

2. Why would thousands of young women go to work in places like the Lowell mills in this era? What was life like for them in the mill and in their living quarters?

Ten.3

Mary Paul, Letters Home
(1845, 1846)

The following documents are letters from Mary Paul, an operative at the Lowell mills, to her father in Claremont, New Hampshire. Mary was fifteen years old, and typical of many of the young women who worked in Lowell and similar mill towns. Mill work offered women like Mary the possibility of independence—Mary herself worked away from home for twelve years before her marriage. And, like Mary Paul, most women did not make a permanent commitment to factory work. Because of this and other factors, rural women proved only to be a temporary fix to the needs of industrialization, and by the 1840s and 1850s they were replaced by immigrant, largely Irish, labor. *

Saturday Sept. 13th 1845

Dear Father

...I want you to consent to let me go to Lowell if you can. I think it would be much better for me than to stay about here. I could earn more to begin with than I can any where about here. I am in need of clothes which I cannot get if I stay about here and for that reason I want to go to Lowell or some other place. We all think if I could go with some steady girl that I might do well. I want you to think of it and make up your mind....

Mary

* From "The Letters of Mary Paul, 1845–1849," in *Vermont History* 48, ed. Thomas Dublin, (Montpelier, VT: Vermont Historical Society, 1980). Reprinted with permission of Vermont Historical Society.

Woodstock Nov 8 1845

Dear Father

As you wanted me to let you know when I am going to start for Lowell, I improve this opportunity to write you. Next Thursday the 13th of this month is the day set or the Thursday afternoon. I should like to have you come down. If you come bring Henry if you can for I should like to see him before I go....

Mary

Lowell Nov 20th 1845

Dear Father

...Went to a boarding house and staid until Monday night. On Saturday after I got here Luthera Griffith went round with me to find a place but we were unsuccessful. On Monday we started again and were more successful. We found a place in a spinning room and the next morning I went to work. I like very well have 50 cts first payment increasing every payment as I get along in work have a first rate overseer and a very good boarding place....It cost me $3.25 to come. Stage fare was $3.00 and lodging at Windsor, 25 cts. Had to pay only 25 cts for board for 9 days after I got here before I went into the mill. Had 2.50 left with which I got a bonnet and some other small articles....

excuse bad writing and mistakes

This from your own daughter

Mary

Lowell Dec 21st 1845

Dear Father

...I am well which is one comfort. My life and health are spared while others are cut off. Last Thursday one girl fell down and broke her neck which caused instant death. She was going in or coming out of the mill and slipped down it being very icy. The same day a man was killed by the [railroad] cars. Another had nearly all of his ribs broken. Another was nearly killed by falling down and having a bale of cotton fall on him. Last Tuesday we were paid. In all I had six dollars and sixty cents paid $4.68 for board. With the rest I got me a pair of rubbers and a pair of 50 cts shoes. Next payment I am to have a dollar a week beside my board....Perhaps you would like something about our regulations about going in and coming out of the mill. At 5 o'clock in the morning the bell rings for the folks to get up and get breakfast. At half past six it rings for the girls to get up and at seven they are called into the mill. At half past 12 we have dinner are called back again at one and stay till half past seven. I get along very well with my work....

This from

Mary S. Paul

Lowell April 12th 1846

Dear Father

...The overseer tells me that he never had a girl get along better than I do and that he will do the best he can by me. I stand it well, though they tell me that I am growing very poor. I was paid nine shillings a week last payment and am to have more this one though we have been out considerable for backwater which will take off a good deal.* The Agent promises to pay us nearly as much as we should have made but I do not think that he will....I have a very good boarding place have enough to eat and that which is good enough. The girls are all kind and obliging. The girls that I room with are all from Vermont and good girls too....

DOCUMENT ANALYSIS

1. How does Mary Paul characterize her life and work in Lowell? Do you think she's being totally honest with her father about her situation?

---

* Mary quoted her wages in English currency, but she was almost certainly paid in American money. Nine shillings would be equal to $1.50. Mary was referring to her wages exclusive of room and board charges. "Backwater" was caused by heavy run-off from rains and melting snow. The high water levels caused water to back up and block the waterwheel.

Chapter Study Questions

1. Why was the Erie Canal such boon to the American economy?

2. How might the *Harbinger* report on Lowell reflect certain assumptions about female work capabilities and the proper place for young women? Based on her own experience at Lowell, do you think Mary Paul would find this report accurate or not? Explain.

Eleven

Slavery and the Old South

A s illustrated in this chapter, the Nat Turner revolt was perhaps the most famous and most violent slave uprising of the antebellum period. It was also the slave revolt that galvanized white fears and antipathy toward their slaves—manumission became increasingly difficult and interest in ending slavery faded soon afterwards. Nat Turner, the leader of the revolt, was a religious, educated slave who believed himself to be on a religious mission. In August 1831, before the revolt was crushed, Turner and his compatriots murdered fifty-five white men, women, and children, including the family of his master, Joseph Travis. Turner was caught and executed. Before he was killed he dictated a confession, excerpted here, to his white lawyer.

Most slaves did not revolt like Nat Turner or other organizers like Denmark Vesey and Gabriel Prosser. A few slaves, however, did try to escape from slavery to the North or to escaped-slave communities in Florida. The narratives of Mrs. James Steward and Mrs. Nancy Howard reveal not only the sufferings and indignities suffered by slave women, but also their attempts to maintain dignity and family ties.

The final two documents in this chapter demonstrate the abolitionist view of slavery and the views of one of slavery's staunchest defenders. In the 1830s, abolitionists had begun to increase their attacks upon the institution. By the 1850s, especially after the passage of the Fugitive Slave Act, the debate became even more heated. In his Independence Day Speech, the escaped slave Frederick Douglass voiced, in his powerful way, the inherent contradiction of celebrating the Fourth of July in a nation which enslaved human beings. But Douglass and others were met with justifications of the institution by men such as George Fitzhugh, who argued that slavery had a biblical basis and was, in fact, humane. But he also argued for expanding the slave system, which was alarming to many Americans.

Eleven.1

Nat Turner, Confession (1831)

This is a selection from Nat Turner's confessions, collected by his white lawyer after he had been apprehended for leading a revolt that culminated in the murder of fifty-five whites and the death of at least that many African Americans from white retaliation. The revolt, intended, in Turner's words, to "carry terror and devastation," was spurred by his divine vision. This selection describes the origins of Turner's sense of his own uniqueness and his divine revelation.*

. . . To a mind like mine, restless, inquisitive and observant of every thing that was passing, it is easy to suppose that religion was the subject to which it would be directed, and although this subject principally occupied my thoughts—there was nothing that I saw or heard of to which my attention was not directed—The manner in which I learned to read and write, not only had great influence on my own mind, as I acquired it with the most perfect ease, so much so, that I have no recollection whatever of learning the alphabet—but to the astonishment of the family, one day, when a book was shewn to me to keep me from crying, I began spelling the names of different objects—this was a source of wonder to all in the neighborhood, particularly the blacks—and this learning was constantly improved at all opportunities—when I got large enough to go to work, while employed, I was reflecting on many things that would present themselves to my imagination, and whenever an opportunity occurred of looking at a book, when the school children were getting their lessons, I would find many things that the fertility of my own imagination had depicted to me before....

[A]ll my time, not devoted to my master's service, was spent either in prayer, or in making experiments in casting different things in moulds made of earth, in attempting to make paper, gun-powder, and many other experiments, that although I could not perfect, yet convinced me of its practicability if I had the means.

* From Thomas R. Gray, *The Confessions of Nat Turner, The Leader of the Late Insurrection in Southamton Virginia* (Baltimore, 1831).

I was not addicted to stealing in my youth, nor have ever been—Yet such was the confidence of the negroes in the neighborhood, even at this early period of my life, in my superior judgment, that they would often carry me with them when they were going on any roguery, to plan for them. Growing up among them, with this confidence in my superior judgment, and when this, in their opinions, was perfected by Divine inspiration, from the circumstances already alluded to in my infancy, and which belief was ever afterwards zealously inculcated by the austerity of my life and manners, which became the subject of remark by white and black.

—Having soon discovered to be great, I must appear so, and therefore studiously avoided mixing in society, and wrapped myself in mystery, devoting my time to fasting and prayer—by this time, having arrived to man's estate, and hearing the scriptures commented on at meetings, I was struck with that particular passage which says: "Seek ye the kingdom of Heaven and all things shall be added unto you." I reflected much on this passage, and prayed daily for light on this subject—As I was praying one day at my plough, the spirit spoke to me, saying "Seek ye the kingdom of Heaven and all things shall be added unto you."

Question—what do you mean by the Spirit? Ans.—The Spirit that spoke to the prophets in former days—and I was greatly astonished, and for two years prayed continually, whenever my duty would permit—and then again I had the same revelation, which fully confirmed me in the impression that I was ordained for some great purpose in the hands of the Almighty.

Several years rolled round, in which many events occurred to strengthen me in this my belief. At this time I reverted in my mind to the remarks made of me in my childhood, and the things that had been shewn me—and as it had been said of me in my childhood by those by whom I had been taught to pray, both white and black, and in whom I had the greatest confidence, that I had too much sense to be raised, and if I was, I would never be of any use to any one as a slave. Now finding I had arrived to man's estate, and was a slave, and these revelations being made known to me, I began to direct my attention to this great object, to fulfill the purpose for which, by this time, I felt assured I was intended.

Knowing the influence I had obtained over the minds of my fellow servants (not by the means of conjuring and such like tricks—for to them I always spoke of such things with contempt) but by the communion of the Spirit whose revelations I often communicated to them, and they believed and said my wisdom came from God. I now began to prepare them for my purpose, by telling them something was about to happen that would terminate in fulfilling the great promise that had been made to me—...

DOCUMENT ANALYSIS

1. How does Turner characterize how it was that he was transformed into the leader of a slave rebellion?

2. What does this excerpt from Turner's confession suggest about the importance of religion to his life?

Benjamin Drew, Narratives of Escaped Slaves (1855)

These two stories of fugitive slaves who escaped from Maryland to freedom in Canada were recorded by Benjamin Drew, an abolitionist. Most runaway slaves were young men, who, like these young women, had suffered physical abuse. Relatively few women were able to make the dangerous journey to freedom because of the difficulty of fleeing with children. These women's stories document some of the sadistic physical abuse many slaves—men and women alike—suffered at the hands of their masters: whippings, brandings, and confinement, for instance. They also provide evidence of the attempt by women to maintain family ties, relationships, and commitments.*

[Mrs. James Steward]

The slaves want to get away bad enough. They are not contented with their situation.

I am from the eastern shore of Maryland. I never belonged but to one master; he was very bad indeed. I was never sent to school, nor allowed to go to church. They were afraid we would have more sense than they. I have a father there, three sisters, and a brother. My father is quite an old man, and he is used very badly. Many a time he has been kept at work a whole long summer day without sufficient food. A sister of mine has been punished by his taking away her clothes and locking them up, because she used to run when master whipped her. He kept her at work with only what she could pick up to tie on her for decency. He took away her child which had just begun to walk, and gave it to another woman—but she went and got it afterward. He had a large farm eight miles from home. Four servants were kept at the house. My master could not manage to whip my sister when she was strong. He waited until she was confined, and the second week after her confinement he said, "Now I can handle you, now you are weak." She ran from him, however, and had to go through water, and was sick in consequence.

---

* From *A Northside View of Slavery: The Refuge, or The Narratives of Fugitive Slaves in Canada, Related by Themselves*, ed. Benjamin Drew (Boston: John P. Jowett, 1856), 41–43, 50–51, 138, 140–141, 224–227.

I was beaten at one time over the head by my master, until the blood ran from my mouth and nose: then he tied me up in the garret, with my hands over my head—then he brought me down and put me in a little cupboard, where I had to sit cramped up, part of the evening, all night, and until between four and five o'clock, next day, without any food. The cupboard was near a fire, and I thought I should suffocate.

My brother was whipped on one occasion until his back was as raw as a piece of beef, and before it got well, master whipped him again. His back was an awful sight.

We were all afraid of master: when I saw him coming, my heart would jump up into my mouth, as if I had seen a serpent.

I have been wanting to come away for eight years back. I waited for Jim Steward to get ready. Jim had promised to take me away and marry me. Our master would allow no marriages on the farm. When Jim had got ready, he let me know—he brought to me two suits of clothes—men's clothes—which he had bought on purpose for me. I put on both suits to keep me warm. We eluded pursuit and reached Canada in safety.

[Mrs. Nancy Howard]

I was born in Anne Arundel County, Maryland—was brought up in Baltimore. After my escape, I lived in Lynn, Mass., seven years, but I left there through fear of being carried back, owing to the fugitive slave law. I have lived in St. Catherines [Ontario, Canada] less than a year.

The way I got away was—my mistress was sick, and went into the country for her health. I went to stay with her cousin. After a month, my mistress was sent back to the city to her cousin's, and I waited on her. My daughter had been off three years. A friend said to me—"Now is your chance to get off." At last I concluded to go—the friend supplying me with money. I was asked no questions on the way north.

My idea of slavery is, that it is one of the blackest, the wickedest things everywhere in the world. When you tell them the truth, they whip you to make you lie. I have taken more lashes for this, than for any other thing, because I would not lie.

One day I set the table, and forgot to put on the carving-fork—the knife was there. I went to the table to put it on a plate. My master said,—"Where is the fork?" I told him "I forgot it." He says,—"You d——d black b——, I'll forget you!"—at the same time hitting me on the head with the carving knife. The blood spurted out—you can see. (Here the woman removed her turban and showed a circular cicatrices denuded of hair, about an inch in diameter, on the top of her head.) My mistress took me into the kitchen and put on camphor, but she could not stop the bleeding. A doctor was sent for. He came but asked no questions. I was frequently punished with raw hides—was hit with tongs and poker and anything. I used when I went out, to look up at the sky, and say, "Blessed Lord, oh, do take me out of this!" It seemed to me I could not bear another lick. I can't forget it. I sometimes dream that I am pursued, and when I wake, I am scared almost to death.

DOCUMENT ANALYSIS

1. What abuses were endured by Mrs. Steward and Mrs. Howard as slaves? How do their experiences refute Southern claims about how the slaves were usually well cared for by their masters?

2. What opportunities arose to allow Mrs. Steward and Mrs. Howard ultimately to escape slavery?

Eleven.3

Frederick Douglass, Independence Day Speech (1852)

Frederick Douglass spent his young years as a slave in Maryland where he was (illegally) taught to read and write. As a young man, he escaped to New York City and later Massachusetts. In his twenties, he became an abolitionist speaker of renown and was the leading black abolitionist of his time. This speech was given in Rochester, New York on Independence Day 1852.*

Fellow citizens above your national, tumultuous joy, I hear the mournful wail of millions! whose chains, heave and grievous yesterday, are, today, rendered more intolerable by the jubilee shouts that reach them. If I do forget, if I do not faithfully remember those bleeding children of sorrow this day, "may my right hand forger her cunning, and may my tongue cleave to the roof of my mouth"! To forget them, to pass lightly over their wrongs, and to chime in with the popular theme would be treason most scandalous and shocking, and would make me a reproach before God and the world. My subject, them, fellow citizens, is *American Slavery*. I shall see this day and its popular characteristics from the slave's point of view. Standing there identified with the American bondman, making his wrongs mine. I do not hesitate to declare with all my soul that the character and conduct of this nation never looked blacker to me than on this Fourth of July! Whether we turn to the declarations of the past or to the professions of the present, the conduct of the nation seems equally hideous and revolting. America is false to the past, false to the present, and solemnly binds herself to be false to the future. Standing with God and the crushed and bleeding slave on this occasion, I will, in the name of humanity which is outraged, in the name of liberty which is fettered, in the name of the Constitution and the Bible which are disregarded and trampled upon, All the emphasis I can command, everything that serves to perpetuate slavery the great sin and shame of America! "I will not equivocate, I will not excuse"; I will use the severest

* Reprinted from *The American Reader. Words That Moved a Nation*, ed. Diane Ravitch (New York: HarperCollins, 1991), 155–156.

of language I can command; and yet not one word shall escape that any man, whose judgment is not blinded by prejudice, or who is not at heart a slaveholder, shall not confess to be right and just.

But I fancy I hear someone of my audience say, "It is just in this circumstance that you and your brother abolitionists fail to make a favorable impression on the public mind. Would you argue more and denounce less, would you persuade more and rebuke less, your cause would be much more likely to succeed." But, I submit, where all is plain, there is nothing to be argued. What point in the antislavery creed would you have me argue? On what branch of the subject do the people of this country need light? Must I undertake to prove that the slave is a man? That point is conceded already. Nobody doubts it. The slaveholders themselves acknowledge it the enactment of laws for their government. They acknowledge it when they punish disobedience on the part of the slave. There are seventy-two crimes in the state of Virginia which, if committed by a black man (no matter how ignorant he be), subject him to the punishment of death, while only two of the same crimes will subject a white man to the like punishment. What is this but the acknowledgment that the slave is a moral, intellectual, and responsible being? The manhood of the slave is conceded.

It is admitted in the fact that the Southern statute books are covered with enactments forbidding, under severe fines and penalties, the teaching of the slave to read or to write. When you can point to any such laws in reference to the beasts of the field, then I may consent to argue the manhood of the slave. When the dogs in your streets, when the fowls of the air, when the cattle on your hills, when the fish of the sea and the reptiles that crawl shall be unable to distinguish the slave from a brute, then will I argue with you that the slave is a man!

For the present, it is enough to affirm the equal manhood of the Negro race. It is not astonishing that, while we are plowing, planting, and reaping, using all kinds of mechanical tools erecting houses, constructing bridges, building ships, working in metals of brass, iron, copper and silver, and gold; that, while we are reading, writing, and ciphering, acting as clerks, merchants and secretaries, having among us lawyers, doctors, ministers, poets, authors, editors, orators, and teachers; that, while we are engaged in all manner of enterprises common to other men, digging gold in California, capturing the whale in the Pacific, feeding sheep and cattle on the hillside, living, moving, acting, thinking, planning, living in families as husbands, wives, and children, and, above all, confessing and worshipping the Christian's God, and looking hopefully for life and immortality beyond the grave, we are called upon to prove that we are men!

Would you have me argue that man is entitled to liberty? That he is the rightful owner of his own body? You have already declared it. Must I argue the wrongfulness of slavery? Is that a question for republicans? Is it to be settled by the rules of logic and argumentation, as a matter beset with great difficulty, involving a doubtful application of the principle of justice, hart to be understood? How should I look today, in the presence of Americans, dividing and subdividing a discourse, to show that men have a natural right to freedom? speaking of it relatively and positively, negatively and affirmatively? To do so would be to make myself ridiculous and to offer an insult to your understanding. There is not a man beneath the canopy of heaven that does not know that slavery is wrong for him.

What, am I to argue that is wrong to make men brutes, to rob them of their liberty, to work them without wages, to keep them ignorant of their relations to their fellow men, to beat them with sticks, to flay their flesh with the last, to load their limbs with irons, to hunt them with dogs, to sell them at auction, to sunder their families, to knock out their teeth, to burn their flesh, to starve them into obedience and submission to their masters? Must I argue that a system them marked with blood, and stained with pollution, is wrong? No! I will not. I have better employment for my time and strength than such arguments would imply.

What, then remains to be argued? Is it that slavery is not divine; that God did not establish it; that our doctors of divinity are mistaken? There is blasphemy in the thought. That which is inhuman cannot be divine? Who can reason on such a proposition? They that can may; I cannot. The time for such argument is past.

At a time like this, scorching iron, not convincing argument, is needed. O! had I the ability, and could I reach the nation's ear, I would today pour out a fiery stream of biting ridicule, blasting reproach, withering sarcasm, and stern rebuke. For it is not light that is needed, but fire; it is not the gentle shower, but thunder. We need the storm, the whirlwind, and the earthquake. The feeling of the nation must be quickened, the conscience of the nation must be startled; the hypocrisy of the nation must be exposed; and its crimes against God and man must be proclaimed and denounced.

What, to the American slave is your Fourth of July? I answer: a day that reveals to him, more than all other days in the year, the gross injustice and cruelty to which he is the constant victim. To him, your celebration is a sham; your boasted liberty an unholy license; your national greatness, swelling vanity; your sound of rejoicing are empty and heartless; your denunciation of tyrants, brass-fronted impudence; your shouts of liberty and equality, hollow mockery; your prayers and hymns, your sermons and thanksgivings with all your religious parade and solemnity, are, to Him, mere bombast, fraud, deception, impiety, and hypocrisy a thin veil to cover up crimes which would disgrace a nation of savages. There is not a nation of savages. There is not a nation on earth guilty of practices more shocking and bloody than are the people of the United States at this very hour.

Go where you may, search where you will, roam through all the monarchies and despotisms of the Old World, travel through South America, search out every abuse, and when you have found the last, lay your facts by the side of the everyday practices of this nation, and you will say with that, for revolting barbarity and shameless hypocrisy, America reigns without a rival.

Document Analysis

1. What accounts for the impassioned anger in Douglass's 1852 Independence Day speech? How does Douglass address those critics who charge that his tone is often too angry?

2. When Douglass states that "America reigns without a rival," to what is he referring? Is this claim fair? Explain.

George Fitzhugh, "The Blessings of Slavery" (1857)

This selection, from Fitzhugh's Cannibals All! or Slaves Without Masters, *is a justification and defense of slavery. In other portions of his radical book, Fitzhugh argued that (as his title implies) work relations made cannibals of everyone and that, ideally, liberty was meant only for the few—that "some were born with saddles on their backs, and others booted and spurred to ride them—and the riding does them good." In justifying slavery in principle rather than as only a natural state for nonwhites, Fitzhugh ran counter to the general ideology of the antebellum period, a time of increasing democratization, expansion, and participation. In doing so, he became fodder for those northerners who were terrified of a "slave power" conspiracy emanating from the South.**

The negro slaves of the South are the happiest, and in some sense, the freest people in the world. The children and the aged and infirm work not at all, and yet have all the comforts and necessaries of life provided for them. They enjoy liberty, because they are oppressed neither by care or labor. The women do little hard work, and are protected from the despotism of their husbands by their masters. The negro men and stout boys work, on the average, in good weather, no more than nine hours a day. The balance of their time is spent in perfect abandon. Besides, they have their Sabbaths and holidays. White men, with so much of license and abandon, would die of ennui; but negroes luxuriate in corporeal and mental repose. With their faces upturned to the sun, they can sleep at any hour; and quiet sleep is the greatest of human enjoyments. "Blessed be the man who invented sleep." 'Tis happiness in itself—and results from contentment in the present, and confident assurance of the future. We do not know whether free laborers ever sleep. They are fools to do so; for, whilst they sleep, the wily and watchful capitalist is devising means to ensnare and exploit them. The free laborer must work or

* From George Fitzhugh, *Cannibals All! or Slaves Without Masters* (Richmond, Va.: A. Morris, 1857), 294–299.

starve. He is more of a slave than the negro, because he works longer and harder for less allowance than the slave, and has no holiday, because the cares of life with him begin when its labors end. He has no liberty and not a single right....

Until the lands of America are appropriated by a few, population becomes dense, competition among laborers active, employment uncertain, and wages low, the personal liberty of all the whites will continue to be a blessing. We have vast unsettled territories; population may cease to increase slowly, as in most countries, and many centuries may elapse before the question will be practically suggested, whether slavery to capital be preferable to slavery to human masters. But the negro has neither energy nor enterprise, and, even in our sparser populations, finds with his improvident habits, that his liberty is a curse to himself, and a greater curse to the society around him. These considerations, and others equally obvious, have induced the South to attempt to defend negro slavery as an exceptional institution, admitting, nay asserting, that slavery, in the general or in the abstract, is morally wrong, and against common right. With singular inconsistency, after making this admission, which admits away the authority of the Bible, of profane history, and of the almost universal practice of mankind—they turn around and attempt to bolster up the cause of negro slavery by these very exploded authorities. If we mean not to repudiate all divine, and almost all human authority in favor of slavery, we must vindicate that institution in the abstract.

To insist that a status of society, which has been almost universal, and which is expressly and continually justified by Holy Writ, is its natural, normal, and necessary status, under the ordinary circumstances, is on its face a plausible and probable proposition. To insist on less, is to yield our cause, and to give up our religion; for if white slavery be morally wrong, be a violation of natural rights, the Bible cannot be true. Human and divine authority do seem in the general to concur, in establishing the expediency of having masters and slaves of different races. In very many nations of antiquity, and in some of modern times, the law has permitted the native citizens to become slaves to each other. But few take advantage of such laws; and the infrequency of the practice establishes the general truth that master and slave should be of different national descent. In some respects the wider the difference the better, as the slave will feel less mortified by his position. In other respects, it may be that too wide a difference hardens the hearts and brutalizes the feeling of both master and slave. The civilized man hates the savage, and the savage returns the hatred with interest. Hence West India slavery of newly caught negroes is not a very humane, affectionate, or civilizing institution. Virginia negroes have become moral and intelligent. They love their master and his family, and the attachment is reciprocated. Still, we like the idle, but intelligent house-servants, better than the hard-used, but stupid outhands; and we like the mulatto better than the negro; yet the negro is generally more affectionate, contented, and faithful.

The world at large looks on negro slavery as much the worst form of slavery; because it is only acquainted with West India slavery. But our Southern slavery has become a benign and protective institution, and our negroes are confessedly better off than any free laboring population in the world. How can we contend that white slavery is wrong, whilst all the great body of free laborers are starving; and slaves, white or black, throughout the world, are enjoying comfort?...

The aversion to negroes, the antipathy of race, is much greater at the North than at the South; and it is very probable that this antipathy to the person of the negro, is confounded with or generates hatred of the institution with which he is usually connected. Hatred to slavery is very generally little more than hatred of negroes.

There is one strong argument in favor of negro slavery over all other slavery; that he, being unfitted for the mechanic arts, for trade, and all skillful pursuits, leaves those pursuits to be carried on by the whites; and does not bring all industry into disrepute, as in Greece and Rome, where the slaves were not only the artists and mechanics, but also the merchants.

Whilst, as a general and abstract question, negro slavery has no other claims over other forms of slavery, except that from inferiority, or rather peculiarity, of race, almost all negroes require masters, whilst only the children, the women, and the very weak, poor, and ignorant, &c., among the whites, need some protective and governing relation of this kind; yet as a subject of temporary, but worldwide importance, negro slavery has become the most necessary of all human institutions.

The African slave trade to America commenced three centuries and a half since. By the time of the American Revolution, the supply of slaves had exceeded the demand for slave labor, and the slaveholders, to get rid of a burden, and to prevent the increase of a nuisance, became violent opponents of the slave trade, and many of them abolitionists. New England, Bristol, and Liverpool, who reaped the profits of the trade, without suffering from the nuisance, stood out for a long time against its abolition. Finally, laws and treaties were made, and fleets fitted out to abolish it; and after a while, the slaves of most of South America, of the West Indies, and of Mexico were liberated. In the meantime, cotton, rice, sugar, coffee, tobacco, and other products of slave labor, came into universal use as necessaries of life. The population of Western Europe, sustained and stimulated by those products, was trebled, and that of the North increased tenfold. The products of slave labor became scarce and dear, and famines frequent. Now, it is obvious, that to emancipate all the negroes would be to starve Western Europe and our North. Not to extend and increase negro slavery, *pari passu*, with the extension and multiplication of free society, will produce much suffering. If all South America, Mexico, the West Indies, and our Union south of Mason and Dixon's line, of the Ohio and Missouri, were slaveholding, slave products would be abundant and cheap in free society; and their market for their merchandise, manufactures, commerce, &c., illimitable. Free white laborers might live in comfort and luxury on light work, but for the exacting and greedy landlords, bosses, and other capitalists.

We must confess, that overstock the world as you will with comforts and with luxuries, we do not see how to make capital relax its monopoly—how to do aught but tantalize the hireling. Capital, irresponsible capital, begets, and ever will beget, the *immedicabile vulnus* of so-called Free Society. It invades every recess of domestic life, infects its food, its clothing, its drink, its very atmosphere, and pursues the hireling, from the hovel to the poor-house, the prison and the grave. Do what he will, go where he will, capital pursues and persecutes him. "*Haeret lateri lethalis arundo!*"

Capital supports and protects the domestic slave; taxes, oppresses, and persecutes the free laborer.

DOCUMENT ANALYSIS

1. How does Fitzhugh contrast slavery to the treatment of free laborers who work in Northern industry? Is Fitzhugh's argument persuasive?

2. How does Fitzhugh characterize the black slaves? How do you think those black slaves might characterize Fitzhugh?

Chapter Study Questions

1. How different was Nat Turner from most other slaves of this period? Why did he think himself qualified to lead a rebellion?

2. In what ways do the experiences of the fugitive slaves documented by Benjamin Drew make it easier to understand why other slaves might follow Nat Turner in rebelling violently against their masters?

3. How would Douglass have reacted to Fitzhugh's claim that "The Negro slaves of the South are the happiest, and in some sense, the freest people in the world"?

Twelve

Shaping America in the Antebellum Age

The election of Andrew Jackson to the presidency in 1828 marked a revolution in American politics. As described in the text, Jackson's era saw a return to the two-party system, now markedly changed since the era of the Federalists and Republicans as a result of the enfranchisement of poorer male white voters, territorial expansion into the West, and the resultant rise of political power there. And while altering the political landscape, expansion also exposed some of the limitations of democracy, as Native Americans were removed from the East and whites moved farther west, bringing slavery with them.

By 1829 it had become clear that America's expansion westward would require a national policy. Since most of the expansion was confined to the areas east of the Mississippi, Americans believed transplanting Native Americas west of the river would solve the problem they presented. In his annual address to Congress included here, Jackson, who had gained fame as a professional Indian fighter, supported the Indian Removal Act and pursued a policy of removing Indians from the path of white settlement.

The Cherokee had attempted to hold their lands by adjusting to white ways. However, in spite of several treaties that had seemed to establish the legitimacy of their government, in 1829 Georgia refused to recognize the Cherokee and passed a law declaring all Cherokee laws void and Cherokee lands part of Georgia. In *Worcester v. Georgia*, the Marshall Supreme Court ruled that the Georgia law was "repugnant to the Constitution" and did not apply to the Cherokee. President Jackson, taking a state's rights position, backed Georgia and defied the Supreme Court. He insisted that no independent nation could exist within the United States. Between 1837 and 1839 the army drove about 15,000 Cherokee to leave Georgia for lands in Oklahoma; about 4,000 died on the way.

Andrew Jackson came into the White House intending to "reform" and "purify" the government. He ushered in a new political culture, one that appeared more egalitarian and democratic, filled with political conventions, rallies, and parades, all engineered to increase voter participation.

Concurrently, American society in the antebellum period experienced many rapid cultural, economic, and social changes. One of the responses to these changes was a "reform" movement that permeated all parts of society. Rooted in the ideals of the Second Great Awakening, many American reformers believed in and strove for the perfectibility of man. While some groups focused on individual reform, others looked toward reforming specific American institutions. Most of the reform groups were located in the North, where the Industrial Revolution had begun to affect all aspects of its society and change was occurring at a far more accelerated rate than in the South. Ironically, while many of these groups wanted to perfect life in America, they would only end up exacerbating the growing tensions and strains between the North and the South.

The wave of religious revivals that ran through New England and the frontier from the turn of the century through the 1830s was reenergized in upstate New York and the Midwest under the influence of a new generation of revivalists like Charles Finney, a former lawyer, who was one of the most compelling speakers of his day. In the 1820s and 1830s, Finney believed anyone could be converted and "saved" through the magical effects of the "powerful excitement" brought on by a revival. The selection included here is Finney's description of revivalism and his defense of revivals to those who would suggest the church pursue its mission in more discreet ways.

As the northern economy industrialized, many began to question industrialization's effect on the people of the region. Like the revivalists, they believed in human perfectibility and did not see industrialization as the path to that ideal. Some withdrew from a world they thought flawed and created their own "utopian" communities. George Ripley, a Boston Unitarian minister, organized Brook Farm in Massachusetts in 1841, believing that self-realization could be found through communal sharing in a pastoral setting. Among the literary figures who came to the farm was Nathaniel Hawthorne, a writer who celebrated the transcendence of the human heart in the face of social intolerance. Hawthorne's letter from Brook Farm to his wife describes his experiences there.

Education reform was another important force in this era, as public schooling became more widely available and popular. Religious groups and private foundations also set up hundreds of colleges and universities across the nation, and teacher training schools were set up in many states as well. Meanwhile, other reformers sought to improve the conditions of those in prisons, hospitals, and asylums. A leading advocate for the mentally ill in this period was Dorothea Dix of Massachusetts, who worked tirelessly to expose often barbaric conditions in insane asylums, and convince state and local authorities to provide humane facilities.

No reform movement, however, had a more dramatic effect on antebellum America than abolitionism. This movement had a long history that began with the Quakers during the colonial period. After 1830, its activity would be centered in the North. While earlier antislavery groups, like the American Colonization Society, had sought amicable solutions for planters and slaves—"gradual abolition," colonization, or humanization of the institution—the new reformers stridently sought immediate abolition of slavery. One of the catalysts for this change was William Lloyd Garrison, the founder of the

New England Anti-Slavery Society and the publisher of *The Liberator*, the leading abolitionist journal. Beginning with the first articles published in the *The Liberator*, Garrison's challenged northern—as well as southern—society to consider its relationship to slavery.

Women, including Angelina and Sarah Grimke, Lucretia Mott, and Elizabeth Cady Stanton, were actively involved in the antislavery movement and through it developed a growing awareness of their own disenfranchisement. Within the abolitionist community, there were considerable misgivings about the equality of women and women's rights. At the World Anti-Slavery Congress in 1840, Elizabeth Cady Stanton and Lucretia Mott were not permitted to speak because they were women. In response, they called a convention at Seneca Falls, New York, in 1848, to advocate the rights of women. The Declaration of Sentiments, reprinted here, resulted from that convention and articulates the women's desire for equality.

Twelve.1

Andrew Jackson,
First Annual Message to Congress
(1829)

In the early nineteenth century, the lands occupied by southeastern and northwestern Native American groups, including the Cherokee, Chickasaw, Choctaw, Seminole, Fox, and Creek, were closed in upon by an expanding frontier of white settlement. In this address, President Jackson, a former frontiersman and Indian fighter, cloaked his argument for the relocation of Native Americans in the language of concern and honor. Indian removal helped bring about economic expansion for the new republic, but at tremendous cost to both the Native Americans who fought displacement and who moved west. *

The condition and ulterior destiny of the Indian tribes within the limits of some of our states have become objects of much interest and importance. It has long been the policy of government to introduce among them the arts of civilization, in the hope of gradually reclaiming them from a wandering life. This policy has, however, been coupled with another wholly incompatible with its success. Professing a desire to civilize and settle them, we have at the same time lost no opportunity to purchase their lands and thrust them farther into the wilderness. By this means they have not only been kept in a wandering state, but been led to look upon us as unjust and indifferent to their fate....

Our conduct toward these people is deeply interesting to our national character. Their present condition, contrasted with what they once were, makes a most powerful appeal to our sympathies. Our ancestors found them the uncontrolled possessors of these vast regions. By persuasion and force they have been made to retire from river to river and from mountain to mountain, until some of the tribes have become extinct and others have left but remnants to preserve for awhile their once terrible names. Surrounded by the whites with their arts of civilization, which, by destroying the

* From *Messages and Papers of the Presidents*, ed. J. D. Richardson, National Archives and Records Administration, (1896), II, 456–459 (Dec. 8, 1829).

resources of the savage, doom him to weakness and decay, the fate of the Mohegan, the Narragansett, and the Delaware is fast overtaking the Choctaw, the Cherokee, and the Creek. That this fate surely awaits them if they remain within the limits of the states does not admit of a doubt. Humanity and national honor demand that every effort should be made to avert so great a calamity....

As a means of effecting this end, I suggest for our consideration the propriety of setting apart an ample district west of the Mississippi, and without [outside] the limits of any state or territory now formed, to be guaranteed to the Indian tribes as long as they shall occupy it, each tribe having a distinct control over the portion designated for its use. There they may be secured in the enjoyment of governments of their own choice, subject to no other control from the United States than such as may be necessary to preserve peace on the frontier and between the several tribes. There the benevolent may endeavor to teach them the arts of civilization, and, by promoting union and harmony among them, to raise up an interesting commonwealth, destined to perpetuate the race and to attest the humanity and justice of this government.

This emigration should be voluntary, for it would be as cruel as unjust to compel the aborigines to abandon the graves of their fathers and seek a home in a distant land. But they should be distinctly informed that if they remain within the limits of the states they must be subject to their laws.

DOCUMENT ANALYSIS

1. Why did Andrew Jackson appeal to "humanity and national honor" while advocating removal of southeastern Indians?

2. In what ways did Jackson acknowledge that American policy toward Native Americans up to 1829 had been unsuccessful? What would Jackson have considered to be a success?

Twelve.2

"Memorial of the Cherokee Nation" (1830)

The Washington administration had established a policy designed to "civilize" the Indians, and the Cherokee, more than any other Native American group, had done so—by codifying their own legal system, printing their own newspapers, and even owning slaves. However, no amount of assimilation helped the Cherokee when the state of Georgia demanded their land. During the "trail of tears," when the Cherokee were forced to march to Oklahoma, more than 4,000 Cherokee died. The "Memorial of the Cherokee Nation" appeared in Nile's Weekly Register *in 1830.**

We are aware that some persons suppose it will be for our advantage to remove beyond the Mississippi. We think otherwise. Our people universally think otherwise. Thinking that it would be fatal to their interests, they have almost to a man sent their memorial to Congress, deprecating the necessity of a removal....It is incredible that Georgia should ever have enacted the oppressive laws to which reference is here made, unless she had supposed that something extremely terrific in its character was necessary in order to make the Cherokees willing to remove. We are not willing to remove; and if we could be brought to this extremity, it would be not by argument, nor because our judgment was satisfied, not because our condition will be improved; but only because we cannot endure to be deprived of our national and individual rights and subjected to a process of intolerable oppression.

We wish to remain on the land of our fathers. We have a perfect and original right to remain without interruption or molestation. The treaties with us, and laws of the United States made in pursuance of treaties, guaranty our residence and our privileges, and secure us against intruders. Our only request is, that these treaties may be fulfilled, and these laws executed.

* Reprinted from "Memorial of the Cherokee Nation," in *Nile's Weekly Register*, 1830.

But if we are compelled to leave our country, we see nothing but ruin before us. The country west of the Arkansas territory is unknown to us. From what we can learn of it, we have no prepossessions in its favor. All the inviting parts of it, as we believe, are preoccupied by various Indian nations, to which it has been assigned. They would regard us as intruders....The far greater part of that region is, beyond all controversy, badly supplied with wood and water; and no Indian tribe can live as agriculturists without these articles. All our neighbors...would speak a language totally different from ours, and practice different customs. The original possessors of that region are now wandering savages lurking for prey in the neighborhood....Were the country to which we are urged much better than it is represented to be,...still it is not the land of our birth, nor of our affections. It contains neither the scenes of our childhood, nor the graves of our fathers.

...We have been called a poor, ignorant, and degraded people. We certainly are not rich; nor have we ever boasted of our knowledge, or our moral or intellectual elevation. But there is not a man within our limits so ignorant as not to know that he has a right to live on the land of his fathers, in the possession of his immemorial privileges, and that this right has been acknowledged by the United States; nor is there a man so degraded as not to feel a keen sense of injury, on being deprived of his right and driven into exile....

Document Analysis

1. Why do the Cherokee reject the idea that their removal to west of the Mississippi River will be good for them?

2. What did the Cherokee expect awaited them in western territory?

Twelve.3

Charles Finney, "Religious Revival" (1835)

Some Christians, including Catholics and upper-class individuals, believed revivalism—with its group conversions, camp meetings, and abundance of religious fervor that sometimes included speaking in tongues, screaming, and dancing—to be an embarrassment or a perversion. Finney, perhaps the most successful revivalist of his day, believed in the possibility of group conversion through the hypnotic work of an effective minister, and thought the revival movement absolutely essential to the future of Christianity. *

It is altogether improbable that religion will ever make progress among *heathen* nations except through the influence of revivals. The attempt is now making to do it by education, and other cautious and gradual improvements. But so long as the laws of mind remain what they are, it cannot be done in this way. There must be excitement sufficient to wake up the dormant moral powers, and roll back the tide of degradation and sin. And precisely so far as our own land approximates to heathenism, it is impossible for God or man to promote religion in such a state of things but by powerful excitements.—This is evident from the fact that this has always been the way in which God has done it. God does not create these excitements, and choose this method to promote religion for nothing, or without reason. Where mankind are so reluctant to obey God, they will not obey until they are excited. For instance, how many there are who know that they ought to be religious, but they are afraid if they become pious they will be laughed at by their companions. Many are wedded to idols, others are procrastinating repentance, until they are settled in life, or until they have secured some favorite worldly interest. Such persons never will give up their false shame, or relinquish their ambitious schemes, till they are so excited that they cannot contain themselves any longer....

It is presupposed that the church is sunk down in a backslidden state, and a revival consists in the return of the church from her backsliding, and in the conversion of sinners.

* From Charles G. Finney, *What a Revival of Religion Is* (1835).

1. A revival always includes conviction of sin on the part of the church. Backslidden professors cannot wake up and begin right away in the service of God, without deep searching of heart. The fountains of sin need to be broken up. In a true revival, Christians are always brought under such convictions; they see their sins in such a light, that often they find it impossible to maintain a hope of their acceptance with God. It does not always go to that extent; but there are always, in a genuine revival, deep convictions of sin, and often cases of abandoning all hope.

2. Backslidden Christians will be brought to repentance. A revival is nothing else than a new beginning of obedience to God. Just as the case of a converted sinner, the first step is a deep repentance, a breaking down of heart, a getting down into the dust before God, with deep humility, and forsaking of sin.

3. Christians will have their faith renewed. While they are in their backslidden state they are blind to the state of sinners. Their hearts are as hard as marble. The truths of the Bible only appear like a dream. They admit it to be all true; their conscience and their judgment assent to it; but their faith does not see it standing out in bold relief, in all the burning realities of eternity. But when they enter into a revival, they no longer see men as trees walking, but they see things in that strong light which will renew the love of God in their hearts. This will lead them to labor zealously to bring others to him. They will feel grieved that others do not love God, when they love him so much. And they will set themselves feelingly to persuade their neighbors to give him their heart. So their love to men will be renewed. They will be filled with a tender and burning love for souls. They will have a longing desire for the salvation of the whole world. They will be in agony for individuals whom they want to have saved; their friends, relations, enemies. They will not only be urging them to give their hearts to God, but they will carry them to God in the arms of faith, and with strong crying and tears beseech God to have mercy on them, and save their souls from endless burning.

4. A revival breaks the power of the world and sin over Christians. It brings them to such vantage ground that they get a fresh impulse towards heaven. They have a new foretaste of heaven, and new desires after union to God; and the charm of the world is broken, and the power of sin overcome.

5. When the churches are thus awakened and reformed, the reformation and salvation of sinners will follow, going through the same stages of conviction, repentance, and reformation. Their hearts will be broken down and changed. Very often the most abandoned profligates are among the subjects. Harlots, and drunkards, infidels, and all sorts of abandoned characters, are awakened and converted. The worst part of human society are softened, and reclaimed, and made to appear as lovely specimens of the beauty of holiness....

You see the error of those who are beginning to think that religion can be better promoted in the world without revivals, and who are disposed to give up all efforts to produce religious excitements. Because there are evils arising in some instances out of great excitements on the subject of religion, they are of opinion that it is best to dispense with them altogether. This cannot, and must not be. True, there is danger of abuses. In cases of great *religious* as well as all other excitements, more or less incidental evils may be expected of course....So in revivals of religion, it is found by experience, that in the present state of the world, religion cannot be promoted to any considerable extent without them.

DOCUMENT ANALYSIS

1. Why did Finney believe that revivals of religion were necessary and served as a positive force?
2. How does Finney answer critics who question the emotionalism of such revivals?

Twelve.4

Nathaniel Hawthorne,
A Letter from Brook Farm
(1841)

Brook Farm was a utopian community dedicated to merging "intellectual and manual labor" founded in Massachusetts by George Ripley and Bronson Alcott, friends of Ralph Waldo Emerson. Hawthorne lived on Brook Farm in 1841 and his later book The Blithedale Romance *(1852) was harshly critical of unflinching and naïve optimism of the community. This letter to his wife, however, provides a detailed and sympathetic account of the daily life of the community.* *

As the weather precludes all possibility of ploughing, hoeing, sowing and other such operations, I bethink me that you may have no objection to hear something of my whereabout and whatabout. You are to know then, that I took up my abode here on the 12th ultimo, in the midst of a snowstorm, which kept us all idle for a day or two. At the first glimpse of fair weather, Mr. Ripley summoned us into the cowyard and introduced me to an instrument with four prongs, commonly called a dung-fork. With this tool, I have already assisted to load twenty or thirty carts of manure, and shall take part in loading nearly three hundred more. Besides, I have planted potatoes and peas, cut straw and hay for the cattle, and done various other mighty works. This very morning, I milked three cows; and I milk two or three every night and morning. The weather has been so unfavorable, that we have worked comparatively little in the fields; but, nevertheless, I have gained strength wonderfully—grown quite a giant, in fact—and can do a day's work without the slightest inconvenience. In short, I am transformed into a complete farmer.

This is one of the most beautiful places I ever saw in my life, and as secluded as if it were a hundred miles from any city or village. There are woods, in which we can ramble all day, without meeting anybody, or scarcely seeing a house. Our house stands apart from the main road; so that we are not troubled even with passengers looking at us.

* Reprinted from *Voices from America's Past*, eds. Richard B. Morris and James Woodress (New York: E. P. Dutton & Co., 1961, 1962, 1963), 2:46–47.

Once in a while, we have a transcendental visitor, such as Mr. [Bronson] Alcott; but, generally, we pass whole days without seeing a single face, save those of the brethren. At this present time, our effective force consists of Mr. Ripley, Mr. Farley (a farmer from the far west), Rev. Warren Burton (author of various celebrated works), three young men and boys, who are under Mr. Ripley's care, and William Allen, his hired man, who has the chief direction of our agricultural labors. In the female part of the establishment there is Mrs. Ripley and two women folks. The whole fraternity eat together; and such a delectable way of life has never been seen on earth, since the days of the early Christians. We get up at half-past four, breakfast at half-past six, dine at half-past twelve, and go to bed at nine.

The thin frock, which you made for me, is considered a most splendid article; and I should not wonder if it were to become the summer uniform of the community. I have a thick frock, likewise; but it is rather deficient in grace, though extremely warm and comfortable. I wear a tremendous pair of cow-hide boots, with soles two inches thick. Of course, when I come to see you, I shall wear my farmer's dress.

We shall be very much occupied during most of this month, ploughing and planting; so that I doubt whether you will see me for two or three weeks. You have the portrait by this time, I suppose; so you can very well dispense with the original. When you write to me (which I beg you will do soon) direct your letter to West Roxbury, as there are two post offices in the town. I would write more; but William Allen is going to the village, and must have this letter; so good-bye.

Nath Hawthorne
Ploughman

DOCUMENT ANALYSIS

1. Based upon this letter, what does Hawthorne find himself engaged in at Brook Farm?

Twelve.5

Dorothea Dix,
Appeal on Behalf of the Insane
(1843)

The spirit of reform led many Americans, including many middle class women, to devote their lives to improving society. One of the most famous reformers of this era was Dorothea Dix, a teacher from Massachusetts, who committed more than thirty years of her life to improving the treatment of the mentally ill. Dix traveled around the country to expose abuses in insane asylums and similar facilities, and to argue for humane care. In this excerpt, Dix makes a successful dramatic appeal to the Massachusetts legislature to provide better facilities for the mentally ill.*

I come to present the strong claims of suffering humanity. I come to place before the Legislature of Massachusetts the condition of the miserable, the desolate, the outcast. I come as the advocate of helpless, forgotten, insane, and idiotic men and women; of beings sunk to a condition from which the most unconcerned would start with real horror; of beings wretched in our prisons, and more wretched in our almshouses. And I cannot suppose it needful to employ earnest persuasion, or stubborn argument, in order to arrest and fix attention upon a subject only the more strongly pressing in its claims because it is revolting and disgusting in its details.

I must confine myself to few examples, but am ready to furnish other and more complete details, if required. If my pictures are displeasing, coarse, and severe, my subjects, it must be recollected, offer no tranquil, refined, or composing features....

I proceed, gentlemen, briefly to call your attention to the *present* state of insane persons confined within this Commonwealth, in *cages, closets, cellars, stalls, pens! Chained, naked, beaten with rods,* and *lashed* into obedience....

Lincoln. A woman in a cage. *Medford.* One idiotic subject chained, and one in a closed stall for seventeen years. *Pepperell.* One often doubly chained, hand and foot; another violent; several peaceable now. *Brookfield.* One man caged, comfortable. *Granville.* One

* From *Old South Leaflets 6* (Boston: 1904) 490–494, 518–519.

often closely confined; now losing the use of his limbs from lack of exercise. *Charlemont.* One man caged. *Savoy.* One man caged. *Lenox.* Two in the jail, against whose unfit condition there the jailer protests.

Dedham. The insane disadvantageously placed in jail. In the almshouse, two females in stalls, situated in the main building; lie in wooden bunks filled with straw; always shut up. One of these subjects is supposed curable. The overseers of the poor have declined giving her a trial at the hospital, as I was informed, on account of expense.

Besides the above, I have seen many who, part of the year, are chained or caged. The use of cages all but universal. Hardly a town but can refer to some not distant period of using them; chains are less common; negligences frequent; wilful abuse less frequent than sufferings proceeding from ignorance, or want of consideration. I encountered during the last three months many poor creatures wandering reckless and unprotected through the country. Innumerable accounts have been sent me of persons who had roved away unwatched and unsearched after; and I have heard that responsible persons, controlling the almshouses, have not thought themselves culpable in sending away from their shelter, to cast upon the chances of remote relief, insane men and women. These, left on the highways, unfriended and incompetent to control or direct their own movements, sometimes have found refuge in the hospital, and others have not been traced....

Gentlemen, I commit to you this sacred cause. Your action upon this subject will affect the present and future conditions of hundreds and thousands.*

DOCUMENT ANALYSIS

1. How do you account for the bad conditions endured by the mentally ill in Massachusetts as described by Dix?

2. How does the appeal made by Dix here echo a broader concern for improving society during this age of ferment?

[* The legislature responded favorably, voting funds to improve conditions at the state's hospital for the insane at Worcester.]

Twelve.6

William Lloyd Garrison, from *The Liberator* (1831)

William Lloyd Garrison was a radical abolitionist from Massachusetts who advocated immedi-ate abolition of slavery. Garrison outraged his contemporaries, was attacked and harassed by mobs, and alienated moderate abolitionists—who advocated "gradual" emancipation. The Liberator *was Garrison's newspaper and this excerpt is from its first issue, declaring its edito-rial stand bravely and unequivocally. **

During my recent tour for the purpose of exciting the minds of the people by a series of discourses on the subject of slavery, every place that I visited gave fresh evidence of the fact that a great revolution in public sentiment was to be effected in the free states—and particularly in New England—than at the South. I find contempt more bitter, opposition more active, detraction more relentless, prejudice more stubborn, and apathy more frozen, than among slaveowners themselves. Of course, there were individual exceptions to the contrary.

This state of things afflicted but did not dishearten me. I determined, at every hazard, to lift up the standard of emancipation in the eyes of the nation, within sight of Bunker Hill and in the birthplace of liberty. That standard is now unfurled; and long may it float, unhurt by the spoliations of time or the missiles of a desperate foe—yea, till every chain be broken, and every bondman set free! Let Southern oppressors tremble—let all the enemies of the persecuted blacks tremble....

Assenting to the "self-evident truth" maintained in the American Declaration of Independence "that all men are created equal, and endowed by their Creator with cer-tain inalienable rights—among which are life, liberty, and the pursuit of happiness," I shall strenuously contend for the immediate enfranchisement of our slave popula-tion....In Park Street Church, on the Fourth of July, 1829, in an address on slavery, I unreflectingly assented to the popular but pernicious doctrine of gradual abolition. I

* *The Liberator* (Boston), Jan. 1, 1831.

seize this opportunity to make a full and unequivocal recantation, and thus publicly to ask pardon of my God, of my country, and of my brethren the poor slaves, for having uttered a sentiment so full of timidity, injustice, and absurdity....

I am aware that many object to the severity of my language; but is there not cause for severity? I will be as harsh as truth, and as uncompromising as justice. On this subject I do not wish to think, or speak, or write, with moderation. No! No! Tell a man whose house is on fire to give a moderate alarm; tell him to moderately rescue his wife from the hands of the ravisher; tell the mother to gradually extricate her babe from the fire into which it has fallen—but urge me not to use moderation in a cause like the present. I am in earnest—will not equivocate—I will not excuse—I will not retreat in a single inch—and I will be heard. The apathy of the people is enough to make every statue leap from its pedestal, and to hasten the resurrection of the dead.

It is pretended that I am retarding the cause of emancipation by the coarseness of my invective and the precipitancy of my measures. The charge is not true. On this question my influence—humble as it is—is felt at this moment to a considerable extent, and shall be felt in coming years—not perniciously, but beneficially—not as a curse, but as a blessing. And posterity will bear testimony that I was right.

DOCUMENT ANALYSIS

1. Why do you think Garrison feels so passionately against slavery?
2. How does Garrison defend himself against those who believe his criticism of slavery is too severe?

Elizabeth Cady Stanton,
Declaration of Sentiments
(1848)

Elizabeth Cady Stanton (1815–1902) along with Lucretia Mott, played a major role in drafting the declaration that was presented at the Seneca Falls convention in 1848. The document paralleled the Declaration of Independence and listed the grievances of women, ending with the controversial request for women's rights. *

When, in the course of human events, it becomes necessary for one portion of the family of man to assume among the people of the earth a position different from that which they have hitherto occupied, but one to which the laws of nature and of nature's God entitle them, a decent respect to the opinions of mankind requires that they should declare the causes that impel them to such a course.

We hold these truths to be self-evident: that all men and women are created equal; that they are endowed by their Creator with certain inalienable rights; that among these are life, liberty, and the pursuit of happiness; that to secure these rights governments are instituted, deriving their just powers from the consent of the governed. Whenever any form of government becomes destructive of these ends, it is the right of those who suffer from it to refuse allegiance to it, and to insist upon the institution of a new government, laying its foundation on such principles, and organizing its powers in such form, as to them shall seem most likely to effect their safety and happiness. Prudence, indeed, will dictate that governments long established should not be changed for light and transient causes; and accordingly all experience has shown that mankind are more disposed to suffer, while evils are sufferable, than to right themselves by abolishing the forms to which they are accustomed. But when a long train of abuses and usurpations, pursuing invariably the same object, evinces a design to reduce them under absolute despotism, it is their duty to throw off such government, and to provide new guards for their future

* From Elizabeth Cady Stanton, Susan B. Anthony, and Matilda J. Gage, eds., "Declaration of Sentiments," in *History of Woman Suffrage* (Rochester, N.Y.: Charles Mann, 1881),1: 67–94.

security. Such has been the patient sufferance of the women under this government, and such is now the necessity which constrains them to demand the equal station to which they are entitled.

The history of mankind is a history of repeated injuries and usurpations on the part of man toward woman, having in direct object the establishment of an absolute tyranny over her. To prove this, let facts be submitted to a candid word.

He has never permitted her to exercise her inalienable right to the elective franchise.

He has compelled her to submit to laws, in the formation of which she had no voice.

He has withheld from her rights which are given to the most ignorant and degraded men—both natives and foreigners.

Having deprived her of this first right of a citizen, the elective franchise, thereby leaving her without representation in the halls of legislation, he has oppressed her on all sides.

He has made her, if married, in the eye of the law, civilly dead.

He has taken from her all right in property, even to the wages she earns.

He has made her, morally, an irresponsible being, as she can commit many crimes with impunity, provided they be done in the presence of her husband. In the covenant of marriage, she is compelled to promise obedience to her husband, he becoming, to all intents and purposes, her master, the law giving him power to deprive her of her liberty, and to administer chastisement.

He has so framed the laws of divorce, as to what shall be the proper causes, and in case of separation, to whom the guardianship of the children shall be given, as to be wholly regardless of the happiness of women—the law, in all cases, going upon a false supposition of the supremacy of man, and giving all power into his hands.

After depriving her of all rights as a married woman, if single, and the owner of property, he has taxed her to support a government which recognizes her only when her property can be made profitable to it.

He has monopolized nearly all the profitable employments, and from those she is permitted to follow, she receives but a scanty remuneration. He closes against her all the avenues to wealth and distinction which he considers most honorable to himself. As a teacher of theology, medicine, or law, she is not known.

He has denied her the facilities for obtaining a thorough education, all colleges being closed against her.

He allows her in Church, as well as in State, but a subordinate position, claiming Apostolic authority for her exclusion from the ministry, and, with some exceptions, from any public participation in the affairs of the Church.

He has created a false public sentiment by giving to the world a different code of morals for men and women, by which the moral delinquencies which exclude women from society are not only tolerated, but deemed of little account in man.

He has usurped the prerogative of Jehovah himself, claiming it as his right to assign for her a sphere of action, when that belongs to her conscience and to her God.

He has endeavored, in every way he could, to destroy her confidence in her own powers, to lessen her self-respect, and to make her willing to lead a dependent and abject life.

Now, in the view of this entire disfranchisement of one-half of the people of this country, their social and religious degradation, in view of the unjust laws above mentioned, and because women do feel themselves aggrieved, oppressed, and fraudulently deprived of their most sacred rights, we insist that they have immediate admission to all the rights and privileges which belong to them as citizens of the United States.

In entering upon the great work before us, we anticipate no small amount of misconception, misrepresentation, and ridicule; but we shall use every instrumentality within our power to effect our object. We shall employ agents, circulate tracts, petition the State and National legislatures, and endeavor to enlist the pulpit and the press on our behalf. We hope this Convention will be followed by a series of Conventions embracing every part of the country.

DOCUMENT ANALYSIS

1. In what ways did the Declaration of Sentiments deny or uphold the view of women's moral superiority?

2. Of the injustices listed in this Declaration, how many have been eliminated or significantly reduced in American society today? Do any of the injustices listed persist? Explain.

Chapter Study Questions

1. How popular do you think Jackson's Indian removal policies were among white voters in the West? In what ways were the Cherokees victims of Jacksonian democracy?

2. What similar assumptions about human nature and society do the reformers and revivalists in this chapter share?

3. In what ways is Finney's revivalist strategy—encouraging "excitement"—reflected in the strategies of other reformers like Garrison and Dix?

4. Are there hints of Hawthorne's later criticisms of utopian communitarianism in his letter from Brook Farm? Why might he believe that he had "gained strength wonderfully" from his farming experience?

5. Why do you think this era gave rise to such zealous reformers as Dix, Garrison, and Stanton?

Thirteen

Moving West

Westward expansion was an integral part of the development of the United States. From the first settlers, Americans assumed it was their destiny to move across the continent. By the 1830s this ideology strongly influenced the policies and actions of the national government. During the next twenty years, through peace and war and by peaceful and aggressive means, the government encouraged and facilitated settlement in what came to be called "manifest destiny." However, each new territorial acquisition in the antebellum era brought debate over whether or not such areas should be free or slave territory.

This chapter of your text examines manifest destiny and its effect on the American nation. The author of the term "manifest destiny" was John L. O'Sullivan. In "The Great Nation of Futurity," he proposed to the American public that they were "a nation…destined to be the great nation of futurity" and glorified America as a nation connected to the future.

During this period, white Southerners (and their slaves) were moving onto Mexican territory in what is now Texas. The selection included here, by José María Sánchez, provides a vivid picture of the mixture of cultures in eastern Texas during in the late 1820s. This westward expansion also led to a conflict with Mexico. Texas had declared its independence in 1836, and in 1845, in a move defended as an expansion of American civilization (or manifest destiny), Texas was annexed by the United States. After losing Texas, Mexico had little interest in selling California and the New Mexico territory to President James Polk. In 1846, a border dispute in Texas provided the opportunity for the United States to send the military to the region and war broke out.

Though it appeared to be a popular undertaking, many Americans were skeptical of the country's motives and feared the consequences of the Mexican-American War. Abraham Lincoln, then a Whig congressman, introduced a resolution demanding to know the exact spot at which American troops had been fired on. Many from the North were afraid of the expansion of slavery into the new territories. Thomas Corwin, a Whig senator from Ohio, argued before Congress that the Mexican-American War would heighten the tensions between pro- and anti-slavery groups in the United States and feared that the external war would lead to a civil war.

A related but broader protest of antebellum society was offered by Henry David Thoreau, the transcendentalist writer most famous for his work, *Walden*. Thoreau celebrated independent living and independent thinking, and found much to criticize about society in the 1840s and 1850s. This chapter includes an excerpt from his famous essay, "Civil Disobedience" in which he criticized the war in Mexico and urged civil disobedience in protest.

Further north, American settlers had been streaming into the Oregon Territory in the early 1840s, while it was still jointly occupied by the United States and Great Britain. In the treaty of 1846, the United States gained sole possession of the lands south of the forty-eighth parallel—opening the way for more settlement of the territory. Settlers in search of their fortune or a new life moved with their families to Oregon and California on torturous overland routes. The journal of Elizabeth Greer, excerpted here, reveals the difficulties of making the journey.

Settlers in virtually all cases were moving into lands that had been occupied by Native American groups, including the Sioux Indians of the Great Plains, and the Blackfoot, Nez Percé, and Crow Indians of the Plateau. Chief Seattle was the leader of six Native American tribes in the Oregon Territory. In 1854 he was told that the United States government wanted to buy his lands and establish reservations for his people. As his oration describes, he accepted the offer, fearing what a bloody war would do to his people.

Thirteen.1

John L. O'Sullivan,
"The Great Nation of Futurity"
(1845)

In this selection from "The Great Nation of Futurity," John O'Sullivan glorified America and proclaimed its destiny to spread its civilization. In his magazine, The United States Magazine and Democratic Review, *O'Sullivan reminded Americans that "America is destined for better deeds" and spread the expansionist doctrine.* *

The American people having derived their origin from many other nations, and the Declaration of National Independence being entirely based on the great principle of human equality, these facts demonstrate at once our disconnected position as regards any other nation; that we have, in reality, but little connection with the past history of any of them and still less with all antiquity, its glories, or its crimes. On the contrary, our national birth was the beginning of a new history, the formation and progress of an untried political system, which separates us from the past and connects us with the future only; and so far as regards the entire development of the natural rights of man, in moral, political, and national life, we may confidently assume that our country is destined to be the great nation of futurity.

It is so destined, because the principle upon which a nation is organized fixes its destiny, and that of equality is perfect, is universal. It presides in all the operations of the physical world, and it is also the conscious law of the soul—the self-evident dictate of morality, which accurately defines the duty of man to man, and consequently man's rights as man. Besides, the truthful annals of any nation furnish abundant evidence that its happiness, its greatness, its duration, were always proportionate to the democratic equality in its system of government.

How many nations have had their decline and fall because the equal rights of the minority were trampled on by the despotism of the majority; or the interests of the many sacrificed to the aristocracy of the few; or the rights and interests of all given up to the

* From *The United States Magazine and Democratic Review*, VI (November, 1839), 2–3, 6.

monarchy of one? These three kinds of government have figured so frequently and so largely in the ages that have passed away that their history, through all time to come, can only furnish a resemblance. Like causes produce like effects, and the true philosopher of history will easily discern the principle of equality, or of privilege, working out its inevitable result. The first is regenerative, because it is natural and right; and the latter is destructive to society, because it is unnatural and wrong.

What friend of human liberty, civilization, and refinement can cast his view over the past history of the monarchies and aristocracies of antiquity, and not deplore that they ever existed? What philanthropist can contemplate the oppressions, the cruelties, and injustice inflicted by them on the masses of mankind and not turn with moral horror from the retrospect?

America is destined for better deeds. It is our unparalleled glory that we have no reminiscences of battlefields, but in defense of humanity, of the oppressed of all nations, of the rights of conscience, the rights of personal enfranchisement. Our annals describe no scenes of horrid carnage, where men were led on by hundreds of thousands to slay one another, dupes and victims to emperors, kings, nobles, demons in the human form called heroes. We have had patriots to defend our homes, our liberties, but no aspirants to crowns or thrones; nor have the American people ever suffered themselves to be led on by wicked ambition to depopulate the land, to spread desolation far and wide, that a human being might be placed on a seat of supremacy.

We have no interest in the scenes of antiquity, only as lessons of avoidance of nearly all their examples. The expansive future is our arena and for our history. We are entering on its untrodden space with the truths of God in our minds, beneficent objects in our hearts, and with a clear conscience unsullied by the past. We are the nation of human progress, and who will, what can, set limits to our onward march? Providence is with us, and no earthly power can. We point to the everlasting truth on the first page of our national declaration, and we proclaim to the millions of other lands that "the gates of hell"—the powers of aristocracy and monarchy—"shall not prevail against it."

The far-reaching, the boundless future, will be the era of American greatness. In its magnificent domain of space and time, the nation of many nations is destined to manifest to mankind the excellence of divine principles; to establish on earth the noblest temple ever dedicated to the worship of the Most High, the Sacred, and the True. Its floor shall be a hemisphere, roof the firmament of the star-studded heavens, and its congregation of Union of many Republics, comprising hundreds of happy millions, calling owning no man master, but governed by God's natural and moral law of equality, the law of brotherhood—of "peace and good will amongst men."

Yes, we are the nation of progress, of individual freedom, of universal enfranchisement. Equality of rights is the cynosure of our union of states, the grand exemplar of the correlative equality of individuals; and, while truth sheds its effulgence, we cannot retrograde without dissolving the one and subverting the other. We must onward to the fulfillment of our mission—to the entire development of the principle of our organization—freedom of conscience, freedom of person, freedom of trade and business pursuits, universality of freedom and equality. This is our high destiny, and in nature's eternal, inevitable decree of cause and effect we must accomplish it. All this will be our future history, to establish on earth the moral dignity and salvation of man—the immutable truth and beneficence of God. For this blessed mission to the nations of the world, which are shut out from the lifegiving light of truth, has America been chosen; and her high example shall smite unto death the tyranny of kings, hierarchs, and oligarchs and carry the glad tidings of peace and good will where myriads now endure in existence scarcely more enviable than that of beasts of the field. Who, then, can doubt that our country is destined to be the great nation of futurity?

DOCUMENT ANALYSIS

1. According to O'Sullivan, what characteristics of the American nation determine its future? How did O'Sullivan contrast the United States to other nations?

2. How might O'Sullivan's rhetoric have helped to propel the expansionism of the antebellum era?

José María Sánchez, from "A Trip to Texas" (1828)

José María Sánchez was sent by the Mexican government to survey and report on conditions in southeastern Texas, where increasing numbers of southern white Americans had settled. The Mexican government had encouraged immigration into their relatively unpopulated borderlands, provided that the settlers convert to Roman Catholicism and become Mexican citizens. Few did neither, however. José María Sánchez's report reveals the increasing tensions in the area.*

The Americans from the north have taken possession of practically all the eastern portion of Texas, in most cases without the permission of the authorities. They immigrate constantly, finding no one to prevent them, and take possession of the site that best suits them without asking leave or going through any formality other than that of building their homes. Thus the majority of inhabitants in the Department are North Americans, the Mexican population being reduced to only Bejar, Nacadoches, and La Bahía del Espíritu Santo, wretched settlements that between them do not number three thousand inhabitants, and the new village of Guadeloupe Victoria that has scarcely more than seventy settlers. The government of the state, with its seat at Saltillo, that should watch over the preservation of its most precious and interesting department, taking measures to prevent its being stolen by foreign hands, is the one that knows the least not only about actual conditions, but even about its territory....

The Mexicans that live here are very humble people and perhaps their intentions are good, but because of their education and environment they are ignorant not only of the customs of our great cities, but even of the occurrences of our Revolution, exception a few persons who have heard about them. Accustomed to the continued trade with the

---

* From José María Sánchez "A Trip to Texas" (1828), trans. Carlos E. Castaneda in *Southwestern Historical Quarterly*, Vol. 29, No. 4, April 1926, 270–273. Reprinted with permission of the Texas State Historical Association.

North Americans, they have adopted their customs and habits and one may say truly that they are not Mexicans except by birth, for they even speak Spanish with marked incorrectness....

This village [San Felipe de Austin] has been settled by Mr. Stephen Austin, a native of the United States of the North. It consists, at present, of forty or fifty wooden houses on the western bank of the large river known as Rio de los Brazos de Dios, but the houses are not arranged symmetrically so as to form streets, but on the contrary, lie in an irregular and desultory manner. Its population is nearly two hundred persons, of which only ten are Mexicans, for the balance are all Americans from the North with an occasional European. Two wretched little stores supply the inhabitants of the colony: one sells only whiskey, rum, sugar, and coffee; the other, rice, flour, lard, and cheap cloth. It may seem that these items are too few for the needs of the inhabitants, but they are not because the American from the North, at least the greater part of those I have seen, eat only salted meat, bread made by themselves out of corn meal, coffee and home-made cheese. To these the greater part of those who live in the village add strong liquor, for they are in general, in my opinion, lazy people of vicious character. Some of them cultivate their small farms by planting corn; but this task they usually entrust to their negro slaves, whom they treat with considerable harshness. Beyond the village in an immense stretch of land formed by rolling hills are scattered the families brought by Stephen Austin, which today number more than two thousand persons. The diplomatic policy of this impresario, evident in all his actions, has, as one may say, lulled the authorities into a sense of security, while he works diligently for his own ends. In my judgment, the spark that will start the conflagration that will deprive us of Texas, will start from this colony. All because the government does not take vigorous measures to prevent it. Perhaps it does not realize the value of what it is about to lose.

DOCUMENT ANALYSIS

1. How does José María Sánchez view the character of the white inhabitants of San Felipe de Austin?

2. What does Sánchez see looming in the near future for Texas, based upon what he observed?

Thirteen.3

Thomas Corwin, Against the Mexican War
(1847)

The Mexican-American war began in early 1846 and ended abruptly—after Americans had marched all the way to Mexico City—less than a year later. The question of who would win the war was never really seriously debated. What was in debate was the character of the American expansion and the question of slavery. Corwin, a Whig senator from Ohio, questioned expansionism and feared that the South would carry slavery wherever it went. *

What is the territory, Mr. President, which you propose to wrest from Mexico? It is consecrated to the heart of the Mexican by many a well-fought battle with his old Castilian master. His Bunker Hills, and Saratogas, and Yorktowns are there! The Mexican can say, "There I bled for liberty! and shall I surrender that consecrated home of my affections to the Anglo-Saxon invaders? What do they want with it? They have Texas already. They have possessed themselves of the territory between the Nueces and the Rio Grande. What else do they want? To what shall I point my children as memorials of that independence which I bequeath to them, when those battlefields shall have passed from my possession?"

Sir, had one come and demanded Bunker Hill of the people of Massachusetts, had England's lion ever showed himself there, is there a man over thirteen and under ninety who would not have been ready to meet him? Is there a river on this continent that would not have run red with blood? Is there a field but would have been piled high with the unburied bones of slaughtered Americans before these consecrated battlefields of liberty should have been wrested from us? But this same American goes into a sister republic, and says to poor, weak Mexico, "Give up your territory, you are unworthy to possess it; I have got one half already, and all I ask of you is to give up the other!"....

* From *The American Reader: Words That Moved a Nation*, ed. Diane Ravitch (New York: HarperCollins, 1991), 77–79.

Sir, look at this pretense of want of room. With twenty millions of people, you have about one thousand millions of acres of land, inviting settlement by every conceivable argument, bringing them down to a quarter of a dollar an acre, and allowing every man to squat where he pleases....

There is one topic connected with this subject which I tremble when I approach, and yet I cannot forbear to notice it. It meets you in every step you take; it threatens you which way soever you go in the prosecution of this war. I allude to the question of slavery. Opposition to its further extension, it must be obvious to everyone, is a deeply rooted determination with men of all parties in what we call the nonslaveholding states. New York, Pennsylvania, and Ohio, three of the most powerful, have already sent their legislative instructions here. So it will be, I doubt not, in all the rest. It is vain now to speculate about the reasons for this. Gentlemen of the South may call it prejudice, passion, hypocrisy, fanaticism. I shall not dispute with them now on that point. You and I cannot alter or change this opinion, if we would. These people only say we will not, cannot consent that you shall carry slavery where it does not already exist. They do not seek to disturb you in that institution as it exists in your states. Enjoy it if you will and as you will. This is their language; this their determination. How is it in the South? Can it be expected that they should expend in common their blood and their treasure in the acquisition of immense territory, and then willingly forgo the right to carry thither their slaves, and inhabit the conquered country if they please to do so? Sir, I know the feelings and opinions of the South too well to calculate on this. Nay, I believe they would even contend to any extremity for the mere right, had they no wish to exert it. I believe (and I confess I tremble when the conviction presses upon me) that there is equal obstinacy on both sides of this fearful question.

If, then, we persist in war, which, if it terminates in anything short of a mere wanton waste of blood as well as money, must end (as this bill proposes) in the acquisition of territory, to which at once this controversy must attach—this bill would seem to be nothing less than a bill to produce internal commotion. Should we prosecute this war another moment, or expend one dollar in the purchase or conquest of a single acre of Mexican land, the North and the South are brought into collision on a point where neither will yield. Who can foresee or foretell the result! Who so bold or reckless as to look such a conflict in the face unmoved! I do not envy the heart of him who can realize the possibility of such a conflict without emotions too painful to be endured. Why, then, shall we, the representatives of the sovereign states of the Union—the chosen guardians of this confederated Republic, why should we precipitate this fearful struggle, by continuing a war the result of which must be to force us at once upon a civil conflict? Sir, rightly considered, this is treason, treason to the Union, treason to the dearest interests, the loftiest aspirations, the most cherished hopes of our constituents. It is a crime to risk the possibility of such a contest. It is a crime of such infernal hue that every other in the catalogue of iniquity, when compared with it, whitens into virtue....

Let us abandon all idea of acquiring further territory and by consequence cease at once to prosecute this war. Let us call home our armies, and bring them at once within our own acknowledged limits. Show Mexico that you are sincere when you say you desire nothing by conquest. She has learned that she cannot encounter you in war, and if she had not, she is too weak to disturb you here. Tender her peace, and, my life on it, she will then accept it. But whether she shall or not, you will have peace without her consent. It is your invasion that has made war; your retreat will restore peace. Let us then close forever the approaches of internal feud, and so return to the ancient concord and the old ways of national prosperity and permanent glory. Let us here, in this temple consecrated to the Union, perform a solemn lustration; let us wash Mexican blood from our hands, and on these altars, and in the presence of that image of the Father of his Country that looks down upon us, swear to preserve honorable peace with all the world and eternal brotherhood with each other.

DOCUMENT ANALYSIS

1. Why Does Corwin consider proceeding with the Mexican War to be "treason to the Union"? Is his argument convincing?

Thirteen.4

Henry David Thoreau, from "Civil Disobedience" (1849)

Henry David Thoreau was a leading transcendentalist writer in the 1840s and 1850s, who celebrated the individual and the rhythms of the natural world. Thoreau's most famous book, Walden, *recounted his retreating to live in the woods, usually alone, independent, growing beans, studying nature, and contemplating life. In his essay "Civil Disobedience," published in 1849, Thoreau articulates his ardent political beliefs and the duty of the individual to reject unjust laws.** *

I heartily accept the motto, "That government is best which governs least"; and I should like to see it acted up to more rapidly and systematically. Carried out, it finally amounts to this, which also I believe—"That government is best which governs not at all"; and when men are prepared for it, that will be the kind of government which they will have. Government is at best but an expedient; but most governments are usually, and all governments are sometimes, inexpedient. The objections which have been brought against a standing army, and they are many and weighty, and deserve to prevail, may also at last be brought against a standing government. The standing army is only an arm of the standing government. The government itself, which is only the mode which the people have chosen to execute their will, is equally liable to be abused and perverted before the people can act through it. Witness the present Mexican war, the work of comparatively a few individuals using the standing government as their tool; for, in the outset, the people would not have consented to this measure.

This American government—what is it but a tradition, though a recent one, endeavoring to transmit itself unimpaired to posterity, but each instant losing some of its integrity? It has not the vitality and force of a single living man; for a single man can bend it to his will. It is a sort of wooden gun to the people themselves. But it is not the

* From Henry David Thoreau, "Civil Disobedience," orig. published in 1849, in *Walden and Civil Disobedience,* ed. by Sherman Paul (Boston: Houghton Mifflin, 1957), pp. 235–236, 238, 245–247.

less necessary for this; for the people must have some complicated machinery or other, and hear its din, to satisfy that idea of government which they have. Governments show thus how successfully men can be imposed on, even impose on themselves, for their own advantage. It is excellent, we must all allow. Yet this government never of itself furthered any enterprise, but by the alacrity with which it got out of its way. *It* does not keep the country free. *It* does not settle the West. *It* does not educate. The character inherent in the American people has done all that has been accomplished; and it would have done somewhat more, if the government had not sometimes got in its way....

How does it become a man to behave toward this American government today? I answer, that he cannot without disgrace be associated with it. I cannot for an instant recognize that political organization as *my* government which is the *slave's* government also....

Under a government which imprisons any unjustly, the true place for a just man is also a prison. The proper place to-day, the only place which Massachusetts has provided for her freer and less desponding spirits, is in her prisons, to be put out and locked out of the State by her own act, as they have already put themselves out by their principles. It is there that the fugitive slave, and the Mexican prisoner on parole, and the Indian come to plead the wrongs of his race should find them; on that separate, but more free and honorable ground, where the State places those who are not *with* her, but *against* her—the only house in a slave State in which a free man can abide with honor. If any think that their influence would be lost there, and their voices no longer afflict the ear of the State, that they would not be as an enemy within its walls, they do not know by how much truth is stronger than error, nor how much more eloquently and effectively he can combat injustice who has experienced a little in his own person. Cast your whole vote, not a strip of paper merely, but your whole influence. A minority is powerless while it conforms to the majority; it is not even a minority then; but it is irresistible when it clogs by its whole weight. If the alternative is to keep all just men in prison, or give up war and slavery, the State will not hesitate which to choose. If a thousand men were not to pay their tax-bills this year, that would not be a violent and bloody measure, as it would be to pay them, and enable the State to commit violence and shed innocent blood. This is, in fact, the definition of a peaceable revolution, if any such is possible. If the tax-gatherer, or any other public officer, asks me, as one has done, "But what shall I do?" my answer is, "If you really wish to do anything, resign your office." When the subject has refused allegiance, and the officer has resigned his office, then the revolution is accomplished. But even suppose blood should flow. Is there not a sort of blood shed when the conscience is wounded? Through this wound a man's real manhood and immortality flow out, and he bleeds to an everlasting death. I see this blood flowing now....

When I converse with the freest of my neighbors, I perceive that, whatever they may say about the magnitude and seriousness of the question, and their regard for the public tranquillity, the long and the short of the matter is, that they cannot spare the protection of the existing government, and they dread the consequences to their property and families of disobedience to it. For my own part, I should not like to think that I ever rely on the protection of the State. But, if I deny the authority of the State when it presents its tax-bill, it will soon take and waste all my property, and so harass me and my children without end. This is hard. This makes it impossible for a man to live honestly, and at the same time comfortably in outward respects. It will not be worth the while to accumulate property; that would be sure to go again. You must hire or squat somewhere, and raise but a small crop, and eat that soon. You must live within yourself, and depend upon yourself always tucked up and ready for a start, and not have many affairs....No: until I want the protection of Massachusetts to be extended to me in some distant Southern port, where my liberty is endangered, or until I am bent solely on building up an estate at home by peaceful enterprise, I can afford to refuse allegiance to Massachusetts, and her right to my property and life. It costs me less in every sense to incur the penalty of disobedience to the State than it would to obey. I should feel as if I were worth less in that case.

DOCUMENT ANALYSIS

1. What price does Thoreau argue one pays for obeying laws you know to be unjust? Do you agree with Thoreau?

2. Why, at this time, does Thoreau consider the American government to be a disgrace?

Thirteen.5

Elizabeth Dixon Smith Greer, Journal
(1847–1850)

Like many during the 1840s and 1850s, Elizabeth Dixon Smith Greer, her husband, and her small children made the journey along the Oregon Trail from Indiana. The migrants' motivations were often complex, but all hoped to improve their lives. Oregon settlers like the Greers were promised 640 acres in the territory. In this selection from her journal, kept for friends back home, Elizabeth Greer documents the difficulties of the overland journey. *

Dear Friends—By your request I have endeavored to keep a record of our journey from "the States" to Oregon, though it is poorly done, owing to my having a young babe and besides a large family to do for; and, worst of all, my education is very limited.

April 21, 1847—Commenced our journey from La Porte, Indiana, to Oregon; made fourteen miles....

November 18—My husband is sick. It rains and snows. We start this morning around the falls with our wagons. We have 5 miles to go. I carry my babe and lead, or rather carry, another through snow, mud and water, almost to my knees. It is the worst road that a team could possibly travel. I went ahead with my children, and I was afraid to look behind me for fear of seeing the wagons turn over into the mud and water with everything in them. My children gave out with cold and fatigue and could not travel, and the boys had to unhitch the oxen and bring them and carry the children on to camp. I was so cold and numb that I could not tell by the feeling that I had any feet at all. We started this morning at sunrise and did not get to camp until after dark, and there was not one dry thread on one of us—not even my babe. I had carried my babe and I was so fatigued that I could scarcely speak or step. When I got here I found my husband lying in Welch's wagon, very sick. He had brought Mrs. Polk down the day before and was

---

* From *The Thirty-fifth Transactions of the Oregon Pioneer Association* (1907), 153, 171–78.

taken sick here. We had to stay up all night, for our wagons are left halfway back. I have not told half we suffered. I am not adequate to the task. Here were some hundreds camped, waiting for boats to come and take them down the Columbia to Vancouver or Portland or Oregon City.

November 19—My husband is sick and can have but little care. Rain all day.

November 20—Rain all day. It is almost an impossibility to cook, and quite so to keep warm or dry. I froze or chilled my feet so that I cannot wear a shoe, so I have to go around in the cold water barefooted.

November 21—Rain all day. The whole care of everything falls upon my shoulders. I cannot write any more at present.

November 30—Raining. This morning I ran about trying to get a house to get into with my sick husband. At last I found a small, leaky concern, with two families already in it. Mrs. Polk had got down before us. She and another widow was in this house. My family and Welch's went in with them, and you could have stirred us with a stick. Welch and my oldest boy was driving the cattle around. My children and I carried up a bed. The distance was nearly a quarter of a mile. Made it down on the floor in the mud. I got some men to carry my husband up through the rain and lay him on it, and he never was out of that shed until he was carried out in his coffin. Here lay five of us bedfast at one time…and we had no money, and what few things we had left that would bring money, I had to sell. I had to give 10 cents a pound for fresh pork, 75 cents per bushel for potatoes, 4 cents a pound for fish. There are so many of us sick that I cannot write any more at present. I have not time to write much, but I thought it would be interesting to know what kind of weather we have in the winter.

1848—January 14—Rain this morning. Warm weather. We suppose it has rained half of the time that I have neglected writing.

January 15—My husband is still alive, but very sick. There is no medicine here except at Fort Vancouver, and the people there will not sell one bit—not even a bottle of wine.

February 1—Rain all day. This day my dear husband, my last remaining friend, died.

February 2—Today we buried my earthly companion. Now I know what none but widows know; that is, how comfortless is a widow's life, especially when left in a strange land, without money or friends, and the care of seven children. Cloudy…

DOCUMENT ANALYSIS

1. What do Greer's journal entries suggest about the sexual division of labor or the flexibility of gender roles on the trail?

2. What difficulties does Greer and her family encounter as they make their way west on the trail?

Thirteen.6

Chief Seattle, Oration
(1854)

Native Americans were devastated by the effects of American expansion: 70,000 Indians died in California alone between 1849 and 1859; the Paiute were shot for sport by trappers. Between 1853 and 1857, the United States forced the secession of 147 million acres of Native American land. This land included those of Chief Seattle, who chose to capitulate to the government rather than risk conflict with an army that had been singularly effective in crushing other Indian groups. *

. . . Yonder sky that has wept tears of compassion upon my people for centuries untold, and which to us appears changeless and eternal, may change. Today is fair. Tomorrow it may be overcast with clouds. My words are like the stars that never change. Whatever Seattle says the great chief at Washington can rely upon with as much certainty as he can upon the return of the sun or the seasons. The White Chief says that Big Chief at Washington sends us greetings of friendship and goodwill. This is kind of him for we know he has little need of our friendship in return. His people are many. They are like the grass that covers vast prairies. My people are few. They resemble the scattering trees of a storm-swept plain. The great, and—I presume—good White Chief sends us word that he wishes to buy our lands but is willing to allow us enough to live comfortably. This indeed appears just, even generous, for the Red Man no longer has rights that he need respect, and the offer may be wise also, as we are no longer in need of an extensive country.

There was a time when our people covered the land as the waves of a wind-ruffled sea cover its shell-paved floor, but that time long since passed away with the greatness of tribes that are now but a mournful memory. I will not dwell on nor mourn over, our

---

* Reprinted from *The American Reader: Words That Moved a Nation*, ed. Diane Ravitch (New York: HarperCollins, 1991), 92–94.

untimely decay, nor reproach my paleface brothers with hastening it as we too may have been somewhat to blame.

Youth is impulsive. When our young men grow angry at some real or imaginary wrong, and disfigure their faces with black paint, it denotes that their hearts are black, and that they are often cruel and relentless, and our old men and old women are unable to restrain them. Thus has ever been. Thus it was when the White Men first began to push our forefathers further westward. But let us hope that the hostilities between us may never return. We would have everything to lose and nothing to gain. Revenge by young men is considered gain, even at the cost of their own lives, but old men who stay at home in times of war, and mothers who have sons to lose, know better.

Our good father at Washington—for I presume he is now our father as well as yours…sends us word that if we do as he desires he will protect us. His brave warriors will be to us a bristling wall of strength, and his wonderful ships of war will fill our harbors so that our ancient enemies far to the northward—the Hydas and Tsimpsians,—will cease to frighten our women, children, and old men. Then in reality will he be our father and we his children. But can that ever be? Your God is not our God! Your God loves your people and hates mine. He folds his strong protecting arms lovingly about the paleface and leads him by the hand as a father leads his infant son—but He has forsaken His red children—if they really are his. Our God, the Great Spirit, seems also to have forsaken us. Your God makes your people wax strong every day. Soon they will fill all the land. Our people are ebbing away like a rapidly receding tide that will never return. The White Man's God cannot love our people or He would protect them. They seem to be orphans who can look nowhere for help. How then can we be brothers? How can your God become our God and renew our prosperity and awaken in us dreams of returning greatness? If we have a common heavenly father He must be partial—for He came to His paleface children. We never saw Him. He gave you laws but had no word for His red children whose teeming multitudes once filled this vast continent as stars fill the firmament. No; we are two distinct races with separate origins and separate destinies. There is little in common between us.

To us the ashes of our ancestors are sacred and their resting place is hallowed ground. You wander far from the graves of your ancestors and seemingly without regret. Your religion was written upon tables of stone by the iron finger of your God so that you could not forget. The Red Man could never comprehend nor remember it. Our religion is the traditions of our ancestors—the dreams of our old men, given them in solemn hours of night by the Great Spirit; and the visions of our sachems, and is written in the hearts of our people.

Your dead cease to love you and the land of their nativity as soon as they pass the portals of the tomb and wander away beyond the stars. They are soon forgotten and never return. Our dead never forget the beautiful world that gave them being. They still love its verdant valleys, its murmuring rivers, its magnificent mountains, sequestered vales and verdant lined lakes and bays, and even yearn in tender, fond affection over the lonely hearted living, and often return from the Happy Hunting Ground to visit, guide, console and comfort them.

Day and night cannot dwell together. The Red Man has ever fled the approach of the White Man, as the morning mist flees before the morning sun.

However, your proposition seems fair and I think that my people will accept it and will retire to the reservation you offer them. Then we will dwell apart in peace....

It matters little where we pass the remnant of our days. They will not be many. The Indians' night promises to be dark. Not a single star of hope hovers above his horizon. Sad-voiced winds moan in the distance. Grim fate seems to be on the Red Man's trail, and wherever he goes he will hear the approaching footsteps of his fell destroyer and prepare stolidly to meet his doom, as does the wounded doe that hears the approaching footsteps of the hunter.

...But why would I mourn at the untimely fate of my people? Tribe follows tribe, and nation follows nation, like the waves of the sea. It is the order of nature, and regret is useless. Your time of decay may be distant, but it will surely come, for even the White Man whose God walked and talked with him as friend with friend, cannot be exempt from the common destiny. We may be brothers after all. We will see.

We will ponder your proposition and when we decide we will let you know. But should we accept it, I here and now make this condition that we will not be denied the privilege without molestation of visiting at any time the tombs of our ancestors, friends, and children....

And when the last Red Man shall have perished, and the memory of my tribe shall have become a myth among the White Men, these shores will swarm with the invisible dead of my tribe, and when your children's children think themselves alone in the field, the store, the ship, upon the highway, or in the silence of the pathless woods, they will not be alone. In all the earth there is no place dedicated to solitude. At night when the streets of your cities and villages are silent and you think them deserted, they will throng with the returning hosts that once filled them and still love this beautiful land. The White Man will never be alone.

Let him be just and deal kindly with my people, for the dead are not powerless. Dead, did I say? There is no death, only a change of worlds.

DOCUMENT ANALYSIS

1. In Chief Seattle's terms, what were the major differences between Native American and white societies?

Chapter Study Questions

1. Compare O'Sullivan's discussion of America's special destiny with the ideas of John Winthrop in chapter three.

2. While O'Sullivan celebrates American expansionism as destined for a great nation, Corwin argues that the nation should "abandon all idea of acquiring further territory." Whose argument is more compelling to you, and why?

3. Compare Corwin's anti-war sentiments to Thoreau's. In what ways are they similar or different? Which offers a more compelling argument? Why?

4. How were the Cherokees and the Mexicans, about whom Jose Maria Sanchez writes, fighting the same phenomenon in this era? How were their situations different?

5. How were pioneers like Greer and her family, who made it all the way to Oregon after overcoming profound obstacles, affecting Chief Seattle and other Native Americans of the Pacific Northwest?

Fourteen

The Union in Peril

The 1850s was a decade of crisis, as the last hopes for peace between the North and South were shattered. As described in this chapter, the Compromise of 1850 quickly proved to be a failure, and as the years progressed, the political system became deadlocked and was unable to deal with the growing sectional divisions. Each day seemed to bring another occasion for Northerners and Southerners to become hardened in their stands. This chapter describes some of the events that inflamed sectional differences.

The Fugitive Slave Act, part of the Compromise of 1850, angered and impassioned many Northerners, including Harriet Beecher Stowe. It inspired Stowe to write her bestselling novel, *Uncle Tom's Cabin*, which sold over 300,000 copies in the first year after its publication in 1852. So influential was it that during the Civil War Abraham Lincoln reported referred to Stowe as "the little lady who started this big war." The selection from *Uncle Tom's Cabin* excerpted here showcases the sensationalist and heartrending aspects of the novel, which brought the ethics of slavery into question for a wide audience.

In the midst of the sectional debate over slavery in the 1850s, one proposal put forward was to annex Cuba and make it part of the United States. This proposal was announced in the Ostend Manifesto of 1854, and, if it had gone through (it didn't), it would have added another area of slave territory to the United States.

While debate raged, the United States Supreme Court had not been directly involved in the sectional conflict. However, a case on appeal from the circuit court afforded the Supreme Court the opportunity to finally render a decision on the constitutionality of the Missouri Compromise. Dred Scott and his wife Harriet sued the state of Missouri for their freedom. They argued that because they had been taken into territories where slavery was prohibited, they should be freed.

The Supreme Court's decision in *Dred Scott v. Sanford* was one of the most controversial events in a decade full of political controversy. Historians have long debated why Chief Justice Roger B. Taney, a staunch Jacksonian and a southern Democrat, would abandon his hesitancy to impose judicial solutions on political problems. Taney's appointment in 1836 roughly coincided with the emergence of slavery as a national issue. At that time, the law, as it related to the status of slaves and free blacks, consisted of the Constitution, a few isolated Supreme Court cases, and a few, similarly isolated, acts of Congress and the executive branch. The Constitution clearly recognized slavery. The three-fifths compromise and the provision prohibiting the outlawing of the African slave trade until 1808 both implicitly recognized the institution of slavery. Moreover, the Constitution specifically provided that persons who owed service or labor in one state and escaped should, upon recapture, be returned to the person to whom such service was due. In the *Dred Scott* decision, Court argued that blacks—whether free or slave—were not citizens and thus could not sue in federal court. In addition, the Court declared that, because Congress did not have the power to ban slavery, the Missouri Compromise was unconstitutional. Dred Scott and his wife remained slaves.

The 1850s ended with one final dramatic event related to slavery. In 1859, the fiery abolitionist John Brown led a raid on a federal arsenal in Harpers Ferry, Virginia, hoping to arm a slave rebellion. Brown and his raiders were caught and tried, and Brown was sentenced to hang for his actions. To some in the North, Brown's extremism in the pursuit of a noble goal—the ending of slavery—justified his violent means, and Brown became a martyr to the abolitionist cause. He also exemplified what slave owners feared most.

Fourteen.1

Harriet Beecher Stowe, from *Uncle Tom's Cabin* (1852)

This selection from Uncle Tom's Cabin *describes a violent exchange between the slave master Simon Legree (a transplanted Connecticut native) and the patient slave Uncle Tom. Southerners criticized Stowe, who had very little (if any) experience of plantation life, for an atypical, distorted perception of slavery. Most Northern readers were taken in by Stowe's tale and its somewhat sensationalized and sentimental portrayal of slavery.* *

"And now," said Legree, "come here, you Tom. You see, I telled ye I didn't buy ye jest for the common work. I mean to promote ye, and make a driver of ye; and tonight ye may jest as well begin to get ye hand in. Now, ye jest take this yer gal and flog her; ye've seen enough on't [of it] to know how." "I beg Mas'r' pardon," said Tom; "hopes Mas'r won't set me at that. It's what I an't used to—never did—and can't do, no way possible."

"Ye'll larn a pretty smart chance of things ye never did know, before I've done with ye!" said Legree, taking up a cowhide and striking Tom a heavy blow across the cheek, and following up the infliction by a shower of blows.

"There!" he said, as he stopped to rest; "now, will ye tell me ye can't do it?"

"Yes, Mas'r," said Tom, putting up his hand, to wipe the blood that trickled down his face. "I'm willin' to work, night and day, and work while there's life and breath in me. But this yer thing I can't feel it right to do; and, Mas'r, I never shall do it—never!"

Tom had a remarkably smooth, soft voice, and a habitually respectful manner that had given Legree an idea that he would be cowardly and easily subdued. When he spoke these last words, a thrill of amazement went through everyone. The poor woman clasped her hands and said, "O Lord!" and everyone involuntarily looked at each other and drew in their breath, as if to prepare for the storm that was about to burst.

---

* From Harriet B. Stowe, *Uncle Tom's Cabin* (Cleveland, 1852).

Legree looked stupefied and confounded; but at last burst forth: "What! Ye blasted black beast! Tell me ye don't think it right to do what I tell ye! What have any of you cussed cattle to do with thinking what's right? I'll put a stop to it! Why, what do ye think ye are? May be ye think ye're a gentleman, master Tom, to be a telling your master what's right, and what an't! So you pretend it's wrong to flog the gal!"

"I think so, Mas'r," said Tom; "the poor crittur's sick and feeble; 'twould be downright cruel, and it's what I never will do, nor begin to. Mas'r, if you mean to kill me, kill me; but, as to my raising my hand again any one here, I never shall—I'll die first!"

Tom spoke in a mild voice, but with a decision that could not be mistaken. Legree shook with anger; his greenish eyes glared fiercely, and his very whiskers seemed to curl with passion. But, like some ferocious beast, that plays with its victim before he devours it, he kept back his strong impulse to proceed to immediate violence, and broke out into bitterly raillery.

"Well, here's a pious dog, at last, let down among us sinners—a saint, a gentleman, and no less, to talk to us sinners about our sins! Powerful holy crittur, he must be! Here, you rascal, you make believe to be so pious—didn't you never hear, out of yer Bible, 'Servants, obey yer masters'? An't I yer master? Didn't I pay down twelve hundred dollars, cash, for all there is inside yer old cussed black shell? An't yer mine, now, body and soul?" he said, giving Tom a violent kick with his heavy boot; "tell me!"

In the very depth of physical suffering, bowed by brutal oppression, this question shot a gleam of joy an triumph through Tom's soul. He suddenly stretched himself up, and, looking earnestly to heaven, while the tears and blood that flowed down his face mingled, he exclaimed, " No! no! no! my soul an't yours, Mas'r! You haven't bought it—ye can't buy it! It's been bought and paid for by One that is able to keep it. No matter, no matter, you can't harm me!"

"I can't!" said Legree, with a sneer; "we'll see—we'll see! Here Sambo, Quimbo, give this dog such a breakin' in as he won't get over this month!"

The two gigantic Negroes that now laid hold of Tom, with fiendish exultation in their faces, might have formed no unapt personification of powers of darkness. The poor woman screamed with apprehension, and all rose, as by a general impulse, while they dragged him unresisting from the place.

DOCUMENT ANALYSIS

1. Despite the melodramatic nature of the story related in this passage, what deep truths is Stowe attempting to show? Do you think her use of melodrama was overdone, or appropriate for the audience of her day?

2. Do you see racial stereotypes embedded in Stowe's characterization of Southern plantation life? Explain.

Fourteen.2

The Ostend Manifesto
(1854)

The war with Mexico in the 1840s divided many in the United States, many of whom were concerned especially with the additional slave territory added to the country following the war. In the contentious 1850s, some in the federal government sought to acquire the island of Cuba, still controlled by Spain, and issued the Ostend Manifesto, detailing why this acquisition was desirable. Although Cuba was not acquired, the debate over the Ostend Manifesto added additional fire to the sectional disputes of the decade leading up to the Civil War.*

SIR:—The undersigned, in compliance with the wish expressed by the President in the several confidential despatches you have addressed to us, respectively, to that effect, have met in conference, first at Ostend, in Belgium, on the 8th, 10th, and 11th instant, and then at Aix la Chapelle in Prussia, on the days next following, up to the date hereof.

We have arrived at the conclusion, and are thoroughly convinced, that an immediate and earnest effort ought to be made by the government of the United States to purchase Cuba from Spain at any price for which it can be obtained...

The proposal should, in our opinion, be made in such a manner as to be presented through the necessary diplomatic forms to the Supreme Constituent Cortes about to assemble. On this momentous question, in which the people both of Spain and the United States are so deeply interested, all our proceedings ought to be open, frank, and public. They should be of such a character as to challenge the approbation of the world.

We firmly believe that, in the progress of human events, the time has arrived when the vital interests of Spain are as seriously involved in the sale, as those of the United States in the purchase, of the island and that the transaction will prove equally honorable to both nations.

* From House Executive Documents, 33 Cong., 2 Sess., Vol. X, pp. 127–136.

Under these circumstances we cannot anticipate a failure, unless possibly through the malign influence of foreign powers who possess no right whatever to interfere in the matter....

Cuba is as necessary to the North American republic as any of its present members, and that it belongs naturally to that great family of States of which the Union is the providential nursery.

From its locality it commands the mouth of the Mississippi and the immense and annually increasing trade which must seek this avenue to the ocean....

The natural and main outlet to the products of this entire population, the highway of their direct intercourse with the Atlantic and the Pacific States, can never be secure, but must ever be endangered whilst Cuba is a dependency of a distant power in whose possession it has proved to be a source of constant annoyance and embarrassment to their interests.

Indeed, the Union can never enjoy repose, nor possess reliable security, as long as Cuba is not embraced within its boundaries....

Extreme oppression, it is now universally admitted, justifies any people in endeavoring to relieve themselves from the yoke of their oppressors. The sufferings which the corrupt, arbitrary, and unrelenting local administration necessarily entails upon the inhabitants of Cuba, cannot fail to stimulate and keep alive that spirit of resistance and revolution against Spain, which has, of late years, been so often manifested. In this condition of affairs it is vain to expect that the sympathies of the people of the United States will not be warmly enlisted in favor of their oppressed neighbors....

It is not improbable, therefore, that Cuba may be wrested from Spain by a successful revolution; and in that event she will lose both the island and the price which we are now willing to pay for it—a price far beyond what was ever paid by one people to another for any province.

It may also be remarked that the settlement of this vexed question, by the cession of Cuba to the United States, would forever prevent the dangerous complications between nations to which it may otherwise give birth.

It is certain that, should the Cubans themselves organize an insurrection against the Spanish government, and should other independent nations come to the aid of Spain in the contest, no human power could, in our opinion, prevent the people and government of the United States from taking part in such a civil war in support of their neighbors and friends....

The United States have never acquired a foot of territory except by fair purchase, or, as in the case of Texas, upon the free and voluntary application of the people of that independent State, who desired to blend their destinies with our own.

Even our acquisitions from Mexico are no exception to this rule, because, although we might have claimed them by the right of conquest in a just war, yet we purchased them for what was then considered by both parties a full and ample equivalent.

Our past history forbids that we should acquire the island of Cuba without the consent of Spain, unless justified by the great law of self-preservation. We must, in any event, preserve our own conscious rectitude and our own self-respect.

Whilst pursuing this course we can afford to disregard the censures of the world, to which we have been so often and so unjustly exposed.

After we shall have offered Spain a price for Cuba far beyond its present value, and this shall have been refused, it will then be time to consider the question, does Cuba, in the possession of Spain, seriously endanger our internal peace and the existence of our cherished Union?

Should this question be answered in the affirmative, then, by every law, human and divine, we shall be justified in wresting it from Spain if we possess the power, and this upon the very same principle that would justify an individual in tearing down the burning house of his neighbor if there were no other means of preventing the flames from destroying his own home....

We have already witnessed the happy results for both countries which followed a similar arrangement in regard to Florida.

Yours, very respectfully,

JAMES BUCHANAN
J. Y. MASON
PIERRE SOULÉ

DOCUMENT ANALYSIS

1. What arguments are made in the Ostend Manifesto to suggest that Spain would be far better off to sell Cuba to the United States?

2. What pressing issue is totally ignored in the language of the Ostend Manifesto? Do you think that omission is intentional? Explain.

Fourteen.3

Dred Scott v. Sanford
(1857)

Dred and Harriet Scott first sued for their freedom in 1846, after their master, a doctor, had brought them from Missouri to Minnesota and Wisconsin. They waited more than ten years before the Supreme Court decision, which ultimately denied them their freedom, was handed down. This excerpt is from Chief Justice Roger Taney's decision. *

The Question is simply this: Can a negro, whose ancestors were imported into this country, and sold as slaves, become a member of the political community formed and brought into existence by the Constitution of the United States, and as such become entitled to all the rights, and privileges, and immunities, guarantied [sic] by that instrument to the citizen? One of which rights is the privilege of suing in a court of the United States in the cases specified in the constitution.

...The only matter in issue before the Court, therefore, is, whether the descendants of such slaves, when they shall be emancipated, or who are born of parents who had become free before their birth, are citizens of a State, in the sense which the word citizen is used in the Constitution....

The words "people of the United States" and "citizens" are synonymous terms. ...They both describe the political body who, according to our republican institutions, form the sovereignty, and who hold the power and conduct the government through their representatives....The question before us is, whether the class of persons described in the plea in abatement compose a portion of this people, and are constituent members of this sovereignty? We think they are not, under the word "citizens" in the Constitution, and can therefore claim none of the rights and privileges which that instrument provides for and secures to citizens of the United States. On the contrary, they were at that time considered as a subordinate and inferior class of beings, who had been subjugated by the dominant race, and whether emancipated or not, yet remained subject to their authority, and had no rights or privileges but such as those who held the power and the government might choose to grant them....

In discussing the question, we must not confound the rights of citizenship which a State may confer within its own limits, and the rights of citizenship as a member of the Union. It does not by any means follow, because he has all the rights and privileges of a citizen of a State, that he must be a citizen of the United States....

In the opinion of the court, the legislation and histories of the times, and the language used in the Declaration of Independence, show, that neither the class of persons who had been imported as slaves, nor their descendants, whether they had become free or not, were then acknowledged as a part of the people, nor intended to be included in the general words used in that memorable instrument....

They had for more than a century before been regarded as beings of an inferior order, and altogether unfit to associate with the white race, either in social or political relations, and so far inferior, that they had no rights which the white man was bound to respect; and that the negro might justly and lawfully be reduced to slavery for his benefit....

...there are two clauses in the constitution which point directly and specifically to the negro race as a separate class of persons, and show clearly that they were not regarded as a portion of the people or citizens of the government then formed.

...upon full and careful consideration of the subject, the court is of opinion, that, upon the facts stated,...Dred Scott was not a citizen of Missouri within the meaning of the constitution of the United States and not entitled as such to sue in its courts....

DOCUMENT ANALYSIS

1. What are the most momentous points made in Taney's opinion in the Dred Scott case? What was your reaction as you read it?

2. How do you suppose Southern supporters of slavery reacted to Taney's opinion?

Fourteen.4

John Brown, Address to the Virginia Court (1859)

The fire of abolitionism burned strong in John Brown, a deeply religious white man who became increasingly fervid in his denunciation of slavery. Brown and his sons fought guerrilla battles in "Bleeding Kansas" in the mid-1850s, then he became renown nationwide in 1859 for masterminding an attempt to start a slave rebellion in Harpers Ferry, Virginia (now West Virginia). After seizing weapons at the federal arsenal, the revolt was quickly put down, and Brown was captured, convicted, and sentenced to death for his role. Most in the North as well as the South viewed him as a dangerous threat to the Union, and there is evidence he may have been mentally unbalanced. A minority of prominent northerners, however, viewed Brown as virtually a biblical prophet, and his speech to the court at his sentencing helped seal his status as a martyr.*

I have, may it please the Court, a few words to say.

In the first place, I deny every thing but what I have already admitted, of a design on my part to free Slaves. I intended, certainly, to have made a clean thing of that matter, as I did last winter, when I went into Missouri, and there took Slaves, without the snapping of a gun on either side, moving them through the country, and finally leaving them in Canada. I desired to have done the same thing again, on a much larger scale. That was all I intended. I never did intend murder, or treason, or the destruction of property, or to excite or incite Slaves to rebellion, or to make insurrection.

I have another objection, and that is, that it is unjust that I should suffer such a penalty. Had I interfered in the manner, and which I admit has been fairly proved,—for I admire the truthfulness and candor of the greater portion of the witnesses who have

* From Pearson Online http://wps.ablongman.com/wps/media/objects/1676/1716309/
documents/doc_t125.html.

testified in this case,—had I so interfered in behalf of the Rich, the Powerful, the Intelligent, the so-called Great, or in behalf of any of their friends, either father, mother, brother, sister, wife, or children, or any of that class, and suffered and sacrificed what I have in this interference, it would have been all right. Every man in this Court would have deemed it an act worthy a reward, rather than a punishment.

This Court acknowledges too, as I suppose, the validity of the Law of God. I saw a book kissed, which I suppose to be the Bible, or at least the New Testament, which teaches me that, "All things whatsoever I would that men should do to me, I should do even so to them." It teaches me further, to "Remember them that are in bonds, as bound with them." I endeavored to act up to that instruction. I say I am yet too young to understand that God is any respecter of persons. I believe that to have interfered as I have done, as I have always freely admitted I have done, in behalf of his despised poor, I have done no wrong, but RIGHT.

Now, if it is deemed necessary that I should forfeit my life, for the furtherance of the ends of justice, and MINGLE MY BLOOD FURTHER WITH THE BLOOD OF MY CHILDREN, and with the blood of millions in this Slave country, whose rights are disregarded by wicked, cruel, and unjust enactments,—I say, LET IT BE DONE.

Let me say one word further: I feel entirely satisfied with the treatment I have received on my trial. Considering all the circumstances, it has been more generous than I expected; but I feel no consciousness of guilt. I have stated from the first what was my intention, and what was not. I never had any design against the liberty of any person, nor any disposition to commit treason, or excite Slaves to rebel, or make any general insurrection. I never encouraged any man to do so, but always discouraged any idea of that kind.

Let me say something, also, in regard to the statements made by some of those who were connected with me. I hear that it has been stated by some of them, that I have induced them to join me; but the contrary is true. I do not say this to injure them, but as regarding their weakness. Not one but joined me of his own accord, and the greater part at their own expense. A number of them I never saw and never had a word of conversation with, till the day they came to me, and that was for the purpose I have stated. Now I have done.

John Brown

DOCUMENT ANALYSIS

1. In what ways does Brown invoke God and the Bible in his address to the court? Is the religious base to his argument compelling? Explain.

Chapter Study Questions

1. How would Harriet Beecher Stowe have reacted to the *Dred Scott* decision?

2. In what ways can novels convey information better than newspapers or other media? Can movies today have the same kind of impact on public opinion as Stowe's?

3. How did the *Dred Scott* decision shake up the entire national debate over slavery? In what ways did it force northerners to take stock of their acceptance of slavery in the South and the status of slaves and former slaves?

4. In what ways was John Brown's 1859 raid on Harpers Ferry an exclamation point for the growing sectional anger in this decade before the Civil War? In what ways was it a sign of greater bloodshed to come?

Fifteen

The Union Severed

The Civil War began in 1861 with an outpouring of support in both the North and the South as thousands of young men rushed to volunteer to fight for the Union or for an independent Confederacy. Troops went off to battle expecting a brief engagement. However, the war was brutal and by the end of the fighting in 1865, over 600,000 men had been killed. In many ways, the Civil War transformed American society. Slavery was ended, the South was physically damaged and forced to adapt its distinctive economic system, and technological advancements and industries became more important in both the North and the South.

Slavery was not part of the rhetoric of the early part of the war. Most Northerners believed the war was being fought to preserve the Union and most Southerners believed they were fighting for self-determination—not over the question of the spread of slavery or the emancipation of slaves. In fact, Lincoln argued that "If I could save the Union without freeing any slave, I would do it; and if I could save it by freeing all the slaves, I would do it." But in 1863, Lincoln did issue the Emancipation Proclamation freeing the slaves. Although the proclamation had little practical effect, it had great symbolic resonance, elevating the war to save the Union into a war to end slavery.

From the beginning of the war, blacks attempted to participate in the war effort, although they were initially rebuffed by the Union side. But by war's end, over 186,000 African Americans had served in the Union forces. They received lower pay, had poorer supplies and equipment, and were led by white officers. In an 1863 letter to President Lincoln, an African American soldier, James Gooding, protested the lower pay received by black soldiers and described the difficulties they encountered in the Union army.

The Confederate States of America were established in 1861, and eventually included eleven states and Indian Territory (present-day Oklahoma). The president of the Confederacy was Jefferson Davis, from Mississippi. In his second inaugural speech from

1862, excerpted here, Davis likened the Confederate cause to that of America's founding fathers.

There were many women who served the army on the field and many more who took on increased responsibilities on the home front. Clara Barton, nicknamed the "Angel of the Battlefield," was one of thousands of women who served as a field nurse. Until the Civil War, nursing was considered "unladylike" and an improper occupation for a well-bred woman, and Barton encountered tremendous resistance to her work during the war. In this selection, she describes her difficulties caring for thousands of suffering men dying on a battlefield in Virginia.

Gettysburg is probably the most famous and arguably the most important battle of the Civil War. In the first three days of July 1863, Union troops, commanded by General George G. Meade turned back a Confederate advance into Pennsylvania. It was the first time the Confederate General Robert E. Lee was clearly beaten on the battle-field and it marked a crucial military turning point. The diary entries of Lieutenant Theodore A. Dodge, a Union soldier from upstate New York who was wounded at Gettysburg, are excerpted in this chapter. After the carnage, the South would never again mount an offensive into northern territory. The following November, Lincoln came to Gettysburg to dedicate a memorial cemetery.

By the fall of 1864, after three bloody years of civil war, the North was finally winning decisively. Abraham Lincoln won re-election that November and supporters of the Union cheered additional battle victories and territorial gains over the next few months. In March of 1865, with the war nearly won, Lincoln took the oath of office for a second term. In that inaugural address, he offered his hopes for quickly reuniting the nation.

Fifteen.1

James Henry Gooding, Letter to President Lincoln (1863)

In this eloquent letter, written after the Emancipation Proclamation, James Henry Gooding wrote to his president, complaining about his ill-treatment and that he had not been paid in over a month. No answer from President Lincoln is recorded. *

Morris Island, S.C.
September 28, 1863

Your Excellency, Abraham Lincoln:

Your Excellency will pardon the presumption of an humble individual like myself, in addressing you, but the earnest solicitation of my comrades in arms besides the genuine interest felt by myself in the matter is my excuse, for placing before the Executive head of the Nation our Common Grievance.

On the 6th of the last Month, the Paymaster of the Department informed us, that if we would decide to receive the sum of $10 (ten dollars) per month, he would come and pay us that sum, but that, on the sitting of Congress, the Regt. (regiment) would, in his opinion, be allowed the other 3 (three). He did not give us any guarantee that this would be, as he hoped; certainly he had no authority for making any such guarantee, and we cannot suppose him acing in any way interested.

Now the main question is, are we Soldiers, or are we Laborers? We are fully armed, and equipped, have done all the various duties pertaining to a Soldier's life, have conducted ourselves to the complete satisfaction of General Officers, who were, if anything, prejudiced against us, but who now accord us all the encouragement and honors due us; have shared the perils an labor of reducing the first strong-hold that flaunted a

* Reprinted from *A Documentary History of the Negro People in the U.S.* ed. Herbert Aptheker (New York: Citadel Press, 1951), 482–484.

Traitor Flag; and more, Mr. President, to-day the Anglo-Saxon Mother, Wife, or Sister are not alone in tears for departed Sons, Husbands, and Brothers. The patient, trusting descendant of Afric's Clime have dyed the ground with blood, in defence of the Union, and Democracy. Men, too, your Excellency, who know in a measure the cruelties of the iron heel of oppression, which in years gone by, the very power their blood is now being spilled to maintain, ever ground them in the dust.

But when the war trumpet sounded o'er the land, when men knew not the Friend from the Traitor, the black man laid his life at the altar of the Nation,—and he was refused. When the arms of the Union were beaten, in the first year of the war, and the Executive called for more food for its ravenous maw, again the black man begged the privilege of aiding his country, in her need, to be again refused.

And now he is in the War, and how has he conducted himself? Let their dusky forms rise up, out of the mires of James Island, and give the answer. Let the rich mould around Wagner's parapet be upturned, and there will be found an eloquent answer. Obedient and patient and solid as a wall are they. All we lack is a paler hue and a better acquaintance with the alphabet.

Now your Excellency, we have done a Soldier's duty. Why can't we have a Soldier's pay? You caution the Rebel chieftain, that the United States knows no distinction in her soldiers. She insists on having all her soldiers of whatever creed or color, to be treated according to the usages of War. Now if the United States exacts uniformity of treatment of her soldiers from the insurgents, would it not be well and consistent to set the example herself by paying all her soldiers alike?

We of this Regt. were not enlisted under any "contraband" act. But we do not wish to be understood as rating our service or more value to the Government than the service of the ex-slave. Their service is undoubtedly worth much to the Nation, but Congress made express provision touching their case, as slaves freed by military necessity, and assuming the Government to be their temporary Guardian. Not so with us. Freemen by birth and consequently having the advantage of thinking and acting for ourselves so far as the Laws would allow us, we do not consider ourselves fit subjects for the Contraband act.

We appeal to you, Sir, as the Executive of the Nation, to have us justly dealt with. The Regt. do pray that they be assured their service will be fairly appreciated by paying them as American Soldiers, not as menial hirelings. Black men, you may well know, are poor; three dollars per month, for a year, will supply their needy wives and little ones with fuel. If you, as Chief Magistrate of the Nation, will assure us of our whole pay, we are content. Our Patriotism, our enthusiasm will have a new impetus, to exert our energy more and more to aid our Country. Not that our hearts ever flagged in devotion, spite the evident apathy displayed in our behalf, but we feel as though our country spurned us, now we are sworn to serve her. Please give this a moment's attention.

DOCUMENT ANALYSIS

1. What was James Gooding's rationale for asking for increased wages from President Lincoln?

Jefferson Davis, Second Inaugural Address as President of the Confederate States of America (1862)

In the months following Republican Abraham Lincoln's election to the presidency in November 1860, several Southern states seceded from the United States and formed their own Confederate States of America. The first capital of the Confederacy was Montgomery, Alabama, but after Virginia seceded, the capital was moved to Richmond. The president of the Confederacy was Jefferson Davis of Mississippi. In his second inaugural address, given at Richmond in early 1862, Davis argued that it was the Confederacy that embodied the ideals of the country's original founding fathers. *

*F*ellow-Citizens: On this the birthday of the man most identified with the establishment of American independence, and beneath the monument erected to commemorate his heroic virtues and those of his compatriots, we have assembled to usher into existence the Permanent Government of the Confederate States. Through this instrumentality, under the favor of Divine Providence, we hope to perpetuate the principles of our revolutionary fathers. The day, the memory, and the purpose seem fitly associated.

It is with mingled feelings of humility and pride that I appear to take, in the presence of the people and before high Heaven, the oath prescribed as a qualification for the exalted station to which the unanimous voice of the people has called me....

When a long course of class legislation, directed not to the general welfare, but to the aggrandizement of the Northern section of the Union, culminated in a warfare on the domestic institutions of the Southern States—when the dogmas of a sectional party, substituted for the provisions of the constitutional compact, threatened to destroy the sovereign rights of the States, six of those States, withdrawing from the Union, confederated together to exercise the right and perform the duty of instituting a Government

* From Jefferson Davis, Second Inaugural Speech, February 22, 1862, Transcribed from Dunbar Rowland, ed. Jefferson Davis, Constitutionalist, Volume 5, pp. 198–203. Summarized in *The Papers of Jefferson Davis*, Volume 8, p. 55. Available online at http://jeffersondavis.rice.edu/resources.cfm?doc_id=1514.

which would better secure the liberties for the preservation of which that Union was established.

Whatever of hope some may have entertained that a returning sense of justice would remove the danger with which our rights were threatened, and render it possible to preserve the Union of the Constitution, must have been dispelled by the malignity and barbarity of the Northern States in the prosecution of the existing war. The confidence of the most hopeful among us must have been destroyed by the disregard they have recently exhibited for all the time-honored bulwarks of civil and religious liberty. Bastiles filled with prisoners, arrested without civil process or indictment duly found; the writ of *habeas corpus* suspended by Executive mandate; a State Legislature controlled by the imprisonment of members whose avowed principles suggested to the Federal Executive that there might be another added to the list of seceded States; elections held under threats of a military power; civil officers, peaceful citizens, and gentle-women incarcerated for opinion's sake—proclaimed the incapacity of our late associates to administer a Government as free, liberal, and humane as that established for our common use.

For proof of the sincerity of our purpose to maintain our ancient institutions, we may point to the Constitution of the Confederacy and the laws enacted under it, as well as to the fact that through all the necessities of an unequal struggle there has been no act on our part to impair personal liberty or the freedom of speech, of thought, or of the press. The courts have been open, the judicial functions fully executed, and every right of the peaceful citizen maintained as securely as if a war of invasion had not disturbed the land.

The people of the States now confederated became convinced that the Government of the United States had fallen into the hands of a sectional majority, who would pervert that most sacred of all trusts to the destruction of the rights which it was pledged to protect. They believed that to remain longer in the Union would subject them to a continuance of a disparaging discrimination, submission to which would be inconsistent with their welfare, and intolerable to a proud people. They therefore determined to sever its bonds and establish a new Confederacy for themselves.

The experiment instituted by our revolutionary fathers, of a voluntary Union of sovereign States for purposes specified in a solemn compact, had been perverted by those who, feeling power and forgetting right, were determined to respect no law but their own will. The Government had ceased to answer the ends for which it was ordained and established. To save ourselves from a revolution which, in its silent but rapid progress, was about to place us under the despotism of numbers, and to preserve in spirit, as well as in form, a system of government we believed to be peculiarly fitted to our condition, and full of promise for mankind, we determined to make a new association, composed of States homogeneous in interest, in policy, and in feeling.

True to our traditions of peace and our love of justice, we sent commissioners to the United States to propose a fair and amicable settlement of all questions of public debt or property which might be in dispute. But the Government at Washington, denying our right to self-government, refused even to listen to any proposals for a peaceful separation. Nothing was then left to do but to prepare for war....

Our people have rallied with unexampled unanimity to the support of the great principles of constitutional government, with firm resolve to perpetuate by arms the right which they could not peacefully secure. A million of men, it is estimated, are now standing in hostile array, and waging war along a frontier of thousands of miles. Battles have been fought, sieges have been conducted, and, although the contest is not ended, and the tide for the moment is against us, the final result in our favor is not doubtful....

It was to be expected when we entered upon this war that it would expose our people to sacrifices and cost them much, both of money and blood. But we knew the value of the object for which we struggled, and understood the nature of the war in which we were engaged. Nothing could be so bad as failure, and any sacrifice would be cheap as the price of success in such a contest.

But the picture has its lights as well as its shadows. This great strife has awakened in the people the highest emotions and qualities of the human soul. It is cultivating feelings of patriotism, virtue, and courage. Instances of self-sacrifice and of generous devotion to the noble cause for which we are contending are rife throughout the land. Never has a people evinced a more determined spirit than that now animating men, women, and children in every part of our country....

Fellow-citizens, after the struggle of ages had consecrated the right of the Englishman to constitutional representative government, our colonial ancestors were forced to vindicate that birthright by an appeal to arms. Success crowned their efforts, and they provided for the posterity a peaceful remedy against future aggression.

The tyranny of an unbridled majority, the most odious and least responsible form of despotism, has denied us both the right and the remedy. Therefore we are in arms to renew such sacrifices as our fathers made to the holy cause of constitutional liberty.

DOCUMENT ANALYSIS

1. How does Davis connect the Confederate cause to America's founding, and the broader historical fight for liberty? Is he convincing? Why, or why not?

Clara Barton, Medical Life at the Battlefield (1862)

Clara Barton was one of many women who worked in support of the war effort by nursing troops, raising funds, and making clothes and bandages. This selection from her memoirs describes her initial ambivalence about going to work in the war effort and the nightmarish conditions she found on the battlefield. *

I was strong and thought I might go to the rescue of the men who fell....What could I do but go with them, or work for them and my country? The patriot blood of my father was warm in my veins. The country which he had fought for, I might at least work for....

But I struggled long and hard with my sense of propriety—with the appalling fact that I was only a woman whispering in one ear, and thundering in the other the groans of suffering men dying like dogs—unfed and unsheltered, for the life of every institution which had protected and educated me!

I said that I struggled with my sense of propriety and I say it with humiliation and shame. I am ashamed that I thought of such a thing.

When our armies fought on Cedar Mountain, I broke the shackles and went to the field....

Five days and nights with three hours sleep—a narrow escape from capture—and some days of getting the wounded into hospitals at Washington, brought Saturday, August 30. And if you chance to feel, that the positions I occupied were rough and unseemly for a *woman*—I can only reply that they were rough and unseemly for *men*. But under all, lay the life of the nation. I had inherited the rich blessing of health and strength of constitution—such as are seldom given to woman—and I felt that some return was due from me and that I ought to be there....

* From Perry H. Epler, *Life of Clara Barton* (Macmillan, 1915), 31–32, 35–43, 45, 59, 96–98.

…Our coaches were not elegant or commodious; they had no seats, no platforms, no steps, a slide door on the side the only entrance, and this higher than my head. For my man attaining my elevated position, I must beg of you to draw on your imaginations and spare me the labor of reproducing the boxes, boards, and rails, which in those days, seemed to help me up and down the world. We did not criticize the unsightly helpers and were thankful that the stiff springs did not quite jostle us out. This need not be limited to this particular trip or train, but will for all that I have known in Army life. This is the kind of conveyance which your tons of generous gifts have reached the field with the freights. These trains through day and night, sunshine and heat and cold, have thundered over heights, across plains, the ravines, and over hastily built army bridges 90 feet across the stream beneath.

At 10 O'clock Sunday (August 31) our train drew up at Fairfax Station. The ground, for acres, was a thinly wooded slope—and among the trees on the leaves and grass, were laid the wounded who pouring in by scores of wagon loads, as picked up on the field the flag of truce. All day they came and the whole hillside was red. Bales of hay were broken open and scattered over the ground littering of cattle, and the sore, famishing men were laid upon it.

And when the night shut in, in the midst and darkness about us, we knew that standing apart from the world of anxious hearts, throbbing over the whole country, we were a little band of almost empty handed workers literally by ourselves in the wild woods of Virginia, with 3,000 suffering men crowded upon the few acres within our reach.

After gathering up every available implement or convenience for our work, our domestic inventory stood 2 water buckets, 5 tin cups, 1 camp kettle, 1 stew pan, 2 lanterns, 4 bread knives, 3 plates, and a 2-quart tin dish, and 3,000 guest to serve.

You will perceive by this, that I had not yet learned to equip myself, for I was no Pallas, ready armed, but grew into my work by hard thinking and sad experience. It may serve to relieve your apprehension for the future of my labors if I assure you that I was never caught so again.

But the most fearful scene was reserved for the night. I have said that the ground was littered with dry hay and that we had only two lanterns, but there were plenty of candles. The wounded were laid so close that it was impossible to move about in the dark. The slightest misstep brought a torrent of groans from some poor mangled fellow in your path.

Consequently here were seen persons of all grades from the careful man of God who walked with a prayer upon his lips to the careless driver hunting for his lost whip,— each wandering about among this hay with an open flaming candle in his hands.

The slightest accident, the mere dropping of a light could have enveloped in flames this whole mass of helpless men.

How we watched and pleaded and cautioned as we worked and wept that night! How we put socks and slippers upon their cold feet, wrapped your blankets and quilts about them, and when we no longer these to give, how we covered them in the hay and left them to their rest!…

The slight, naked chest of a fair-haired lad caught my eye. Dropping down beside him, I bent low to draw the remnant of his blouse about him, when with a quick cry he threw his left arm across my neck and, burying his face in the folds of my dress, wept like a child at his mother's knee. I took his head in my hands and held it until great burst of grief passed away. "And do you know me?" he asked at length, "I am Charley Hamilton, we used to carry your satchel home from school!" My faithful pupil, poor Charley. That mangled right hand would never carry a satchel again.

About three o'clock in the morning I observed a surgeon with a little flickering candle in hand approaching me with cautious step up in the wood. "Lady," he said as he drew near, "will you go with me? Out on the hills is a poor distressed lad, mortally wounded, and dying. His piteous cries for his sister have touched all our hearts none of us can relieve him but rather seem to distress him by presence."

By this time I was following him back over the bloody track, with great beseeching eyes of anguish on every side looking up into our faces, saying so plainly, "Don't step on us."

DOCUMENT ANALYSIS

1. What does Barton encounter as she lends her nursing help at night in the aftermath of the battle of Cedar Mountain?

2. Why might Clara Barton's nursing activity have been considered improper or unladylike?

Fifteen.4

Theodore A. Dodge, from Civil War Diary (1863)

One of the thousands who fought at the bloody battles of Gettysburg in early July 1863 was Lieutenant Theodore Ayrault Dodge, a well-educated young volunteer from upstate New York, who kept a diary of his experiences as a soldier. Dodge was only nineteen when he began fighting in the Union's Army of the Potomac a year earlier, and had already seen many awful battles, including Chancellorsville. Unlike 7,000 Union and Confederate troops who died at Gettysburg, Dodge survived; but, like so many thousands of others, he was severely wounded. *

July 1st [1863], 9 A.M.

Early this morning a circular came from General Meade, calling upon every man and officer to do his duty in the approaching battle. This is the first we have heard of the Rebels being in our vicinity. At 7 A.M. we were on the road to Gettysburg, where the enemy are supposed to be. We know however nothing of movements. There is more taciturnity on the subject than usual in this Corps. Well, if we are to have a battle, I hope it may be such a one as will annihilate Lee's Army. But what dare we hope?

10 A.M.—

We have now crossed the border and are in Pennsylvania. The 11th Corps has arrived in the free states, on a hostile movement. I believe we are on the left of the line this time. The country round here is very rocky, and not so well cultivated on that account as the section we have passed through since we crossed the Potomac. There are more roads too. The marching is wretched and the atmosphere so oppressively close that the men scarcely make any way at all. If we march ten miles today we shall do well.

Noon, 2 miles from Gettysburg—

There is firing in the front. They say the 1st, 3rd and 5th Corps are engaged. May they be successful! There is more infantry than artillery firing. It is not as yet very heavy.

* From Stephen W. Sears, ed. *On Campaign with the Army of the Potomac: The Civil War Diary of Theodore Ayrault Dodge* (New York: Cooper Square Press, 2001), pp. 303–306.

2 P.M. Beyond Gettysburg—

We are engaged. We lie in column supporting a battery (Dilger's) with skirmishers in front. Shells are flying and bursting at a considerable rate. The Rebels are about half a mile off. The country is open and we can see everything. We see their batteries and the men at work very plainly. Our batteries are working hard. Reynolds has fallen, and in him we have lost much, but he died bravely and took 1,200 prisoners before he fell. Our Corps is to hold this position of Gettysburg. God grant we may have victory!

July 2nd [1863], 7 P.M.

I am lying on a bed at the house of a Mr. Benner's, 1 ½ miles from Gettysburg. The action of yesterday was short and sharp, Ewell's (late Jackson's) Corps again driving the Germans with fearful strength from the town. I was hit by a minié ball through the ankle just as we started, fell, and was taken prisoner. I fear my foot will be stiff for life, for although the bone is not fractured, it is considerably injured. The Confederates treated me kindly.

July 3rd [1863], 4 P.M.

The battle has raged incessantly since I came to Mr. Benner's. We are within shelling distance, but have a red flag (hospital) hung out, and till now, thank God, no shells have struck us. I am unable to use my right leg at all; have lost all muscular control over it, and it is rather painful, but I thank a kind Providence it is no worse. I suppose I shall be paroled and sent to the Union lines whenever this battle is over. I suspect the slaughter must be fearful. Such cannonading I have not heard since Malvern Hill; last evening it was more like rattling of musketry at short range, so quick was the firing.

I must tell you a queer little incident. There is a Confederate General in this house. His negro servant came into the room just now and looked round without saying anything, until his eye caught some new pennies on the table. He asked me if it was silver. I told him, No, they were cents, and gave him one. He then said, "Would you like some chicken for dinner?" I said I would pay him for anything he would bring me. Shortly after he brought me some stewed chicken and some coffee, which was a great luxury, as I could get none anywhere else. He says he will fetch me some supper....

After I was hit, day before yesterday, I lay for some time between the two fires, our men having retreated, and the Confederates making a pause. It was not a pleasant position. After their line had passed me and I was a prisoner, my sword and belt was taken away. I then cut off my boot and bound up my ankle with my pocket handkerchief. After a while an orderly Sergeant of the 119th, who was also taken prisoner, came up to me, and with the help of a Confederate soldier, got me to a grove in the rear. Here he helped me bind up my wound afresh, and then I waited till after dark, when they came and carried me on a stretcher to Mr. Benner's. I was very lucky all the way through, one of our drummers, also being a prisoner and with me, keeping my foot wet from his canteen while I was on the field. When I got here, I lay down on the floor on a blanket, and with the aid of a dose of morphine, passed a tolerably comfortable night. Yesterday was the longest day I ever remember. The ¼ hours seemed whole days. The firing began early, ceased towards noon, and at 5 P.M. was recommenced in a tremendous style.

There is a French boy of the 107th Pa. Vols., Francois by name, who waits on me, and as I can talk French with him, likes to make me comfortable. So you see that I am pretty well off.

July 4th [1863], 7 A.M.

Still at Mr. Benner's. The Confederates have, it would seem, evacuated the vicinity of this place, whether or not the town, I cannot say. Part of their cavalry pickets have just left, but a few straggling shots still indicate their presence on the Chambersburg Pike west of the town, on which they are probably marching.

I have just seen a couple of slightly wounded boys from our Regiment. They tell me that Colonel Lockman was wounded. Also that many of our officers and men were killed and wounded. I have sent them into town, to see if they can't bring a doctor out here. I much want to get to some civilized hospital. I fear inflammation is setting in my foot.

DOCUMENT ANALYSIS

1. What sense do you get of the fighting at Gettysburg from Dodge's brief diary entries?

Abraham Lincoln, Gettysburg Address
(1863)

In this memorial speech, Lincoln, with characteristic rhetorical power, connected the sufferings of individual soldiers with the larger purposes of the Civil War—to preserve the Union and to preserve freedom for all. Although Lincoln spoke of "all men being equal" it is not quite clear how "equal" he found African Americans to be.*

Four score and seven years ago our fathers brought forth on this continent a new nation, conceived in liberty, and dedicated to the proposition that all men are created equal.

Now we are engaged in a great civil war, testing whether that nation, or any nation so conceived and so dedicated, can long endure. We are met on a great battlefield of that war. We have come to dedicate a portion of that field as a final resting-place for those who here gave their lives that nation might live. It is altogether fitting and proper that we should do this.

But, in a larger sense, we cannot dedicate—we cannot consecrate—we cannot hallow—this ground. The brave men, living and dead, who struggled here, have consecrated it far above our poor power to add or detract. The world will little note nor long remember what we say here, but it can never forget what they did here. It is for us, the living, rather, to be dedicated here to the unfinished work which they who fought here have thus far so nobly advanced. It is rather for us to be here dedicated to the great task remaining before us—that from these honored dead we take increased devotion to that cause for which they gave the last full measure of devotion; that we here highly resolve that these dead shall not have died in vain; that this nation, under God, shall have a new birth of freedom; and that government of the people, by the people, for the people, shall not perish from the earth.

* From *Abraham Lincoln, Complete Works…*, eds. John G. Nicolay and John Hay (New York, 1905), ix, 209–210.

DOCUMENT ANALYSIS

1. In this very short speech, what did Abraham Lincoln ask of his countrymen in the aftermath of the bloody battle of Gettysburg?

2. Why is the Gettysburg Address one of the great symbols of the Civil War and American history? To whom did Lincoln extend new "freedom"?

Fifteen.6

Abraham Lincoln, Second Inaugural Address (1865)

In March of 1865, the Civil War was almost over. The Confederacy had held out for longer than most expected, but much of the South was now under Union control and General Robert E. Lee's forces were losing ground in Virginia at last. With victory in sight, Abraham Lincoln gave a brief speech to commemorate his inauguration for a second term as President. In this speech, he laid out his hopes for a better nation emerging from the end of the war. Only six weeks after this speech, Lee would surrender, the Union would celebrate victory, and Lincoln would be assassinated.*

*F*ellow-countrymen:

At this second appearing to take the oath of the presidential office, there is less occasion for an extended address than there was at the first. Then a statement, somewhat in detail, of a course to be pursued, seemed fitting and proper. Now, at the expiration of four years, during which public declarations have been constantly called forth on every point and phase of the great contest which still absorbs the attention and engrosses the energies of the nation, little that is new could be presented. The progress of our arms, upon which all else chiefly depends, is as well known to the public as to myself; and it is, I trust, reasonably satisfactory and encouraging to all. With high hope for the future, no prediction in regard to it is ventured.

On the occasion corresponding to this four years ago, all thoughts were anxiously directed to an impending civil war. All dreaded it—all sought to avert it. While the inaugural address was being delivered from this place, devoted altogether to saving the

---

* From Abraham Lincoln, Second Inaugural Address, March 4, 1865, accessible online at http://www.ourdocuments.gov/doc.php?doc=38 or at http://wps.ablongman.com/wps/media/objects/1676/1716309/documents/doc_d16d01.html.

Union without war, insurgent agents were in the city seeking to destroy it without war—seeking to dissolve the Union, and divide effects, by negotiation. Both parties deprecated war; but one of them would make war rather than let the nation survive; and the other would accept war rather than let it perish. And the war came.

One-eighth of the whole population were colored slaves, not distributed generally over the Union, but localized in the Southern part of it. These slaves constituted a peculiar and powerful interest. All knew that this interest was, somehow, the cause of the war. To strengthen, perpetuate, and extend this interest was the object for which the insurgents would rend the Union, even by war; while the government claimed no right to do more than to restrict the territorial enlargement of it.

Neither party expected for the war the magnitude or the duration which it has already attained. Neither anticipated that the cause of the conflict might cease with, or even before, the conflict itself should cease. Each looked for an easier triumph, and a result less fundamental and astounding. Both read the same Bible, and pray to the same God; and each invokes his aid against the other. It may seem strange that any men should dare to ask a just God's assistance in wringing their bread from the sweat of other men's faces; but let us judge not, that we be not judged. The prayers of both could not be answered—that of neither has been answered fully.

The Almighty has his own purposes. "Woe into the world because of offenses! for it must needs be that offenses come; but woe to that man by whom the offense cometh." If we shall suppose that American slavery is one of those offenses which, in the providence of God, must needs come, but which, having continued through his appointed time, he now wills to remove, and that he gives to both North and South this terrible war, as the woe due to those by whom the offense came, shall we discern therein any departure from those divine attributes which the believers in a living God always ascribe to him? Fondly do we hope—fervently do we pray—that this mighty scourge of war may speedily pass away. Yet, if God wills that it continue until all the wealth piled by the bondman's two hundred and fifty years of unrequited toil shall be sunk, and until every drop of blood drawn with the lash shall be paid by another drawn with the sword, as was said three thousand years ago, so still it must be said, "The judgments of the Lord are true and righteous altogether."

With malice toward none; with charity for all; with firmness in the right, as God gives us to see the right, let us strive on to finish the work we are in; to bind up the nation's wounds; to care for him who shall have borne the battle, and for his widow, and his orphan—to do all which may achieve and cherish a just and lasting peace among ourselves, and will all nations.

DOCUMENT ANALYSIS

1. What does Lincoln say about slavery in his second inaugural address?

2. In what ways does Lincoln invoke God's power and judgment in the course of this speech? Do his religious references appeal to you or not? Explain.

Chapter Study Questions

1. Why would James Gooding and other African-American soldiers continue to fight in this war even if their pay was not equalized to that of whites?

2. Given what Clara Barton saw on the battlefield, how fortunate was Lt. Dodge in how he fared following his serious injury?

3. Compare Lincoln's Gettysburg Address, and his sense of the meaning of this conflict, with Jefferson Davis's inaugural address.

4. If Fox, CNN, MSNBC, and other networks had been around to provide constant coverage of the grizzly nature of the Civil War, do you think the Union and Confederacy would have been more or less likely to find some earlier resolution? Explain.

5. In his second inaugural address, Lincoln encouraged "malice toward none" in rebuilding the war-torn country. Why do you think that would prove so difficult during the Reconstruction era?

Sixteen

The Union Reconstructed

At the end of Civil War, the nation remained in crisis. The most pressing questions involved reconstructing the Union—what should be done with the newly emancipated slaves and in what capacity and under what conditions should the rebellious states be readmitted? While these issues were debated nationally, the South quickly attempted to find solutions for the economic and social disruptions that had occurred as a result of the war.

Based upon an agrarian economy, the South had depended on the land and slave labor for its wealth. The war had destroyed much of the land and had eliminated the institution of slavery. In the first years after the war ended, the white power structure devised new political and economic arrangements to revive the economy. Black Codes were instituted by some southern legislatures immediately following the war as a means of reestablishing white dominance and assuaging white fear. These laws defined the relationship between African American and white Southerners, describing exactly what rights newly emancipated slaves were entitled to.

The continued dependence on an agricultural economy and the loss of the dependable labor pool provided by slavery forced the South to look for a replacement, while the freedmen did not have the necessary capital to develop an independent farming system. As a result, legal slavery was replaced throughout the South with the economic bondage known as sharecropping. Included in this chapter is a typical contractual agreement between a landowner and a sharecropper.

The Radical Republicans reacted quickly to the legal and economic changes being made in the South. Unlike the executive branch, which believed a quick and expedient readmission of the South to the Union was possible, these legislators thought that the white South was insufficiently repentant for the war and deserved punishment. They attempted to institute their own plans for Reconstruction, which included federal protection for the freedmen. The Fourteenth Amendment was intended to guarantee the political rights of freedmen and punish white Southerners who had actively partici-pated in war. Congress secured ratification by making readmission to the Union depend-ent upon it.

During the period in which the federal government controlled the South, some white Southerners sought extralegal ways to maintain control. Among the organizations that developed was the Ku Klux Klan, a quasi-secret society dedicated to using violence to intimidate and influence the political actions of the freedmen. Included here is an excerpt from a congressional report on the Ku Klux Klan, published in 1872. This doc-ument is an example of the intimidation tactics used by the Klan and other groups to thwart Republican power in Southern states.

By the mid-1870s, Congress and the Northern public had tired of the focus on the post-war reconstruction of the South. As one final attempt to protect the freed slaves, however, Congress passed the Civil Rights Act of 1875, aimed at enforcing the equal protection clause of the Fourteenth Amendment by penalizing those who discriminated against blacks. In 1883, however, the U.S. Supreme Court overturned the Civil Rights Act of 1875 in a decision known as the *Civil Rights Cases*. The document here provides an excerpt from the majority opinion as well as the opinion of one dissenting judge.

Mississippi Black Codes
(1865)

The Mississippi Black Codes are an example of the manner by which the old order was main-tained in the South while African Americans were given limited new rights. Many in the North and the Republicans in Congress were alarmed by the Black Codes. Reaction to the codes helped to radicalize Congress and catalyzed its attempt to seize control of Reconstruction from the president.*

The Civil Rights of Freedmen in Mississippi

Section 1. Be it enacted by the legislature of the State of Mississippi, That all freedmen, free Negroes, and mulattoes may sue and be sued, implead and be impleaded in all the courts of law and equity of this state, and may acquire personal property and chooses in action, by descent or purchase, and may dispose of the same, in the same manner, and to the same extent that white persons may: Provided that the provisions of this section shall not be so construed as to allow any freedman, free Negro, or mulatto to rent or lease any lands or tenements, except in incorporated town or cities in which places the corporate authorities shall control the same.

Sec. 2. Be it further enacted, That all freedmen, free Negroes, and mulattoes may inter-marry with each other, in the same manner and under the same regulations that are pro-vided by law for white persons: Provided, that the clerk of probate shall keep separate records of the same.

Sec. 3. Be it further enacted, That all freedmen, free Negroes, and mulattoes, who do now and have heretofore lived and cohabited together as husband and wife shall be

* From *Mississippi, Laws of the State*...,1865 (Jackson, Miss., 1896), 82–96.

taken and held in law as legally married, and the issue shall be taken and held as legitimate for all purposes. That it shall not be lawful for any freedman, free Negro, or mulatto to intermarry with any white person; nor for any white person to intermarry with any freedman, free Negro, or mulatto; any person who shall so intermarry shall be deemed guilty of felony and, on conviction thereof, shall be confined in the state penitentiary for life; and those shall be deemed freedmen, free Negroes, and mulattoes who are of pure Negro blood, and those descended from a Negro to the third generation inclusive, though one ancestor of each generation may have been a white person.

Sec. 4. Be it further enacted, That in addition to cases in which freedmen, free Negroes, and mulattoes are now by law competent witnesses, freedmen, free Negroes, or mulattoes shall be competent in civil cases when a party or parties to the suit, either plaintiff or plaintiffs, defendant or defendants, also in cases where freedmen, free Negroes, and mulattoes is or are either plaintiff or plaintiffs, defendant or defendants, and a white person or white persons is or are the opposing party or parties, plaintiff or plaintiffs, defendant or defendants. They shall also be competent witnesses in all criminal prosecutions where the crime charged is alleged to have been committed by a white person upon or against the person or property of a freedman, free Negro, or mulatto: Provided that in all cases said witnesses shall be examined in open court on the stand, except, however, they may be examined before the grand jury, and shall in all cases be subject to the rules and tests of the common law as to competency and credibility.

Sec. 5. Be it further enacted, That every freedman, free Negro, and mulatto shall, on the second Monday of January, one thousand eight hundred and sixty-six, and annually thereafter, have a lawful home or employment....

Sec. 6. Be it further enacted, That all contracts for labor made with freedmen, free Negroes, and mulattoes for a longer period than one month shall be in writing and in duplicate, attested and read to said freedman, free Negro, or mulatto, by a beat, city or county officers, or two disinterested white persons of the country in which the labor is to be performed, of which each party shall have one; and said contracts shall be taken and held as entire contracts, and if the laborer shall quit the service of the employer, before expiration of his term of service, without good cause, he shall forfeit his wages for that year, up to the time of quitting.

Sec. 7. Be it further enacted, That every civil officer shall, and every person may, arrest and carry back to his or her legal employer any freedman, free Negro, or mulatto who shall have quit the service of his or her employer before the expiration of his or her term of service without good cause, and said officer and person shall be entitled to receive for arresting and carrying back every deserting employee aforesaid, the sum of five dollars, and ten cents per mile from the place of arrest to the place of delivery, and the same shall be paid by the employer, and held as a set-off for so much against the wages of said deserting employee.

Sec. 8. Be it further enacted, That upon affidavit made by the employer of any freedman, free Negro, or mulatto, or other credible person, before any justice of the peace or member of the board of police, that any freedman, free Negro, or mulatto, legally employed by said employer, has illegally deserted said employment, such justice of the peace or member of the board of police shall issue his warrant or warrants, returnable before himself, or other such officer, directed to any sheriff, constable, or special deputy, commanding him to arrest said deserter and return him or her to said employer, and the like proceedings shall be had as provided in the preceding section....

Sec. 9. Be it further enacted, That if any person shall persuade or attempt to persuade, entice, or cause any freedman, free Negro, or mulatto to desert from the legal employment of any person, before the expiration of his or her term of service, or shall knowingly employ any such deserting freedman, free Negro, or mulatto, or shall knowingly give or sell to any such deserting freedman, free Negro, or mulatto, any food, raiment, or other thing, he or she shall be guilty of a misdemeanor and, upon conviction, shall be fined not less than twenty-five dollars and not more then two hundred dollars and the costs, and, if said fine and costs shall not be immediately paid, the court shall sentence said convict to not exceeding two months' imprisonment in the county jail, and he or she shall moreover be liable to the party injured in damages....

Sec. 10. Be it further enacted, That it shall be lawful for any freedman, free Negro, or mulatto to charge any white person, freedman, free Negro, or mulatto, by affidavit, with any criminal offense against his or her person or property and upon such affidavit the proper process shall be issued and executed as if said affidavit was made by a white person, and it shall be lawful for any freedman, free Negro, or mulatto, in any action, suit, or controversy pending, or about to be instituted, in any court of law or equity of this state, to make all needful and lawful affidavits, as shall be necessary for the institution, prosecution, or defense of such suit or controversy.

Sec. 11. Be it further enacted, That the penal laws of this state, in all cases not otherwise specially provided for, shall apply and extend to all freedmen, free Negroes, and mulattoes....

Approved November 25, 1865

DOCUMENT ANALYSIS

1. How was the post–Civil War relationship between whites and blacks in Mississippi defined by the Black Codes?
2. What privileges did freedmen gain and lose in the Black Codes?

A Sharecrop Contract
(1882)

This is a typical contractual agreement between a landowner and sharecropper. The system ensured that the sharecropper remained poor and in debt to the owner and that the sharecropper might never become an independent farmer. *

To every one applying to rent land upon shares, the following conditions must be read, and agreed to.

To every 30 and 35 acres, I agree to furnish the team, plow, and farming implements, except cotton planters, and I do not agree to furnish a cart to every cropper. The croppers are to have half of the cotton, corn, and fodder (and peas and pumpkins and potatoes if any are planted) if the following conditions are complied with, but—if not—they are to have only two-fifths (⅖). Croppers are to have no part or interest in the cotton seed raised from the crop planted and worked by them. No vine crops of any description, that is, no watermelons, muskmelons,…squashes or anything of that kind, except peas and pumpkins, and potatoes, are to be planted in the cotton or corn. All must work under my direction. All plantation work to be done by the croppers. My part of the crop to be housed by them, and the fodder and oats to be hauled and put in the house. All the cotton must be topped about 1st August. If any cropper fails from any cause to save all the fodder from his crop, I am to have enough fodder to make it equal to one-half of the whole if the whole amount of fodder had been saved.

For every mule or horse furnished by me there must be 1000 good sized rails…hauled, and the fence repaired as far as they will go, the fence to be torn down and put up from the bottom if I so direct. All croppers to haul rails and work on fence whenever I may order. Rails to be split when I may say. Each cropper to clean out every ditch in his crop, and where a ditch runs between two croppers, the cleaning out of that

---

* From *Grimes Family Papers* (#3357), 1882. Held in the Southern Historical Collection, University of North Carolina, Chapel Hill.

ditch is to be divided equally between them. Every ditch bank in the crop must be shrubbed down and cleaned off before the crop is planted and must be cut down every time the land is worked with his hoe and when the crop is "laid by," the ditch banks must be left clean of bushes, weeds, and seeds. The cleaning out of all ditches must be done by the first of October. The rails must be split and the fence repaired before corn is planted.

Each cropper must keep in good repair all bridges in his crop or over ditches that he has to clean out and when a bridge needs repairing that is outside of all their crops, then any one that I call on must repair it.

Fence jams to be done as ditch banks. If any cotton is planted on the land outside of the plantation fence, I am to have three-fourths of all the cotton made in those patches, that is to say, no cotton must be planted by croppers in their home patches.

All croppers must clean out stable and fill them with straw, and haul straw in front of stable whenever I direct. All the cotton must be manured, and enough fertilizer must be brought to manure each crop highly, the croppers to pay for one-half of all manure bought, the quantity to be purchased for each crop must be left to me.

No cropper is to work off the plantation when there is any work to be done on the land he has rented, or when his work is needed by me or other croppers. Trees to be cut down on Orchard, house field, & Evanson fences, leaving such as I may designate.

Road field is to be planted from the very edge of the ditch to the fence, and all the land to be planted close up to the ditches and fences. No stock of any kind belonging to croppers to run in the plantation after crops are gathered.

If the fence should be blown down, or if trees should fall on the fence outside of the land planted by any of the croppers, any one or all that I may call upon must put it up and repair it. Every cropper must feed or have fed, the team he works, Saturday nights, Sundays, and every morning before going to work, beginning to feed his team (morning, noon, and night every day in the week) on the day he rents and feeding it to including the 31st day of December. If any cropper shall from any cause fail to repair his fence as far as 1000 rails will go, or shall fail to clean out any part of his ditches, or shall fail to leave his ditch banks, any part of them, well shrubbed and clean when his crop is laid by, or shall fail to clean out stables, fill them up and haul straw in front of them whenever he is told, he shall have only two-fifths ($\frac{2}{5}$) of the cotton, corn, fodder, peas, and pumpkins made on the land he cultivates.

If any cropper shall fail to feed his team Saturday nights, all day Sunday and all the rest of the week, morning/noon, and night, for every time he so fails he must pay me five cents.

No corn or cotton stalks must be burned, but must be cut down, cut up and plowed in. Nothing must be burned off the land except when it is impossible to plow it in.

Every cropper must be responsible for all gear and farming implements placed in his hands, and if not returned must be paid for unless it is worn out by use.

Croppers must sow & plow in oats and haul them to the crib, but must have no part of them. Nothing to be sold from their crops, nor fodder nor corn to be carried out of the fields until my rent is all paid, and all amounts they owe me and for which I am responsible are paid in full.

I am to gin & pack all the cotton and charge every cropper an eighteenth of his part, the cropper to furnish his part of the bagging, ties, & twine.

The sale of every cropper's part of the cotton to be made by me when and where I choose to sell, and after deducting all they owe me and all sums that I may be responsible for on their accounts, to pay them their half of the net proceeds. Work of every description, particularly the work on fences and ditches, to be done to my satisfaction, and must be done over until I am satisfied that it is done as it should be.

No wood to burn, nor light wood, nor poles, nor timber for boards, nor wood for any purpose whatever must be gotten above the house occupied by Henry Beasley—nor must any trees be cut down nor any wood used for any purpose, except for firewood, without my permission.

DOCUMENT ANALYSIS

1. How did the sharecropping system differ from slavery?

Sixteen.3

Congressional Testimony
on the Actions of the Ku Klux Klan
(1872)

In the post–Civil War South, some whites who opposed Reconstruction formed secret vigilante organizations such as the Ku Klux Klan. The Klan resorted to violence and terror—including murder—to intimidate former slaves from participating in politics. The Klan and similar organizations did not terrorize only African Americans, however, they also attacked whites who supported the Republican Party. Congress passed legislation in 1871 to go after the Klan, and held hearings in 1871 and 1872 on how the Klan operated in various states. This testimony from those hearings shows how the Klan accomplished its goals. *

The actual existence of the Klan in South Carolina in 1870 is shown by the testimony of W. K. Owens, already referred to, who was initiated before Christmas, 1870. He gives the oath, the signs, the pass-words; the fact that they are bound to obey all the orders of their chief; that if ordered to commit murder, the penalty for refusal is death; that they are bound to deny their membership, even as witnesses in court, and to clear each other by their testimony or as jurors; that it is organized all over the State; that he had recognized members in Columbia, Winnsborough, and Spartanburgh; also, members from North Carolina, thus showing the organization to be the same in both States. He speaks of murders committed in York County as communicated to him by his chief; of a raid upon which he went to arrest and murder the county treasurer of York, who escaped from them; gives the names of chiefs and members in the town of York; describes their disguises; states that it was part of their business to disarm negroes, and that their object was political—"to carry the negro for the democratic party"... (pp. 1363–1370.)

This testimony is so entirely in accordance with the acts committed by the Ku-Klux, with their declarations when committing them, and with the experience of the commu-

---

* From *Report of the Joint Select Committee to Inquire into The Condition of Affairs in the Late Insurrectionary States, Made to the Two Houses of Congress*, February 19, 1872 (Washington: Government Printing Office, 1872), pp. 30–32, accessible online at http://www.hti.umich.edu/.

nities in which they operate, that all who are conversant with these acts would ask for no further corroboration....

The order has sought to accomplish its purposes by coercing republicans publicly to renounce their political faith; by whippings, other indignities, and murder. In the county of Spartanburgh, forty-five persons had, during a few months after the election of 1870, published in the Spartan, the democratic newspaper, notices of such renunciation, one of which, as a specimen of the whole, is here given, (page 573):

[COMMUNICATED.]

MR. EDITOR: I desire to make this public announcement of my withdrawal from all affiliation with the republican party, with which I have heretofore acted. I am prompted to take this step from the conviction that the policy of said party, in encouraging fraud, bribery, and excessive taxation, is calculated to ruin the country; and that I did not vote at the last election, because I entertained my present opinion of the republicans, and have been so for the last twelve months.

Respectfully,

SAMUEL F. WHITE.

Mr. White is a respectable white man, a carpenter and millwright; fifty-four years of age, and a native of the county.

The value of public sentiment affected by such publications, as well as the sincerity of such political conversions, will be appreciated by learning from Mr. White's testimony the persuasive means that were used to obtain that card, (pp. 571, 572):

Question. Have you been visited at any time by the Ku-Klux?
Answer. Yes, sir.
Question. When?
Answer. It was the week of the court that was at Spartanburgh,...
Question. Of what month?
Answer. Of April last. It was on Wednesday night, I know.
Question. Go on and tell what they said and did.
Answer. They came there and surrounded the house in the night. I was asleep. They got around each door and demanded of me to make a light and to open the door. They were all around the house, some at one door and some at the other. I did not have much fire, and was slow getting it made up, when they commenced lamming at the back door. After I got up the light I walked to the front door and opened it, and the men there hollered to the others at the back door to stop lamming, and they stopped. They then ordered me to cross my hands; I did so. They asked for a rope; I told them there was none. I reckon one of them went up the stairs with a light to get a piece of rope—an old bed-cord or something, and they took a pillow-slip and slipped it over my head and led me into the yard. They asked me my principles, and I told them. They said, "That was what I thought you were."
Question. What did they say?

Answer. They asked if I was a Union man or a democrat. I told them I had always been a Union man. They said they thought so. They carried me off seventy-five or eighty yards from the house. They said, "Here is a limb," and they asked me whether I would rather be shot, hung, or whipped. I told them if it had to be one, I would have to take a whipping. They ordered me to run; I told them I did not wish to do that. Then they commenced on me.

Question. What did they do?

Answer. They whipped me.

Question. How?

Answer. They took little hickories and one thing or another.

Question. Was the whipping a severe one?

Answer. Yes, sir.

Question. How many strokes did they strike?

Answer. I suppose some thirty or forty.

Question. Did it bruise or cut your flesh?

Answer. Yes, sir.

Question. How many men were there?

Answer. I can't say as to that; I thought, from the number around the house, there were twenty or thirty.

Question. How were they dressed?

Answer. They were disguised.

Question. How were they disguised?

Answer. With horns and everything over their faces.

Question. Could you tell who any of them were?

Answer. No, sir.

Question. What time of night was it?

Answer. I think it was about 11 o'clock, as well as I can recollect.

Question. What was done after they were through whipping you?

Answer. They just untied my hands, got on their horses, and went out.

Question. Did they leave you there?

Answer. Yes, sir. He told me I must publish my principles.

Question. What did you understand by that?

Answer. I think they wanted me to alter my principles to a democrat.

Question. Did you make any such publication? Did you put anything of the kind in the paper.

Answer. Yes, sir. They told me I must do it against the next Wednesday.

Question. In what paper?

Answer. In "The Spartan" paper. They did not particularly mention it, but I put it in "The Spartan" paper; Mr. Trimmier's paper.

Question. What led you to do that?

Answer. They said if I did not publish it, they would come and see me again....

Question. Would you have published any card of this kind if these men had not required it?

Answer. No, sir.

Question. Do you know of others with whom that course has been taken in your part of the county—whipping?

Answer. I have heard of a good many. Dr. Winsmith was shot the same night, because they went off in that direction.

Other witnesses were examined to the same effect.

DOCUMENT ANALYSIS

1. What does Samuel White's testimony suggest about the effectiveness of the Ku Klux Klan's intimidation techniques? In what ways was White's experience less brutal than it might have been had he been an African American?

Sixteen.4

The Civil Rights Cases
(1883)

The last major piece of Reconstruction legislation passed by Congress was the Civil Rights Act of 1875. It was aimed at preventing discrimination based upon race in public accommodations, such as railroads, hotels, restaurants, music halls, etc. Congress was tiring of Reconstruction by the time this law was passed, but this legislation was aimed at protecting the freed slaves against possible abuse, and Congress felt it was merely enforcing the equal protection clause of the Fourteenth Amendment, which had already gone into effect. In reviewing a series of cases in 1883, the U.S. Supreme Court ruled the Civil Rights Act of 1875 was unconstitutional, thus establishing a precedent for their ruling in 1896 in Plessy v. Ferguson. *

Justice Bradley delivered the opinion of the Court.

Has Congress constitutional power to make such a law? Of course, no one will contend that the power to pass it was contained in the Constitution before the adoption of the last three amendments. The power is sought, first, in the 14th Amendment. It is State action of a particular character that is prohibited....Individual invasion of individual rights is not the subject-matter of the amendment. It nullifies and makes void all State legislation, and State action of every kind, which impairs the privileges and immunities of citizens of the United States, or which injures them in life, liberty or property without due process of law, or which denies to any of them the equal protection of the laws. The last section of the amendment invests Congress with power to enforce it by appropriate legislation. To enforce what? To enforce the prohibition. To adopt appropriate legislation for correcting the effects of such prohibited State laws and State acts, and thus to render them effectually null, void, and innocuous. This is the legislative power conferred upon Congress, and this is the whole of it. It does not invest Congress

* From 109 U.S. 3 (1883).

with power to legislate upon subjects which are within the domain of State legislation; but to provide modes of relief against State legislation, or State action, of the kind referred to. It does not authorize Congress to create a code of municipal law for the regulation of private rights; but to provide modes of redress against the operation of State laws, and the action of State officers executive or judicial, when these are subversive of the fundamental rights specified in the amendment. And so in the present case, until some State law has been passed, or some State action through its officers or agents has been taken, adverse to the rights of citizens sought to be protected by the 14th Amendment, no legislation of the United States under said amendment, nor any proceeding under such legislation, can be called into activity: for the prohibitions of the amendment are against State laws and acts done under State authority....

An inspection of the law shows that it proceeds *ex directo* to declare that certain acts committed by individuals shall be deemed offences, and shall be prosecuted and punished by proceedings in the courts of the United States. It does not profess to be corrective of any constitutional wrong committed by the States; it applies equally to cases arising in States which have the justest laws respecting the personal rights of citizens, and whose authorities are ever ready to enforce such laws, as to those which arise in States that may have violated the prohibition of the amendment. In other words, it steps into the domain of local jurisprudence, and lays down rules for the conduct of individuals in society towards each other, and imposes sanctions for the enforcement of those rules, without referring in any manner to any supposed action of the State or its authorities.

Civil rights, such as are guaranteed by the Constitution against State aggression, cannot be impaired by the wrongful acts of individuals, unsupported by State authority in the shape of laws, customs, or judicial or executive proceedings. The wrongful act of an individual, unsupported by any such authority, is simply a private wrong, or a crime of that individual....The abrogation and denial of rights, for which the States alone were or could be responsible, was the great seminal and fundamental wrong which was intended to be remedied. And the remedy to be provided must necessarily be predicated upon that wrong. Of course, these remarks do not apply to those cases in which Congress is clothed with direct and plenary powers of legislation over the whole subject as in the regulation of commerce. It is clear that the law in question cannot be sustained by any grant of legislative power made to Congress by the 14th Amendment. This is not corrective legislation; it is primary and direct....

But the power of Congress to adopt direct and primary, as distinguished from corrective legislation on the subject in hand, is sought, in the second place, from the Thirteenth Amendment. Such legislation may be primary and direct in its character; for the amendment is not a mere prohibition of State laws establishing or upholding slavery, but an absolute declaration that slavery or involuntary servitude shall not exist in any part of the United States....

It would be running the slavery argument into the ground to make it apply to every act of discrimination which a person may see fit to make as to the guests he will entertain, or as to the people he will take into his coach or cab or car, or admit to his concert or theatre, or deal with in other matters of intercourse or business. Innkeepers and public carriers, by the laws of all the States, so far as we are aware, are bound, to the extent of their facilities, to furnish proper accommodation to all unobjectionable persons who in good faith apply for them. If the laws themselves make any unjust discrimination, amenable to the prohibitions of the 14th Amendment, Congress has full power to afford a remedy under that amendment and in accordance with it. When a man has emerged from slavery, and by the aid of beneficent legislation has shaken off the inseparable con- comitants of that state, there must be some stage in the progress of his elevation when he takes the rank of a mere citizen, and ceases to be the special favorite of the laws....

Justice Harlan, dissenting.

The opinion in these cases proceeds, it seems to me, upon grounds entirely too nar- row and artificial. I cannot resist the conclusion that the substance and spirit of the recent amendments of the Constitution have been sacrificed by a subtle and ingenious verbal criticism. Was it the purpose...simply to destroy the institution...and then remit the race, theretofore held in bondage, to the several States for such protection, in their civil rights, necessarily growing out of freedom, as those States, in their discretion, might choose to provide?...

But what was secured to colored citizens of the United States—as between them and their respective States—by the national grant to them of State citizenship? With what rights, privileges, or immunities did this grant invest them? There is one, if there be no other—exemption from race discrimination in respect of any civil right belonging to citizens of the white race in the same State. It is fundamental in American citizenship that, in respect of such rights, there shall be no discrimination by the State, or its offi- cers, or by individuals or corporations exercising public functions or authority.

But if it were conceded that the power of Congress could not be brought into activ- ity until the rights specified in the act of 1875 had been abridged or denied by some State law or State action, I maintain that the decision of the court is erroneous. In every material sense applicable to the practical enforcement of the 14th Amendment, railroad corporations, keepers of inns, and managers of places of public amusement are agents or instrumentalities of the State, because they are charged with duties to the public, and are amenable, in respect of their duties and functions, to governmental regulation. It seems to me a denial, by these instrumentalities of the State, to the citizen, because of his race, of that equality of civil rights secured to him by law, is a denial by the State, within the meaning of the 14th Amendment I agree that if one citizen chooses not to hold social intercourse with another, he is not and cannot be made amenable to the law; no legal right of a citizen is violated by the refusal of others to maintain merely social rela- tions with him, even upon grounds of race. The rights which Congress, by the act of 1875, endeavored to secure and protect are legal, not social rights.

DOCUMENT ANALYSIS

1. On what basis did the Supreme Court rule that the Civil Rights Act of 1875 was unconstitutional?

2. What is the main point made in Justice Harlan's dissenting opinion?

Chapter Study Questions

1. Why did many former slaves enter into sharecropping contracts following the Civil War? What was the alternative? To what extent did the Black Codes encourage such a labor arrangement, and why?

2. How did the Mississippi Black Codes in 1865, and the actions of the Ku Klux Klan throughout the South in subsequent years, seek to overturn the outcome of the Civil War?

3. Why did the *Civil Rights Cases* decision by the Supreme Court in 1883 not result in a massive public outcry in the North? Would the reaction have been as muted had the decision been made several years earlier? Explain.

Credits

Grateful acknowledgment is made for permission to reprint:

CHAPTER 6

Page 88. "Petition for Equal Education," 1787, in *A Documentary History of the Negro People in the United States*, ed. Herbert Aptheker (Secaucus, NJ: Carol Publishing Group, 1951). Copyright © 1951 by Carol Publishing Group. A Citadel Press Book.

CHAPTER 8

Page 114. Excerpts from *The Journals of Lewis and Clark*, edited by Bernard DeVoto. Copyright © 1953 by Bernard DeVoto. Copyright © renewed 1981 by Avis DeVoto. Reprinted by permission of Houghton Mifflin Company. All rights reserved.

CHAPTER 10

Page 138. From "The Letters of Mary Paul, 1845–1849" in *Vermont History*, ed. Thomas Dublin (Montpelier, VT: Vermont Historical Society, 1980). Reprinted with permission of the Vermont Historical Society.

CHAPTER 13

Page 182. From José María Sánchez "A Trip to Texas (1828)" trans. Carlos E. Casteneda in *Southwestern Historical Quarterly*, Vol. 29, No. 4, April 1926, 270–273. Reprinted by permission of the Texas State Historical Association.